THE FORGE
AND
THE CRUCIBLE

① metals (in
religion, folklore
etc.

② alchemy

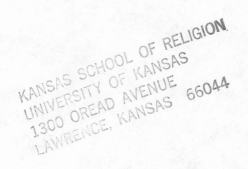

THE FORGE
AND
THE CRUCIBLE

Second Edition

MIRCEA ELIADE

Translated from the French by
STEPHEN CORRIN

THE UNIVERSITY OF CHICAGO PRESS
Chicago and London

This book was originally published by Flammarion under the title
Forgerons et Alchimistes. Copyright © 1956 by Ernest Flammarion

Metals (in Religion, folklore, etc
Alchemy)

'Alchemy in the Period of the Renaissance and the Reformation'
(Appendix O) originally appeared as part of a longer article in
Parabola.

The University of Chicago Press, Chicago 60637
The University of Chicago Press, Ltd., London

Published 1962. Phoenix Edition 1978
Printed in the United States of America

82 81 80 79 78   987654321

ISBN: 0-226-20390-5
LCN: 78-55040

Contents

Foreword

The first section of this small volume presents (through the eyes of a historian of religions) a group of myths, rites and symbols peculiar to the craft of the miner, smith and metal-worker. It goes without saying that I am very much in the debt of the historians of science and technology; their findings have proved invaluable. But my purpose in the present work has been totally different from theirs. My aim has been to attempt to gain an understanding of the behaviour of primitive societies in relation to Matter and to follow the spiritual adventures in which they became involved when they found themselves aware of their power to change the mode of being of substances. It would perhaps have been more worth while to study the demiurgic experiences of the primeval potter, since it was he who was the first to modify the state of matter; these experiences have, however, left little or no trace in the mythological record. I have, therefore, perforce been obliged to take as my starting point the relationship of primitive man to mineral substances, with special emphasis on the ritualist behaviour of the smith and the iron-worker.

The reader should not expect to find here a cultural history of metallurgy, analysing the devious ways by which it spread throughout the world and describing the myths which accompanied it in the course of its propagation. Such a history, even if it were possible, would run into some thousands of pages. But it is extremely doubtful whether it could in fact be written. The principal sources for the myths and rites connected with metals are Africa, Indonesia and Siberia, and these are areas whose cultural history and mythology are either largely unknown or only just beginning to become known. Furthermore, there are considerable gaps in our knowledge of the history of the general spread of metallurgical techniques.

Wherever possible, the historico-cultural context of the various metallurgical complexes has been taken into account; but my main concern has been to pierce through to the mental world which lies behind them. Mineral substances shared in the sacredness attaching to the Earth-Mother. Very early on we are confronted with the notion that ores 'grow' in the belly of the earth after the manner of embryos. Metallurgy thus takes on the character of obstetrics. Miner and metalworker intervene in the unfolding of subterranean embryology: they accelerate the rhythm of the growth of ores, they collaborate in the work of Nature and assist it to give birth more rapidly. In a word, man, with his various techniques, gradually takes the place of Time: his labours replace the work of Time.

To collaborate in the work of Nature, to help her to produce at an ever-increasing tempo, to change the modalities of matter—here, in our view, lies one of the key sources of alchemical ideology. We do not, of course, claim that there is an unbroken continuity between the mental world of the alchemist and that of the miner, metal-worker and smith (although, indeed, the initiation rites and mysteries of the Chinese smiths form an integral part of the traditions later inherited by Chinese Taoism and alchemy). But what the smelter, smith and alchemist have in common is that all three lay claim to a particular magico-religious experience in their relations with matter; this experience is their monopoly and its secret is transmitted through the initiatory rites of their trades. All three work on a Matter which they hold to be at once alive and sacred, and in their labours they pursue the transformation of matter, its perfection and its transmutation. These summary formulations will later be more fully and accurately expounded. But, to repeat what has already been stated, this ritualist attitude towards matter involves, in one form or another, man's intervention in the temporal rhythm peculiar to 'living' substances. And it is here that we find the point of contact between the alchemist and the artisan metal-worker of primitive societies.

The ideology and techniques of alchemy constitute the main theme of the second part of this work. We have dwelt at some length on Chinese and Indian alchemy not only because they are less well known but also because they present in clear form both the experimental and mystical character of its technique. It must be emphasized at the outset that alchemy was not, in its origins, an empirical science, a rudimentary chemistry. This it did not become till later when, for the majority of its practitioners, its mental world had lost its validity and its *raison d'être*. The history of science recognizes no absolute break between alchemy and chemistry; the one, like the other, works on the same mineral substances, uses the same apparatus and, generally speaking, applies itself to the same experiments. In so far as one acknowledges the validity of the investigations into the origins of science and technology, the perspective of the historian of chemistry is perfectly defensible: chemistry was born from alchemy, or, more precisely, it was born from the disintegration of the ideology of alchemy. But if we view it from the standpoint of the history of the human spirit we see the matter quite differently. Alchemy posed as a sacred science, whereas chemistry came into its own when substances had shed their sacred attributes. Now there must, of necessity, be a break of continuity between the sacred and the profane plane of experience.

One example will suffice to bring out the difference. The 'origin' of the drama (both of Greek tragedy and of the dramatic spectacles of the ancient Near East and of Europe) has been traced back to certain seasonal rituals which, broadly speaking, presented the following sequence: conflict between two antagonistic principles (Life and Death, God and the Dragon, etc.), tragic suffering of the God, lamentation at his death and jubilation to greet his 'resurrection'. Gilbert Murray has even shown that the structure of certain of the tragedies of Euripides (not only the *Bacchantes* but also *Hyppolytus* and *Andromache*) retain the pattern of these old ritual spectacles. If such indeed is the true origin of the drama —if, in fact, it became an autonomous phenomenon as a result of the use of the material of the seasonal rites—one is justified in talking of the sacred origins of the secular theatre. But the qualitative difference between the two categories is none the less evident: the ritual spectacle belonged to the sphere of holy things; it unleashed religious experiences; it involved the 'salvation' of the entire community. The secular drama, on the other hand, once it had set the limits of its own spiritual world and defined its system of values, gave rise to experiences of quite a different order; it inspired aesthetic emotions and pursued an ideal of formal perfection quite alien to the values of religious experience. And thus, although the theatre continued in a semi-sacred atmosphere over a period of many centuries, there is a break of continuity between the two dramatic planes. There is an immeasurable gulf between those who participate, in a religious spirit, in the sacred mystery of the liturgy, and those who derive a purely aesthetic pleasure from the beauty of its spectacle and the accompanying music.

Of course, alchemical operations were not symbolic; they were physical operations carried out in laboratories. Yet their purpose was not that of the practical chemist. The latter

carries out his exact observations of physico-chemical phenomena and performs systematic experiments in order to penetrate to the structure of matter. The alchemist, on the other
hand, is concerned with the 'passion', the 'death' and the
'marriage' of substances in so far as they will tend to transmute
matter and human life. His goals were the Philosopher's Stone
and the Elixir Vitae. Jung has shown that the symbolism of
alchemical processes is re-enacted in the dreams and talk of
patients completely ignorant of alchemy. Jung's observations
are of interest not only to depth psychology; they also indirectly confirm the soteriological function which is one of
the main constituents of alchemy.

It would be unwise to try to estimate the original qualities
of alchemy from the manner of its impact on the beginnings
and triumph of chemistry. From the alchemist's point of
view, chemistry represented a 'Fall' because it meant the
secularization of a sacred science. This is not to make an
'apologia' for alchemy but to obey the elementary require-
ments of a history of culture. There is, indeed, only one way
of understanding a cultural phenomenon which is alien to
one's own ideological pattern, and that is to place oneself at
its very centre and from there to track down all the values
that radiate from it. Only by looking at things from the
standpoint of the alchemist will we succeed in gaining an
insight into his mental world and thereby appraise the extent
of its originality. The same methodological requirement
would apply to any primitive or exotic cultural phenomenon.
Before we proceed to judge it we must fully understand it
and become imbued, as it were, with its ideology, whatever
form it may take—myth, symbol, rite, social attitude. . . .

Some strange sort of inferiority complex seems to inhibit
us—the representatives of European culture—from talking
about primitive cultures in just and unprejudiced terms. If we

attempt to describe the logical coherence of an archaic culture and discuss its nobility or humanity without stressing the less favourable aspects of its sociological, economic or hygienic practices, we run the risk of being suspected of evasion or even obscurantism. For close on two centuries the European scientific spirit has made prodigious efforts to explain the world so as to conquer and transform it. Ideologically, this triumph of science has manifested itself in a faith in unlimited progress and in the idea that the more 'modern' we become the more likely we are to approach absolute truth and the full plenitude of human dignity. However, for some time now the investigations of ethnologists and orientalists have revealed the existence of highly estimable societies in the past (and in the present too, for that matter) which, although quite devoid of scientific prowess (in the modern sense) or any aptitude for industrial achievement, had nevertheless worked out their own systems of metaphysics, morality and even economics, and these systems have been shown to be perfectly valid in their own right. But our own culture has become so excessively jealous of its values that it tends to regard with suspicion any attempt to boost the achievements of other, primitive or exotic cultures. Having for so long (and so heroically!) followed the path which we believed to be the best and only one worthy of the intelligent, self-respecting individual, and having in the process sacrificed the best part of our soul in order to satisfy the colossal intellectual demands of scientific and industrial progress, we have grown suspicious of the greatness of primitive cultures. The stalwarts of European culture have now reached the point where they wonder whether their own work (since it may no longer be regarded as the peak of man's spiritual achievement or the *only* culture possible to the twentieth century) has been worth all the effort and sacrifice expended upon it.

This sense of inferiority, however, is being rapidly rendered out of date by the course of history itself. Non-European civilizations are now being studied and investigated in their own right. And likewise it is to be hoped that those periods in the history of the European spirit which are closer to traditional cultures and are clearly marked off from everything that was achieved in the West after the triumph of the scientific method will no longer be judged in that polemically partisan spirit characteristic of the eighteenth and nineteenth centuries. Alchemy is one of those creations of the pre-scientific era and the historiographer who would attempt to present it as a rudimentary phase of chemistry or, indeed, as a secular science, would be treading on very shaky ground. The historian's perspective has been vitiated by his eagerness to demonstrate the beginnings of experiment and observation found in certain alchemical works and consequently he has assigned an exaggerated importance to those texts which revealed the first rough gropings towards the scientific method while ignoring others in which the alchemical perspective proper was patently more valuable. In other words, these interpretations of alchemical writings paid less attention to the theoretical world of which they were part than to those values which properly belong to the historian of chemistry of the nineteenth and twentieth centuries, the values, that is, of experimental science.

This work has been dedicated to the memory of three great historians of science: Sir Praphulla Chandra Ray, Edmund von Lippmann and Aldo Mieli, who guided my researches between 1925 and 1932. Two small volumes published in Rumanian, *Alchimia Asiatica* (Bucharest, 1935) and *Cosmologie babiloniana* (Bucharest, 1937), had already presented the essential material concerning Indian, Chinese and Babylonian alchemy. Some fragments of the first book have been translated into French and published in a monograph on Yoga (cf. *Yoga. Essais sur les Origines de la mystique indienne*, Paris-Bucharest, 1936, pp. 254–75; see also *Le Yoga, Immortalité et Liberté*, Paris, 1954, pp. 274–91); one part (revised and enlarged) of *Cosmologie si Alchimie babiloniana* was published in English in 1938 under the title of *Metallurgy, Magic and Alchemy* (*Zalmoxis*, I, pp. 85–129, and separately in the first of the *Cahiers de Zalmoxis*). In the present work I have taken up most of the material already used in my previous studies, taking into account those works that have appeared since 1937, particularly the translations of Chinese alchemical texts, articles in *Ambix* and the publications of Professor Jung. A number of chapters have been added and the whole work has been rewritten to bring it in line with the most recent views on the subject. Footnotes have been reduced to the very minimum. Details of the latest research, essential bibliography and the discussion of more specialized aspects of the problem have been grouped together in appendices at the end of the volume.

A research scholarship awarded by the Bollingen Foundation, New York, has enabled me to bring this work to a successful conclusion: to the trustees of that Foundation I hereby express my gratitude. I am also indebted to my friend Mme Olga Froebe-Kapteyn, who was kind enough to put at my disposal the collections of the Archiv für Symbolforschung which she has established in Ascona; and to my friends Dr. Henri Hunwald, Marcel Leibovici and Nicolas Morcovescou, who helped me with the research and documentation: to them too I express my sincere thanks. The friendship of Dr. René Laforgue, Delia Laforgue, Dr. Roger Godel and Alice Godel has enabled me to work at their homes in Paris and Val d'Or, and it is a great pleasure to me to be able to record my heartfelt thanks to them here.

Preface to the Phoenix Edition

The French edition of this book was published in 1956, and the English translation came out in 1962. A few years later, I published a critical and biographical *mise au point* entitled 'The Forge and the Crucible: A Postscript', in *History of Religions* 8 (1968): 74–88. This article was also included in the Harper Torchbook edition brought out in 1968. I have taken the opportunity of the present reissue of the book to correct a number of misprints.

Some important works on Chinese alchemy have been published in the last few years—first and foremost, Nathan Sivin, *Chinese Alchemy: Preliminary Studies* (Cambridge, Mass., 1968; see my review in *History of Religions* 10 [1970]: 178–82), and Joseph Needham, *Science and Civilization in China*, vol. 5, parts 2 and 3 (Cambridge, 1974 and 1977). I would also note such stimulating recent books on Renaissance and post-Renaissance alchemy as Allen G. Debus, *The Chemical Dream of the Renaissance* (Cambridge, 1968); Peter J. French, *John Dee: The World of an Elizabethan Magus* (London, 1972); Frances Yates, *The Rosicrucian Enlightenment* (London, 1972); J. W. Montgomery, *Cross and Crucible: Johann Valentin Andreae (1586–1654), Phoenix of the Theologians* (The Hague, 1973); R. J. W. Evans, *Rudolf II and His World: A Study in Intellectual History, 1576–1612* (London, 1975); and Betty J. Dobbs, *The Foundation of Newton's Alchemy* (Cambridge, 1975). I have discussed some of their findings in Note O of the Appendices.

Although I have not viewed the subject of alchemy from the perspective of the history of technique or the history of science, my manner of approach has been received favorably by a number of specialists. It is especially gratifying to note that these include such diverse scholars as R. P. Multhauf and A. G. Debus, historians of early chemistry; J. Needham and N. Sivin, historians of Chinese science; W. Schneider, historian of Western alchemy and pharmacology; S. H, Nasr, historian of Islamic science; and W. E. Peuckert, specialist of *Pansophia.*

THE FORGE
AND
THE CRUCIBLE

1

Meteorites and Metallurgy

I T W A S inevitable that meteorites should inspire awe.
They came from some remote region high up in the heavens
and possessed a sacred quality enjoyed only by things celestial.
In certain cultures there was a time when men thought the
sky was made of stone,[1] and even today the Australian aborigines believe the vault of heaven to be made of rock crystal
and the throne of the heavenly deity of quartz. Rock crystals,
supposedly broken away from the heavenly throne, do in
fact play a special role in the shamanic initiation ceremonies
of the Australian aborigines, among the Negritos of Malacca,
in North America, and elsewhere.[2] These 'stones of light', as
they are called by the maritime Dyaks of Sarawak, reflect
everything that happens on earth. They disclose to the shaman
what has taken place in the sick man's soul and the destination
to which his soul takes flight. There is no need to remind the
reader that the shaman is he who 'sees', because he is endowed
with a supernatural vision. He sees just as far into space as
into time. Likewise he can perceive what is invisible to the
layman—spirits, gods, the soul. When he is being initiated
the future shaman is fed with crystals of quartz. In other
words, his capacity as a visionary, as well as his 'science',

---

[1] See Note A at end of volume.
[2] See M. Eliade, *Le Chamanisme et les techniques archaïques de l'extase*, pp. 135 sq.

comes to him, at least in part, from a mystic solidarity with heaven.[1]

We shall do well to bear in mind the early religious significance attaching to aeroliths. They fall to earth charged with celestial sanctity; in a way, they represent heaven. This would suggest why so many meteorites were worshipped or identified with a deity. The faithful saw in them the 'first form', the immediate manifestation of the godhead. The Palladium of Troy was supposed to have dropped from heaven, and ancient writers saw it as the statue of the goddess Athena. A celestial origin was also accorded to the statue of Artemis at Ephesus and to the cone of Heliogabalus at Emesus (Herodian, v, 3, 5). The meteorite at Pessinus in Phrygia was venerated as the image of Cybele and, following an injunction by the Delphic Oracle, it was transported to Rome shortly after the Second Punic War. A block of hard stone, the most ancient representation of Eros, stood side by side with Praxiteles' sculptured image of the god (Pausanias, ix, 27, i). Other examples could easily be found, the most famous being the *Ka'aba* in Mecca. It is noteworthy that a certain number of meteorites are associated with goddesses, especially fertility goddesses such as Cybele. And here we come up against a transference of sanctity: the celestial origin is forgotten, to the advantage of the religious notion of the *petra genitrix*. We shall deal later with this motif of the fertility of stones.

But the heavenly, and hence masculine, essence of the meteorites is none the less beyond dispute, for certain silex and neolithic tools were subsequently given names like 'thunderstones', 'thunderbolt teeth' or 'God's axes'. The sites where they were found were thought to have been struck by a thunderbolt,[2] which is the weapon of the

[1] It will be seen later that on another cultural level it was not rock crystal but metal which conferred these special qualities on the shaman (cf. p. 84).

[2] See bibliography in Note A at end of volume.

God of Heaven. When this God was ousted by the God of Storms, the thunderbolt became the sign of the sacred union between the God of the Hurricane and the Goddess Earth. This may account for the large number of double-axes discovered in this period in the clefts and caves of Crete. These axes, like the thunderbolt and the meteorites, 'cleaved' the earth;[1] they symbolized, in other words, the union between heaven and earth. Delphi, most famous of the clefts of ancient Greece, owed its name to this mythical image; 'delphi' signifies in fact the female generative organ. As will be seen later, many other symbols and appellations liken the earth to a woman. But this analogy served as a kind of archetypal model in which priority was given to the cosmos. Plato reminds us (*Menex.*, 238A), that in the matter of conception it is the woman who imitates the earth and not the earth woman.

Primitive peoples worked with meteoric iron for a long time before learning how to use ferrous ores.[2] It is known, moreover, that prehistoric peoples, before the discovery of smelting, treated certain ores as though they were stones, that is, they looked upon them as raw materials for the making of stone tools. A similar technique was applied until recently by certain peoples having no knowledge of metallurgy; they worked the meteorite with silex hammers and fashioned objects whose shape resembled, in all respects, their stone models. This was how the Greenland Eskimos made their knives out of meteoric iron.[3] When Cortez enquired of the Aztec chiefs whence they obtained their knives they simply pointed to the sky.[4] Like the Mayas of Yucatan and the Incas

---

[1] W. F. Jackson Knight, *Cumaean Gates* (Oxford, 1936), p. 101.
[2] Cf. G. F. Zimmer, 'The Use of Meteoric Iron by Primitive Man' (*Journal of the Iron and Steel Institute*, 1916, pp. 306 sq). The discussion on the use of meteoric iron by primitive and ancient peoples, begun in 1907 in the Zeitschrift für Ethnologie, was taken up again by Montelius, Prähistorische Zeitung, 1913, pp. 289 sq.
[3] Richard Andrée, *Die Metalle bei den Naturvölkern*, pp. 129–31.
[4] T. A. Rickard, *Man and Metals*, vol. 1, pp. 148–9.

of Peru, the Aztecs used only meteoric iron, which they rated higher than gold. They knew nothing about the smelting of ores. Archaeologists have found no trace of iron in the pre-historic deposits of the New World.[1] Metallurgy as such, in Central and South America, is probably Asiatic in origin. Most recent researches tend to relate it to the south Chinese culture of the Chou epoch (middle and late eighth to fourth centuries B.C.). That would make it more or less of Danubian origin, for it was Danubian metallurgy which, in the ninth to eighth centuries B.C., arrived via the Caucasus in China.[2]

The peoples of the ancient Orient in all probability shared similar ideas. The Sumerian word AN.BAR, the oldest word designating iron, is made up of the pictograms 'sky' and 'fire'. It is usually translated 'celestial metal' or 'star-metal'. Campbell Thompson renders it as 'celestial lightening (of meteorite)'. The etymology of the other Mesopotamian name for iron, the Assyrian *parzillu*, is a matter of controversy. Some scholars derive it from the Sumerian BAR.GAL, 'great metal' (e.g. Persson, p. 113), but most of them suppose it to have an Asiatic origin because of the ending -ill. (Forbes, p. 465. Bork and Goertz have suggested a Caucasian origin, see Forbes, *ibid.*)[3]

We shall not deal with the very complex problem of the metallurgy of ancient Egypt. For a long time meteoric iron was the only kind known to the Egyptians. Iron deposits do not appear to have been made use of till the eighteenth dynasty and the New Empire (Forbes, p. 429). It is true that articles made of telluric iron have been found between the blocks of the Great Pyramid (2900 B.C.) and in a sixth-century pyramid at Abydos, though the Egyptian origin of these

---

[1] R. G. Forbes, *Metallurgy in Antiquity*, p. 401.
[2] R. Heine-Geldern, 'Die asiatische Herkunft der südamerikanischen Metall-technik' (*Pcideuma*, V, 1954), especially pp. 415–16.
[3] See Note A.

articles has not been fully established. The term '*biẓ-n.pt*', 'iron from heaven', or, more exactly, 'metal from heaven', clearly points to their meteorite origin. It is possible, however, that the term was first applied to copper (cf. Forbes, p. 428). We find the same situation with the Hittites: a fourteenth-century text declares that the Hittite kings used 'black iron from the sky' (Rickard, *Man and Metals*, I, p. 149). Meteoric iron was known in Crete from the Minoan era (2000 B.C.) and iron objects have been found in the tombs at Knossos.[1] The 'celestial' origin of iron is perhaps attested by the Greek *sideros*, which has been related to *sidus,-eris*, meaning 'star', and the Lithuanian *svidu*, 'to shine', and *svideti*, 'shining'.

The use of meteorites was not, however, calculated to promote an Iron Age proper. While it lasted the metal remained rare (it was as precious as gold), and its use was more or less ritualistic. Before a new landmark in his evolution could be inaugurated with the Age of Metals, man had to await the discovery of smelting. This is especially true of iron. Unlike copper and bronze, the metallurgy of iron very soon became industrialized. Once the secret of smelting magnetite or hematite was learnt (or discovered) there was no difficulty in procuring large quantities of metal because deposits were rich and easy to exploit. But the handling of telluric ores differed from that of meteoric iron as it did also from the smelting of copper and bronze. It was not until after the discovery of furnaces, and particularly after the perfecting of the technique of the hardening of metal brought to white heat, that iron achieved its dominant position. The beginnings of this metallurgy on an industrial scale can be fixed at a period between 1200–1000 B.C. in the mountains of Armenia. From

[1] Cf. Note A. Iron industry was never important in Crete. Greek myths and legends on iron work in Crete are probably the result of a confusion between the Cretan Mount Ida and the Phrygian mountain of the same name, where there was indeed a very strong iron industry; cf. Forbes, *op. cit.*, p. 385.

there the secret of smelting spread across the Near East, the Mediterranean and central Europe, although, as we have just noted, iron, whether of meteorite origin or from superficial deposits, was known in the third millennium in Mesopotamia (Tell Asmar, Tell Chagar Bazar, Mari), in Asia Minor (Alaca Huyuk) and probably also in Egypt (Forbes, pp. 417). Until fairly late, ironwork was faithfully modelled on Bronze Age styles (just as the Bronze Age at first continued the stylistic morphology of the Stone Age). Iron appears in the form of ornaments, amulets and statuettes. For long it retained a sacred value which still survives among many primitive peoples.

It is not our concern to deal with the various phases of ancient metallurgy nor to demonstrate its influence through the course of history. Our purpose is solely to reveal the symbolisms and magico-religious complexes which became a reality during the Metal Age, especially after the industrial triumph of iron. For the Iron Age, before it became a factor in the military and political history of humanity, gave rise to spiritual creations. As is often the case, the image, the symbol and the rite anticipate—sometimes even make possible—the practical applications of a discovery. Before providing a means of transport, the chariot was the vehicle of ritual processions; it was used to parade the symbol of the sun or the image of the solar god. Besides, the 'discovery' of the chariot only became feasible when the symbolism of the solar wheel was understood. Before changing the face of the world the Iron Age engendered a large number of rites, myths and symbols which have reverberated throughout the spiritual history of humanity. It is only after the industrial success of iron that it is proper to speak of the metallurgical age of man. The discovery and subsequent progress of iron smelting gave a new significance to traditional metallurgical techniques. It was the metallurgy of telluric iron which rendered this metal fit for everyday use.

This fact had important consequences. In addition to the inherent celestial sanctity of meteorites, we now have a terrestrial holiness shared by mines and ores. The metallurgy of iron naturally profited from the technical discoveries in the metallurgy of copper and bronze. It is known that from the time of the Neolithic Age (sixth–fifth millennia), man had made sporadic use of the copper which he could find near the earth's surface, but he handled it as though it were stone or bone, being as yet ignorant of the specific properties of the metal. Not until later did the application of heat to copper become a known technique, and copper-smelting proper dates only from about 4000 to 3500 B.C. (Al Ubeid and Uruk periods). Even so, one cannot speak of an Age of Copper, for only minute quantities of the metal were produced.

The belated appearance of iron, followed by its industrial triumph, had a tremendous influence on the rites and symbols of metallurgy. A whole series of taboos and magical uses of iron are due to this victory and to the fact that it superseded bronze and copper, which were representative of other 'ages' and other mythologies. The smith is first and foremost a worker in iron, and his nomadic condition—for he is constantly on the move in his quest for raw metal and for orders for work—puts him in touch with differing populations. The smith becomes the principal agent in this spread of myths, rites and metallurgical mysteries. This ensemble of facts introduces us to a vast new mental world, and it is this 'spiritual' universe which we propose to present to the readers in the pages that follow.

It would be difficult and perhaps ill-advised to begin by taking a comprehensive view of this historical process. It would be more satisfactory to approach this new metallurgical world by easy stages. We shall encounter a certain number of

rites and mysteries bound up with magico-religious conceptions which are sometimes part and parcel of one another,
sometimes run parallel but which at times are even antagonistic.
We shall try to list them briefly so as to have a view of the
main outline of our enquiry. We shall present a series of
documents concerning the ritual function of the smithy,
the ambivalent character of the smith and the links existing
between the 'magical' mastery of fire, the smith and the
secret societies. On the other hand, when we come to consider
mining and metallurgy, we find ourselves confronted with
specific concepts relating to the earth as mother, to the sexualization of the mineral world and its tools, and to the inter-
relationship of metallurgy, gynaecology and obstetrics. We
shall start by explaining certain of these concepts in order the
better to understand the world of the metallurgist and the
smith. We shall discover, bound up with the myths on the
origin of metals, mythico-ritual complexes embracing the
notion of genesis by means of the sacrifice or self-sacrifice of a
god; the connections between the agricultural mystique,
metallurgy and alchemy; and, finally, the ideas of natural
growth, forced growth and 'perfection'. Following upon this
we shall be in a position to estimate the importance of these
ideas in the establishment of alchemy.

2

Mythology of the Iron Age

WE SHALL not dwell at length on the supposedly
sacred quality of iron. Whether it had fallen from the heavenly
vault or been extracted from the bowels of the earth, it was
still considered to be charged with sacred power. Even among
populations with a high level of culture we still find this
attitude of awe and reverence towards the metal. It is not very
long since the kings of Malaya kept a sacred block of iron
which was part of their regalia and surrounded it with an
extraordinary veneration mingled with a superstitious terror.[1]
By the primitives, ignorant of metal-work, iron tools were
venerated even more. The Bhil, a primitive people of India,
used to offer their first fruits to the points of arrows obtained
from neighbouring tribes.[2] It was not a question of fetishism
or of the worship of an object in itself or for its own sake; it
was not a matter of superstition but a sacred respect for a
strange object outside their own familiar world, an object
coming from elsewhere and hence a sign or token of the
'beyond', a near-image of the transcendental. This is evident
in cultures which have long been familiar with telluric (i.e.
non-celestial) iron, but the legendary memory of the 'heavenly
metal' still persists as does the belief in its occult marvels.
The Bedouins of Sinai are convinced that the man who is

[1] A. C. Kruyt, quoted by W. Perry, *The Children of the Sun* (London, 1927),
p. 391.
[2] R. Andrée, *Die Metalle bei den Naturvölkern*, p. 42.

successful in making a sword of meteoric iron becomes invulnerable in battle and assured of overcoming all his opponents.[1] The celestial metal is foreign to the earth, hence it is
'transcendent'; it comes from 'up above'. That is why to the
contemporary Arab iron is in the nature of a marvel; it can
perform miracles. This may well be the consequence of a
memory heavily weighted with myth and deriving from an
epoch when man used only meteoric iron. Here, too, we are
in the presence of an image of the transcendental, for myths
preserve the memory of that legendary era when there were
men endowed with extraordinary powers, almost demi-gods.
There is a hiatus between these mythical times (*illud tempus*)
and historical times proper—and every hiatus of this sort
indicates, in the sphere of traditional spirituality, a transcendence
which disappeared with the 'fall'.

Iron still retains its extraordinary magico-religious
prestige even among peoples which have a fairly advanced
and complex history. Pliny wrote that iron is effective against
noxia medicamenta and also *adversus nocturnas limphationes*
(*Nat. Hist.*, XXXIV, 44). Similar beliefs are to be found in
Turkey, Persia, India, among the Dayaks and others. In 1907
J. Goldziher was already accumulating a mass of documents
concerning the use of iron for warding off demons. Twenty
years later Seligman had increased the number of references
tenfold. The dossier on the subject is in fact practically limitless. It is the knife, more than anything else, that carries out
the job of keeping away demons. In north-east Europe articles
of iron protect crops not only against the vagaries of the
weather but also against spells and the evil eye.[2] The prestige
of the youngest of metals—the last in the Metal Ages—survives

---

[1] W. E. Jennings-Bramley, *The Bedouins of the Sinai-Peninsula* (Palestine Explora-
tion Fund, 1906, p. 27), quoted by R. Eisler, 'Das Qainzeichen' (*Le Monde Oriental*,
29, 1929, pp. 48–112), p. 55.
[2] On the role of iron in magic, agriculture and popular medicine, etc., see Note B.

in a wealth of myth covering customs, taboos and superstitions, largely unexplored. But, like the smiths, iron retains
its ambivalent character, for it can also embody the spirit of
the devil. The idea vaguely persists that iron has been doubly
victorious: victorious through civilization (through agriculture) and victorious through war. The military triumph will
sometimes be the counterpart of a demoniac triumph. To the
Wa Chagga, iron contains in itself a magic force which is the
enemy of life and of peace.[1]

The tools of the smith also share this sacred quality. The
hammer, the bellows and the anvil are revealed to be animate
miraculous objects. They were regarded as capable of operating by their own magico-religious force, unassisted by the
smith. The smith in Togo, speaking of his tools, describes
them as the 'hammer and its family'. In Angola the hammer is
venerated because it forges the instruments necessary to
agriculture; it is treated like a prince and pampered like a
child. The Ogowe, who are unacquainted with iron and
hence do not work with it, venerate the bellows belonging to
smiths in neighbouring tribes. The Mossengere and the Ba
Sakate believe that the dignity of the master-smith is concentrated in his bellows.[2] As for the furnaces, their construction
is wrapped in mystery and constitutes a genuine ritual (see
later, pp. 57 sq.).

All these beliefs do not stop at the sacred power of the
metals but extend to the magic of the instruments. The art of
creating tools is essentially superhuman—either divine or
demoniac (for the smith also forges murderous weapons).
Remnants of ancient myths belonging to the Stone Age have
probably been added to, or woven into, the mythology of
metals. The stone tool and the hand-axe were charged with a

[1] Walter Cline, *Mining and Metallurgy in Negro Africa* (Paris, 1937), p. 117.
[2] R. Andree, *op. cit.*, p. 42; W. Cline, *op. cit.*, p. 124; R. J. Forbes, *Metallurgy in Antiquity*, p. 83.

mysterious power; they struck, inflicted injury, caused explosions, produced sparks, as did the thunderbolt. The ambivalent magic of stone weapons, both lethal and beneficent, like the thunderbolt itself, was transmitted and magnified in the new instruments forged of metal. The hammer, successor to the axe of the Stone Age, becomes the emblem of powerful gods, the gods of the storm. This enables us to understand why these storm gods and the gods of agricultural fecundity are sometimes conceived as smith-gods. The T'ou-jen of Kuang-si sacrifice goats to the god Däntsien Sân, who uses their heads as anvils. During storms, Däntsien forges his iron between the horns of the sacrificed beast; lightning and a hail of sparks fall upon the earth and lay low the demons. In his capacity as smith this god defends man and his crops. Däntsien Sân is a god of storm, corresponding to the Tibetan *dam-can* and hence to rDorje-legs(pa) who rides a goat and who seems to be an ancient *bon* deity. Now rDorje-legs(pa) is a smith-god; his cult is connected with storms, with agriculture and the goat.[1] We find a similar situation among the Dogons. It is the heavenly smith who fills the role of civilizing hero; he brings down grain from heaven and reveals agriculture to mankind.

Let us glance for the moment at this sequence of mythical images: the storm-gods strike the earth with 'thunderstones'; their emblem is the double axe and the hammer; the storm is the signal for the heaven-earth hierogamy. When striking their anvils smiths imitate the primordial gesture of the strong god; they are in effect his accessories. All the mythology woven round agrarian fertility, metallurgy and work is, moreover, of relatively recent origin. Of later date than pottery and agriculture, metallurgy is set in the framework of

---

[1] Dominik Schroder, 'Zur Religion der Tujen' (*Anthropos*, 1952), pp. 828 sq.; H. Hoffman, *Quellen zur Geschichte der tibetischen Bon Religion* (Mainz, 1951) p. 164.

a spiritual universe where the heavenly god, who was still present in the ethnological phases of food-gathering and small-game hunting, is finally ousted by the strong God, the fertilizing Male, spouse of the terrestrial Great Mother. It is known, of course, that on this religious plane, the conception of a *'creatio ex nihilo'*, accomplished by a supreme heavenly deity, has been overshadowed and superseded by the idea of creation by hierogamy and blood sacrifice; we pass from the idea of *creation* to that of *procreation*. This is one of the reasons why, in the mythology of metallurgy, we come up against the motifs of ritual union and blood sacrifice. It is important to grasp the significance of the novelty represented by the idea that creation is effected by immolation or self-immolation. Previous mythologies know only of a creation *ex nihilo* or from some primordial substance fashioned by God. The making of the blood sacrifice into a condition of creation—cosmogony as well as anthropogeny—reinforces not only the homologies between man and the cosmos (for the universe itself derives from a primordial giant—a Macranthrope), but also introduces the idea that life can only be engendered from another life that has been immolated. These kinds of cosmogony and anthropogeny will have considerable consequences; the stage will be reached where creation or fabrication will be inconceivable without previous sacrifice. During building rites, for example, the 'life' or 'soul' of the victim is transferred into the building itself; the building becomes the new body, structurally speaking, of the sacrificed victim.[1]

From the body of the sea-monster Tiamat, whom he has vanquished, Marduk creates the universe. Similar themes are found elsewhere: in Germanic mythology the giant Ymir constitutes primal matter, as do P'anku and Purusha in

---

[1] This idea finds its echo today in the conception that nothing can be created without the sacrifice of something very important, usually one's own being. Every vocation implies the supreme sacrifice of the self.

Chinese and Indian mythology. *Purusha* signifies 'man', showing indeed that human sacrifice filled a cosmogonic function in certain Indian traditions. But such a sacrifice was the prototype, as it were; the immolated human victim embodied the divine, primordial Macranthrope. It was always a god that was sacrificed, a god represented by a man. This symbolism springs not only from mythological traditions associated with the creation of man, but also from myths concerned with the origin of alimentary plants. To create man, Marduk immolates himself: 'I shall make my blood solid, I will make bones therefrom. I shall raise up Man, indeed, Man will be . . . I shall construct man, inhabitant of the earth. . . .' King, who was the first to translate this text, sought to link it with the Mesopotamian tradition of creation handed down by Berosus (fourth century B.C., author of a valuable Chaldean history, written in Greek, but now lost). 'And Bêl, seeing that the earth was deserted but fertile, commanded one of the gods to cut off his head [i.e. Bêl's head] to mix his blood with earth and to fashion men and animals capable of supporting the air.'[1] Similar cosmological notions are to be found in Egypt. The profound sense of all these myths is clear enough: creation is a sacrifice. One can put life into what one has created only by giving to it one's own life (blood, tears, sperm, 'soul', etc.). Yet another series of myths which are morphologically connected with this theme speak of the origin of alimentary plants which have issued from the self-sacrifice of a god or goddess. To ensure the existence of man, a divine being—a woman, girl, man or child—is sacrificed; from his (or her) body sprout the different kinds of nutritive plants. This myth provides the model for the rites which must

---

[1] King, *The Seven Tablets of Creation*, p. 86, quoted by S. Langdom, *Le Poème sumérien du Paradis, du Déluge et de la Chute de l'homme*, pp. 33–4. See also Edouard Dhorme, *Les Religions de Babylonie et d'Assyrie* (Paris, 1945, coll. Mana), pp. 302, 307. See also Note C at end of volume.

be periodically celebrated. This is the significance of the human sacrifices made for the benefit of the harvest crops: the victim is put to death, cut up and the pieces strewn over the earth to make it fertile.[1] As we shall see later, according to certain traditions, metals are also supposed to have issued from the flesh or blood of some immolated primordial, semi-divine being.

Such cosmological conceptions reinforce the homology between man and universe, and several lines of thought carry on and develop this homology in various directions. From these conceptions emerges the 'sexualization' of the vegetable and mineral kingdom and of the tools and objects in the surrounding world. In direct relation with this sexual symbolism we must recall the multiple images relating to the belly of the earth—the mine compared to the uterus and ores to embryos, all of which are images conferring an obstetric and gynaelogical significance upon the rituals associated with mines and metallurgy.

Concerning these mythical motifs and the rites deriving from them, see Eliade, *Traité d'Histoire des Religions*, pp. 293 sq., and Eliade, 'La Terre-Mère et les Hiéro-gamies cosmiques' (*Eranos-Jahrbuch*, XXII, 1954), pp. 87 sq.

3

The World Sexualized

WHEN we talk of the 'sexualization' of the vegetable world it is necessary to be clear as to the precise meaning of the term. It is not a question of the actual phenomenon of the fertilization of plants but of a qualitative 'morphological' classification, which is the culmination and expression of an experience of mystical sympathy with the world. It is the idea of life which, projected on to the cosmos, sexualizes it. It is not a matter of making objective or scientific observations but of arriving at an appraisal of the world around us in terms of life, and in terms of anthropocosmic destiny, embracing sexuality, fecundity, death and rebirth. Not that men in primitive societies were incapable of objectively observing the life of plants. The proof of this is the discovery of the artificial fertilization and grafting of date trees and fig trees in Mesopotamia. These processes had long been known, for at least two paragraphs of the Hammurabi Code legislate on this point. This practical knowledge was afterwards handed down to the Hebrews and the Arabs.[1] But the artificial fertilization of fruit trees was not looked upon as a horticultural technique, efficient in itself, but as a ritual; the fact that it involved vegetable fertility implied man's sexual participation. Orgiastic practices associated with earthly fertility or with agriculture

[1] See Note D.

34

have been abundantly attested in the history of religions (see Eliade, *Traité*, pp. 271 sq., 303 sq.).

It will suffice to quote one example connected with the grafting of citrus and orange trees in order to illustrate the ritualistic character of this process. Ibn Washya, in his *Book concerning Nabean Agriculture*, has depicted for us the customs of the peasants of Mesopotamia, Persia and Egypt. The book is now lost, but from the fragments quoted by Maimonides, it is possible to appreciate the nature of the superstitions surrounding the fertilization and grafting of fruit trees in the Near East. According to Maimonides, Jews were forbidden to use lemons from grafted trees in order to safeguard them against the possible imitation of the orgiastic practices obtaining among neighbouring peoples. Ibn Washya—and he is not the only oriental writer to allow himself to be carried away by such images—speaks of fantastic graftings ('contrary to Nature') between differing vegetable species. He says, for instance, that the grafting of a branch of a lemon tree on to a laurel or olive tree would produce very small lemons, the size of olives. But he makes it clear that the graft could succeed only if it was performed in the ritual manner and at a certain conjunction of the sun and moon. He explains the rite thus: 'the branch to be grafted must be held in the hands of a very beautiful maiden, while a man is having shameful and unnatural sexual intercourse with her; during coitus the girl grafts the branch on to the tree'.[1] The significance is clear: in order to ensure an 'unnatural' union in the vegetable world an unnatural sexual union between human beings was necessary.

This way of looking at the universe differs radically, of course, from one which permits and encourages the objective observation of the life of plants. Like other peoples of the

[1] Texts reproduced and commented on by S. Tolkowsky, *Hesperides, A History of the Culture and Use of Citrus Fruits*, pp. 56, 129–30.

ancient Orient, the Mesopotamians employed the terms 'male' and 'female' in their classification of vegetable species, but this classification took into account the apparent morphological criteria (e.g. resemblances to human genitalia) and the place held by any given plant in certain magical operations. It was thus, for example, that the cypress and mandragora (NAMTAR) were male, while the shrub *nikibtu* (*liquidambar orientalis*) was considered 'male' or 'female' according to the form or ritual function assigned to it.[1] Analogous conceptions are to be found in ancient India; for example, Caraka (*Kalpasthāna*, v, 3) knows the sexuality of plants but Sanskrit terminology makes quite clear to us the primordial intuition which had led to this discovery: it was the comparison of vegetable species with human genital organs.[2]

We are here dealing therefore with a general conception of cosmic reality seen as *Life* and consequently endowed with sex; sexuality being a particular sign of all living reality. Starting from a certain cultural level, the entire world—the world of nature as well as the world of things and tools made by man—is presented as endowed with sex. The examples which follow have been expressly selected from different cultural milieux so as to show how widespread and persistent such conceptions are. The Kitara divided ores into male and female: the former, hard and black, are found on the surface; the latter, soft and red, are extracted from inside the mine. The mingling of the two 'sexes' is indispensable to fruitful fusion.[3] This is of course an objectively arbitrary classification, for neither the colour nor the hardness of ores always corresponds to their 'sexual' qualification. But it was the total union of reality which mattered, for it justified the rite, namely the

[1] R. Campbell Thompson, *The Assyrian Herbal* (London, 1934), pp. XIX–XX.
[2] Cf. Eliade, 'Cunostintele botanice in vechea Indie' (*Buletinul Societatii de Stiinte din Cluj*, VI, 1931, pp. 221–37), pp. 234–5.
[3] Cline, *Mining and Metallurgy in Negro Africa*, p. 117.

'marriage of the metals', and this last made possible a birth. Similar ideas are found in ancient China. Yu the Great, the primeval smelter, could distinguish male from female metals. And for this reason he saw a parallel between his boilers and the two cosmological principles *yang* and *yin*.[1] We shall return later to the subject of Chinese metallurgical traditions, for the marriage of metals is a very ancient idea which was continued and brought to a conclusion in the *mysterium conjunctionis* of alchemy.

Apart from ores and metals, stones and precious stones have likewise been endowed with sex. The Mesopotamians divided them into male and female, according to their shape, colour and brilliance. An Assyrian text, translated by Boson, speaks of 'the *musa* stone, masculine (in shape), and copper stone, feminine (in shape)'. Boson adds the information that the 'masculine stones' had a more vivid colour while the 'feminine' ones were rather pale.[2] (Even today jewellers distinguish the sex of diamonds according to their brilliance.) With the beginnings of Babylonian ritual writings we find the same division for salts and ores and this has been preserved in medical texts.[3] The sexual classification of ores and stones was maintained in the alchemical writings and lapidaries of the Middle Ages;[4] the *lapis judaicus*, for example, is 'male' or 'female', etc.

The Jewish mystic and exegete, Bahya ben Asher (d. 1340), wrote: 'Not only among palm trees do male and female exist: they exist among all vegetable species, and likewise among

[1] Marcel Granet, *Danses et Legendes de la Chine ancienne* (Paris, 1926), p. 496.

[2] G. Boson, *Les metaux et les pierres dans les inscriptions assyro-babyloniennes* (Munich, 1914), p. 73.

[3] R. Eisler, *Die chemische Terminologie der Babylonier*, p. 116; Kunz, *The Magic of Jewels and Charms* (Philadelphia–London, 1915), p. 188.

[4] The Syrian alchemical texts speak, for example, of 'female magnesium' (ed. von Lippmann, *Entstehung und Ausbreitung der Alchemie*, i, p. 393). The 'sexuality' of stones in the lapidaries: Julius Ruska, *Das Steinbuch des Aristoteles* (Heidelberg, 1912), pp. 18, 165. Sexuality of minerals in the ideas of classical antiquity: Nonnos' *Dionysiaca* (ed. Loeb, Classical Library), i, p. 81. On the 'living stone' in the ideas of antiquity and Christendom, cf. J. C. Plumpe, 'Vivum Saxum, vivi Lapides, (*Traditio*, I, 1943, pp. 1–14).

minerals do we find the natural division between male and female.' The sexuality of minerals is likewise mentioned by Sabattai Donnolo (tenth century). The Arabian scholar and mystic, Ibn Sina (980–1037), declared that 'romantic love (*al'-ishaq*) is not peculiar to the human species but permeates all things, heavenly, elemental, vegetable and mineral, and its sense is neither perceived nor known; it is rendered even more obscure by the explanations made to account for it'.[1] The notion of romantic love applied to metals magnificently completes their 'animation', already ensured by the ideas of sexuality and marriage.

Tools are likewise endowed with sex. 'What is the best weapon?' exclaimed the poet Ibn Errûmi. 'Only a sabre well sharpened with its cutting-edge male and its blade female.'[2] The Arabs call hard iron 'man' (*dzakar*) and soft iron 'woman' (*anît*).[3] The smiths of Tanganyika make several kinds of holes in the kiln. The widest bears the name of 'mother' (*nyina*); 'it is through this that at the end of the operation of roasting you will bring out dross, slag, roasted ore, etc. The opposite hole is the *isi* (the father); to this they will attach one of the best bellows: the intermediaries are the *aana* (children).'[4] In European metallurgical terminology the kiln where enamelling material was smelted (*schmelzofen*) was designated by the name of matrix or maternal bosom (*Mutterschoss*). The comparison of human work, in which fire was used (metallurgy, forging, cooking, etc.), with the growth of the embryo inside the mother, still survives,

---

[1] Salomon Gandz, *Artificial fertilisation of date palms in Palestine and Arabia*, p.246.

[2] F. W. Schwartzlose, *Die Waffen der alten Araber aus ihren Dichtern dargestellt*, p. 142; cf. E. von Lippmann, *Enstehung und Ausbreitung der Alchemie*, p. 403; Concerning 'sexuated' swords in China, see Granet, *Danses et Légendes*, p. 496. Drums and bells are likewise sexed; cf. Max Kaltenmark, 'Le Dompteur des flots' (Han-Hiue. *Bulletin du Centre d'Etudes Sinologiques de Pékin*, III, 1948, pp. 1–113), p. 39, n. 141.

[3] Leo Wiener, *Africa and the discovery of America* (Philadelphia, 1922), vol. III, pp. 11–12.

[4] R. P. Wyckaert, 'Forgerons païens et forgerons chrétiens au Tanganyka' (*Anthropos*, 9, 1914, pp. 371–80), p. 372. The furnaces of the Mashona and Alunda are 'gynecomorphic'; cf. Cline, *op. cit.*, p. 41.

obscurely, in European vocabulary (cf. *Mutterkuchen*, placenta, *Kuchen*, gâteau).[1] It was against a mental background such as this that beliefs were crystallized concerning fertilizing and gynaecological stones and rain stones.[2] A more primitive belief preceded them; the belief in the *petra genitrix*.

When there is a heavy fall of rain the Dayaks know that it is masculine.[3] As for 'Cosmic Waters', the book of Enoch (LIII, 9–10) divides them up thus: 'The upper water will fill the role of man, the lower that of woman.' A well fed by a stream symbolizes the union of man and woman (*The Zohar*, folio 14b, 11, 152). In Vedic India the sacrificial altar (*vedi*) was looked upon as female and the ritual fire (*agni*) as male and 'their union brought forth offspring'. We are in the presence of a very complex symbolism which cannot be reduced to a single plane of reference. For, on the one hand, the *vedi* was compared to the navel (*nabhi*) of the Earth, the symbol *par excellence* of the 'centre'. But the *nabhi* was also established as being the womb of the Goddess (cf. Shatapatha-Brahmana, I, 9, 2, 21). On the other hand, fire itself was looked upon as the result (the progeny) of a sexual union: it was born as a result of the to-and-fro motion (compared to copulation) of a stick (representing the male organ), in a notch made in a piece of wood (female organ; cf. *Rig Veda*, III, 29, 2 sq.; V, 11, 6; VI, 48, 5). The same sexual symbolism of fire is found in a number of primitive societies.[4] But all these sexual terms convey a cosmological conception with a hierogamous base. It is from a 'centre' (navel) that the

---

[1] Cf. R. Eisler, *Die chemische Terminologie der Babylonier*, p. 115.

[2] For bibliographical details, see Eliade, *Traite d'Histoire des Religions*, pp. 208–10. Concerning the gynecological stones, cf. G. Boson, 'I metalli e le Pietri nelle inscrizioni sumero-assiro-babilonesi' (*Rivista di Studi Orientali*, III, 379–420), pp. 413–14; B. Laufer, The Diamond (Chicago, 1915), pp. 9 sq.

[3] A. Bertholet, *Das Geschlecht der Gottheit* (Tübingen, 1934), p. 23. A number of other documents concerning the 'sexualization' of the material world will be found in this little volume.

[4] See Note E.

creation of the world starts and, in solemnly imitating this primary model, every 'construction', every 'fabrication', must operate from a starting 'centre'. The ritual production of fire reproduces the birth of the world. Which is why at the end of the year all fires are extinguished (a re-enactment of the Cosmic night), and rekindled on New Year's Day (this is an enactment of the Cosmogony, the rebirth of the world). For all this, fire does not lose its ambivalent character: it is either of divine origin or 'demoniac' (for, according to certain primitive beliefs, it is engendered magically in the genital organ of the sorceress); we shall return to the subject of this ambivalence before dealing with the marvels associated with the smith.

As was to be expected, the most transparent sexual and gynaecological symbolism is to be found in the images concerned with the Earth-Mother. This is not the place to recall the myths and legends concerning the birth of men on earth (see Eliade, *Traité d'Histoire des Religions*, pp. 216 sq.). Sometimes the anthropogeny is described in terms of embryology and obstetrics. According to the Zuni myths, for example, primitive humanity was born (as a result of the heaven-earth hierogamy) in the deepest of the four chtonian 'cavern-wombs'. Guided by mythical twins, humans climb from one of these 'wombs' to another until they reach the earth's surface. In this kind of myth, the image of the earth corresponds exactly to that of the mother and this anthropogeny is presented in terms of ontogeny. The formation of the embryo and childbirth repeat the primeval fact of the birth of humanity, looked upon as an emergence from the deepest chtonian cavern-matrix.[1] In the form of legend, superstition or mere metaphor, similar beliefs still survive in parts of Europe. There are regions where almost every town and village know of a

[1] Concerning the zuni myth and parallel versions, cf. Eliade, *La Terre-Mère et les hiérogamies cosmiques*, pp. 60 sq.

rock or spring which 'bring' children (*Kinderbrunner, Kinder-teiche, Bubenquellen,* etc.).

But what is especially important to bring into relief are the beliefs relative to the 'gynecomorphic' birth of ores and, hence, the comparison of caves and mines to the womb of the Earth-Mother. The sacred rivers of Mesopotamia were supposed to have their source in the generative organ of the Great Goddess. The source of rivers was indeed considered as the vagina of the earth. In Babylonian the term *pû* signifies both 'source of a river' and 'vagina'. The Sumerian *buru* means both 'vagina' and 'river'. The Babylonian *nagbu*, 'stream', is related to the Hebrew *neqeba*, 'female'. In Hebrew the word 'well' is also used with the meaning of 'woman', 'spouse'. In Egyptian the word *bi* means 'uterus' *and* 'gallery of a mine'.[1] It is worth remembering, too, that the caves and caverns were compared to the matrix of the Earth-Mother. The ritualistic role played by 'caves', attested in prehistoric times, could likewise be interpreted as a mystic return to the mother, which would also help to explain the sepultures in the caves as well as the initiation rites practised in these same places. Such primitive intuitions die hard. We have seen that the designation *delph* (uterus) had been preserved in the name of the most sacred sanctuary of Hellenism, Delphi. W. F. Jackson Knight has remarked (in *Cumaean Gates,* p. 56) that in the three sites where the Sybils were located there was red earth: near Cumae, Marpessos and at Epirus. The Sybils were, of course, intimately connected with the cult of the caves. The red earth symbolized the blood of the Goddess.

An analogous symbolism was connected with the triangle. Pausanias (II, 21) speaks of a place in Argos called *delta* which was considered to be the sanctuary of Demeter. Fick

[1] W. F. Allbright, 'Some Cruces in the Langdon Epic' (*Journ. Americ. Orient. Soc.,* 39, 1919, 65–90), pp. 69–70.

and Eisler have interpreted the triangle as meaning 'vulva', and this interpretation is valid if the term is allowed to retain its first sense of 'matrix' or source. It is known that for the Greeks *delta* was a symbol for woman. The Pythagoreans regarded the triangle as the *arché geneseoas* because of its perfect form and because it represented the archetype of universal fertility. A similar symbolism for the triangle is to be found in India.[1]

For the moment let us remember the following: if streams, galleries of mines, and caves are compared to the *vagina* of the Earth-Mother, everything that lies in the belly of the earth is alive, albeit in the state of gestation. In other words, the ores extracted from the mines are in some way *embryos*: they grow slowly as though in obedience to some temporal rhythm other than that of vegetable and animal organisms. They nevertheless do grow—they 'grow ripe' in their telluric darkness. Their extraction from the bowels of the earth is thus an operation executed before its due time. If they had been permitted the time to develop (i.e. the *geological rhythm of time*), the ores would have become ripe metals, having reached a state of 'perfection'. We shall shortly be citing concrete examples of this embryological conception of ores. But we are in a position to appreciate even at this point the responsibility assumed by the miners and metallurgists by their intervention in the obscure processes of mineral growth. They had at all costs to justify their intervention, and to do this they had to claim that they were, by their metallurgical procedures, superseding the work of Nature. By accelerating the process of the growth of metals, the metallurgist was precipitating temporal growth: geological tempo was by him changed to living tempo. This bold conception, whereby man defends his full responsibility *vis-à-vis* Nature, already gives us a glimpse of something of the work of the alchemist.

[1] See Note F.

4

Terra Mater. Petra Genitrix

FROM the immense mass of lithic mythology, two kinds of belief concern our research: the myths concerning men born from stone and the beliefs regarding the generation and ripening of stones and ores in the bowels of the earth. Both beliefs have implicit in them the notion that stone is the source of life and fertility, that it lives and procreates human creatures just as it has itself been engendered by the earth.

The stone parentage of the first men is a theme which occurs in a large number of myths. The theme recurs in the great civilizations of Central America (Inca, Maya), in the traditions of certain tribes of Southern America, among the Greeks, the Semites, in the Caucasus, and generally from Asia Minor right down to Oceania.[1] Deucalion threw the 'bones of his mother' behind his back to repopulate the world. These 'bones' of the Earth-Mother were stones; they represented the *Urgrund*, indestructible reality, the matrix whence a new mankind was to emerge. That the stone is an archetypal image expressing *absolute reality*, life and holiness is proved by the fact that numerous myths recount the story of gods born from the *petra genitrix* analogous to the Great Goddess, the *matrix mundi*. The Old Testament preserved the *paleo-semitic* tradition of the birth of men from stones but it is even more striking to see Christian religious folklore take up

[1] See Note G.

43

this image in a more exalted way and apply it to the Saviour. Certain Rumanian Christmas carols speak of the Christ who is born from stone.[1]

The second group of beliefs, those relating to the generation of ores and stones in the belly of the earth—deserve particular attention. Rock engenders precious stones. The Sanscrit name for Emerald is *açmagarbhaja*, 'born from rock', and the Indian mineralogical treatises describe its presence in the rock as being in its 'matrix'.[2] The author of the *Jawaher · nameh* (The Book of Precious Stones) distinguishes diamond from crystal by a difference in age expressed in embryological terms: the diamond is *pakka*, i.e. 'ripe', while the crystal is *kaccha*, 'not ripe', 'green', insufficiently developed.[3] A similar conception was preserved in Europe up to the seventeenth century. De Rosnel wrote in the *Le Mercure Indien* (1672, p. 12): 'The ruby, in particular, gradually takes birth in the ore-bearing earth; first of all it is white and gradually acquires its redness in the process of ripening. Thus it is that there are some which are completely white, others half white, half red. . . . Just as the infant is fed on blood in the belly of its mother so is the ruby formed and fed.'[4] Bernard Palissy himself believed in the maturation of minerals. Like all fruits of the earth, he wrote, 'minerals have a different colour at maturity from that at their beginning'.[5]

De Rosnel's comparison between the 'child fed by blood inside its mother's belly' and the ruby ripening in the earth finds

[1] See Note G. It is unnecessary for our purpose to recall the beliefs connected with fertilizing stones and the 'sliding' rituals. Their meaning is clear: force, reality, fecundity, holiness, are incarnate in everything around man which appears as *real* and *existing*. Invulnerable and irreducible, the stone became the image and symbol of being.

[2] R. Garbe, *Die indische Mineralien* (Leipzig, 1882), p. 76.

[3] G. F. Kunz, *The Magic of Jewels and Charms*, p. 134.

[4] Quoted by P. Sébillot, *Les travaux publics et les mines dans les traditions et les superstitions de tous les peuples* (Paris, 1894), p. 395.

[5] Quoted by Gaston Bachelard, *La Terre et les rêveries de la volonté* (Paris, 1948), p. 247.

unexpected confirmation in certain shamanic beliefs and rituals. The Cheroki shamans, for example, possess a crystal which asks to be fed, twice a year, with the blood of an animal: if this is lacking, the crystal flies through the air and attacks human beings. After 'drinking' blood the crystal falls into a peaceful sleep.[1]

For long the idea that metals grow in the bosom of the mine had a place in the mineralogical speculations of Western writers. 'Metallic materials,' writes Cardan, 'are to mountains no other than trees and have their roots, trunk, branches and leaves.' 'What is a mine if not a plant covered with earth?'[2] Bacon writes: 'Some of the ancients report that on the island of Cyprus there is to be found a kind of iron which, having been cut into small pieces and buried in the soil and frequently watered, vegetates therein in some manner so that these same pieces become much bigger.'[3] It is not without interest that these primitive conceptions of the growth of metals were very long in dying out; they withstood centuries of technical experience and rational thought (one has only to recall the mineralogical ideas acceptable to Greek science). Might not the explanation for this be that traditional images, such as these, seem, in the final instance, to be *more true* than the result of exact and precise observations of the mineral kingdom? *More true* because of the noble mythology of the Stone Ages which transmitted them and gave them significance.

For a similar reason, mines were allowed to rest after a period of active exploitation. The mine, matrix of the earth, required time in order to generate the new. Pliny (*Nat. Hist.*, XXXIV, 49) wrote that the galena mines of Spain 'were

---

[1] Cf. J. Mooney, *Myths of the Cherokees*, quoted by Perry, *The Children of the Sun*, p. 401. We are dealing here with the coalescence of several beliefs. To the idea of spirits auxiliary to the shaman was added the notion of 'living stone' and magic stones with which the shaman's body was stuffed; cf. Eliade, *Le Chamanisme*, pp. 133 sq. and *passim*.

[2] *Les Livres de Hierome Cardanus*, trans. 1556, pp. 106, 108, quoted by G. Bachelard, pp. 245, 244.

[3] Bacon, *Sylva sylvarum*, III, p. 153, quoted by G. Bachelard, p. 244.

reborn' after a certain time. Similar indications are to be found in Strabo (*Geography*, V, 2), and Barba, the seventeenth-century Spanish writer, also refers to them: an exhausted mine is capable of re-creating its deposits if it is suitably blocked up and allowed to rest for fifteen years. For, adds Barba, those who think that metals were created at the beginning of the world are grossly mistaken: metals 'grow' in mines.[1] The same notion was in all likelihood shared by African metal-lurgists and this would account for the blocking-up of the ancient mines in the Transvaal.[2]

Ores 'grow' and 'ripen'; this picture of subterranean life is sometimes described in terms of life in the vegetable world. The chemist Glauber goes so far as to say 'that if the metal reaches its final perfection and is not extracted from the earth, which is no longer providing it with nourishment, it may well, at this stage, be compared to an old and decrepit man. . . . Nature maintains the same rhythm of birth and death in metals as in vegetables and animals.'[3] For, as Bernard Palissy writes in '*Récepte véritable par laquelle tous les hommes de la France pourraiment appendre à multiplier et augmenter leurs trésors*'* (La Rochelle, 1563), 'God did not create all these things in order to leave them idle. The stars and the planets are not idle . . . the sea is in constant motion . . . the earth likewise is not idle . . . what is naturally consumed within her, she renews and refashions forthwith, if not in one way then in another. Everything, including the exterior of the Earth, exerts itself to bring something forth; likewise, the interior and matrix strains itself in order to reproduce.'[4]

[1] Quoted by P. Sébillot, *Les travaux publics et les mines*, p. 398.
[2] Cline, *African Mining and Metallurgy*, p. 59.
* Translator's note: True Recipe by which all men of France can learn to increase and multiply their treasures.
[3] Quoted by G. Bachelard, p. 247.
[4] Fragments reproduced in A. Daubrée, 'La génération des minéraux dans la pratique des mineurs du Moyen Age' (*Journal des savants*, 1890, 379–92; 441–52), p. 382.

Indeed, metallurgy, like agriculture—which also presupposes the fecundity of the Earth-Mother—ultimately gave to man a feeling of confidence and pride. Man feels himself able to collaborate in the work of Nature, able to assist the processes of growth taking place within the bowels of the earth. He jogs and accelerates the rhythm of these slow chtonian maturations. In a way he does the work of Time. It is this which makes an eighteenth-century writer declare: 'What Nature did in the beginning we can do equally well by following Nature's processes. What perhaps Nature is still doing, assisted by the time of centuries, in her subterranean solitudes, we can make her accomplish in a single moment, by helping her and placing her in more congenial circumstances. As we make bread, so we will make metals. Without us, the harvest would not ripen in the fields; without our millstones the corn would not turn to flour; nor the flour to bread by stirring and baking. Let us then co-operate with nature in its mineral as well as in its agricultural labours, and treasures will be opened up to all.'[1]

Alchemy, as we shall see, takes its place in the same spiritual category: the alchemist takes up and perfects the work of Nature, while at the same time working to 'make' himself. It is indeed interesting to follow the symbiosis of metallurgical and alchemical traditions at the close of the Middle Ages. On this subject we possess an exceedingly precious document in the *Bergbüchlein*, the first German book ever published on this topic and printed in Augsburg in 1505. In the preface to his *De re Metallica*, 1530, Agricola attributes the *Bergbüchlein* to Colbus Fribergius, a distinguished doctor —*non ignobilis medicus*—who lived in Freiburg among the miners whose beliefs and practices he expounds and interprets

[1] Jean Reynand, *Études encyclopédiques*, vol. IV, p. 487, quoted by Daubrée, *La génération des minéraux métalliques*, p. 383.

in the light of alchemy. This little book, extremely rare and particularly recondite (*liber admodum confusus*, says Agricola), was translated by A. Daubrée in collaboration with a Coblenz mining engineer and published in 1890 in *The Journal des Savants*. It consists of a dialogue between Daniel, a specialist in mineralogical traditions (*der Bergverstanding*), and a young mining apprentice (*Knappius der Jung*). Daniel explains to him the secret of the birth of ores and talks to him about mines—their sites, their technology and exploitation. 'It is to be noted that for the growth or generation of a metal-ore there must be a begetter and some subject material capable of receiving the generative action.'[1] The author recalls the belief, widespread in the Middle Ages, that ores are generated by the union of two principles, sulphur and mercury. 'There are others, too, who allege that metals are not engendered by mercury because metal ores are found in many regions where there is no mercury; in the place of mercury they presuppose a humid, cold and mucous matter, without sulphur, which is extracted from the earth as its sweat and by which, with the copulation of sulphur, all metals are said to be engendered' (*ibid.*, p. 387). 'Furthermore, in the union of mercury and sulphur with the ore, the sulphur behaves like the male seed and the mercury like the female seed in the conception and birth of a child' (*ibid.*, p. 388). The smooth birth of the ore demands the 'quality peculiar to a natural vessel, just as the lodes are natural in which the ore is produced' (*ibid.*, p. 388). 'Convenient ways or approaches are also required by means of which the metal or mineral power may have access to the natural vessel, such as animal hair' (*ibid.*, p. 388). The orientation and inclination of the lodes are connected with the points of the compass. The *Bergbüchlein* recalls the traditions according to which the stars control the formation of metals. Silver

---

[1] A. Daubrée, *op. cit.*, p. 387.

grows under the influence of the moon. And the lodes are more or less argentiferous, according to their situation in relation to the 'perfect direction', marked by the position of the moon (*ibid.*, p. 422). The ore of gold, as might be expected, grows under the influence of the sun. 'According to the opinions of the Sages, gold is engendered from a sulphur, the clearest possible, and properly rectified and purified in the earth, by the action of the sky, principally of the sun, so that it contains no further humour which might be destroyed or burnt by fire nor any liquid humidity which might be evaporated by fire . . .' (p. 443). The *Bergbüchlein* likewise explains the birth of copper ore by the influence of the planet Venus, that of iron by the influence of Mars and that of lead by the influence of Saturn.[1]

This text is important. It bears witness to a whole complex of mining traditions, deriving on the one hand from the primitive conception of mineral embryology and, on the other, from Babylonian astrological speculations. These latter are subsequent, obviously, to the belief in the generation of metals in the bosom of the Earth-Mother, as is, too, the alchemical notion taken up by the *Bergbüchlein*, of the formation of ores resulting from the union between sulphur and mercury. In the *Bergbüchlein* a clear line of demarcation is drawn between the contribution made by primitive and popular tradition—the fertility of the Earth-Mother—and that made by learned tradition which has emanated from Babylonian doctrines—cosmological and astrological. The coalescence of these two streams is attested fairly widely in Hellenistic and Western alchemy. In other words, at least a part of the 'prehistory' of alchemy must be sought not in the

---

[1] A. Daubrée, pp. 445–6. See other alchemical texts touching on the influence of the stars on the formation and growth of metals, in John Read, *Prelude to Chemistry* (London, 1939), pp. 96 sq., and Albert-Marie Schmidt, *La Poésie scientifique en France au XVIe siècle* (Paris, 1938), pp. 321 sq.

learned traditions deriving from Mesopotamia but in primitive myth and ideology.

This venerable heritage includes, as we have noted, the embryological notion of the origin of ores. It is indeed remarkable that traditions, as numerous as they are widespread, should bear witness to this belief in the finality of nature. If nothing impedes the process of gestation, all ores will, in time, become gold. 'If there were no exterior obstacles to the execution of her designs,' wrote a Western alchemist, 'Nature would always complete what she wished to produce. . . . That is why we have to look upon the births of imperfect metals as we would on abortions and freaks which come about only because Nature has been, as it were, misdirected, or because she has encountered some fettering resistance or certain obstacles which prevent her from behaving in her accustomed way. . . . Hence although she wishes to produce only one metal, she finds herself constrained to create several. Gold and only gold is the child of her desires. Gold is her legitimate son because only gold is a genuine production of her efforts.'[1] Belief in the natural metamorphosis of metals is of very ancient origin in China and it is also found in Annam, in India and in the Indian archipelago. The peasants of Tonkin have a saying: 'Black bronze is the mother of gold.' Gold is engendered naturally by bronze. But this transmutation can materialize only if the bronze has lain a sufficiently long period in the bosom of the earth. 'Thus the Annamites are convinced that the gold found in the mines is formed slowly *in situ* over the centuries and that if one had probed the earth originally one would have discovered bronze in the places where gold is found today.'[2] The notion of an accelerated

---

[1] *Bibliothèque des Philosophies chimiques* by M. J. M. D. R. New edition, Paris, 1741. Preface pp. xxviii and xxix, text quoted by G. Bachelard, *La Terre et les rêveries de la volonté*, p. 247.

[2] Jean Przyluski, 'L'or, son origine et ses pouvoirs magiques' (*Bull. Ec. Ex.-Or.*, 14, 1914, 1–16), p. 3. The belief that stones grow and develop in the earth is widespread in Annam; cf. R. Stein, Jardins en miniature d'Extrême-Orient, p. 76.

metamorphosis of metals is already supported by a Chinese text belonging to the year 122 B.C., the *Huai-nan tzu*.[1] Alchemy only accelerated the growth of metals; like his western colleague, the Chinese alchemist contributes to Nature's work by precipitating the rhythm of Time. Left in their subterranean matrix all ores would become gold but only after hundreds and thousands of centuries. Like the metallurgist who transforms embryos (i.e. ores) into metals by accelerating the growth already begun inside the Earth-Mother, the alchemist dreams of prolonging this acceleration and crowning it by the final transmutation of all 'base' metals into the 'noble' metal which is gold.

In the *Summa Perfectionis*, a work on alchemy of the fourteenth century,[2] we read that 'what Nature cannot perfect in a vast space of time we can achieve in a short space of time by our art'. The same idea is clearly expounded by Ben Jonson in his play, *The Alchemist* (Act II, Sc. 2). One of the characters, Surly, hesitates to share the alchemistic opinion which compares the growth of metals to the processes of animal embryology, whereby, like the chicken hatching out from the egg, any metal would ultimately become gold as a result of the slow maturation which goes on in the bowels of the earth. For, says Surly, 'The egg's ordained by Nature to that end, and is a chicken in potentia.' And Subtle replies: 'The same we say of lead and other metals, which would be gold if they had time.' Another character, Mammon, adds: 'And that our art doth further.'

The 'nobility' of gold is thus the fruit at its most mature; the other metals are 'common' because they are crude; 'not ripe'. In other words, Nature's final goal is the completion of

[1] See fragments translated by H. Dubs, *The Beginnings of Alchemy*, pp. 71–3. This text conceivably originates from the school of Tsou Yen, if not from the Master himself (contemporary of Mencius, fourth century); cf. Dubs, p. 74.

[2] The book was for long attributed to Geber, but J. Ruska has proved this tradition to be not authentic. Cf. John Read, *Prelude to Chemistry*, p. 48.

the mineral kingdom, its ultimate 'maturation'. The natural transmutation of metals into gold is inscribed in their destiny. The tendency of Nature is to perfection. But since gold is the bearer of a highly spiritual symbolism ('Gold is immortality', say the Indian texts repeatedly),[1] it is obvious that a new idea is coming into being: the idea of the part assumed by the alchemist as the brotherly saviour of Nature. He assists Nature to fulfil her final goal, to attain her 'ideal', which is the perfection of its progeny—be it mineral, animal or human—to its supreme ripening, which is absolute immortality and liberty (gold being the symbol of sovereignty and autonomy).

The alchemico-soteriological speculations, which paved the way for the above ideas, abound in the alchemistic literature of the West. Jung, for example, has magnificently demonstrated their importance and magnitude. For our part, we prefer to emphasize the extreme antiquity of the premises of this alchemical soteriology. The image of the Earth-Mother pregnant with every kind of embryo, preceded the image of Nature, as the image of the Earth-Mother had preceded that of the Sofia. It is, therefore, important to return now to this exceedingly ancient symbolism in which the earth is compared to the belly of the mother, the mines to her matrix and the ores to embryos. A whole series of mineral and metallurgical rites derives from it.

---

[1] Maitrâyani-samhitâ, II, 2, 2; Satapatha Brâhmana, III, 8, 2, 27; Aitareya-Brâhana, VII, 4, 6; etc.

5

Rites and Mysteries in Metallurgy

A MINE or an untapped vein is not easily discovered; it is for the gods and divine creatures to reveal where they lie and to teach human beings how to exploit their contents. These beliefs were held in European countries until quite recently. The Greek traveller Nucius Nicander, who had visited Liège in the sixteenth century, brings back the legend of the discovery of the coal mines of northern France and Belgium. An angel had appeared in the guise of a venerable old man and had shown the mouth of a gallery to a smith who had until then fed his furnace with wood. In Finistère a fairy (*groac'k*) is believed to have disclosed to man the existence of silver-bearing lead. And it was Péran, the patron saint of mines, who was the first to devise the manner of smelting metals.[1]

I shall not dwell upon the mythological substrata which, in the sacred writings concerning St. Peran, are given a new significance. In other traditions it is also a demi-god or a civilizing hero, a divine messenger, who is the originator of mining and metallurgy. This comes out very vividly in the Chinese legends of Yu the Great, the 'piercer of mountains'. Yu was a happy miner who gave health to the earth instead of disease. He knew the rites of the trade.[2] Nor shall I dwell on the rich mining folklore still alive in Europe; on mysterious beings such as

[1] Paul Sébillot, *Les travaux publics et les mines dans les traditions et les superstitions de tous les pays*, pp. 406, 410 sq.
[2] Marcel Granet, *Danses et Légendes de la Chine ancienne*, p. 496. Cf. pp. 610 sq.

'Master Hoemmerling', known also as the 'Monk of the Mountain'; or 'The White Lady', whose appearance was followed by landslips; or the innumerable 'genies', phantoms and subterranean spirits.[1]

It is sufficient to recall that the sinking of a mine or the construction of a furnace are ritual operations, often of an astonishing primitivism. Mining rites persisted in Europe up to the end of the Middle Ages: every sinking of a new mine was accompanied by religious ceremonies (Sébillot, *op. cit.*, p. 421). But we must look elsewhere in order to estimate the antiquity and complexity of these traditions. For the expression of these rites, their purpose, their underlying ideology, vary at different cultural levels. In the first instance, one notes the desire to appease the spirits guarding or inhabiting the mine. 'The Malayan miner,' writes A. Hale, 'has peculiar ideas about tin and its properties. Above all, he believes that tin is under the orders and protection of certain spirits which he finds it necessary to appease. Likewise he believes that tin is alive and possesses many of the properties of living matter. It can, by itself, move from one spot to another; it can reproduce itself and it has special sympathies, perhaps affinities, for certain people and things, and vice-versa. And so it is urged that the ore of tin be treated with a certain respect, that note be taken of its special qualities and, what is perhaps still more curious, that the exploitation of the mine be directed in such a way that the tin ore may be extracted without its knowledge.'[2]

Let us note in passing the animal behaviour of the ore: it is alive, it moves at will, hides, shows sympathy or antipathy to human beings—a conduct not dissimilar from that shown by game towards its hunter. Although Mohammedanism is

---

[1] P. Sébillot, *op. cit.*, pp. 479–93 and *passim*. On the literary mythology and imagery of the mines, see C. Bachelard, *La Terre et les rêveries de la volonté*, pp. 183 sq. and *passim*.

[2] A. Hale, quoted by W. W. Skeat, *Malay Magic* (London, 1920), pp. 259–60.

strongly entrenched in Malaya, this 'alien' religion has proved powerless in its efforts to secure the success of mining operations. For it is the ancient deities of the soil which keep watch over the mines and have control of the ores. It is thus absolutely necessary to have recourse to a priest of the old religion, the one which has been ousted by Islam. Appeals are addressed to a Malayan *pawang*, sometimes even to a Sakai shaman (i.e. one belonging to the most ancient pre-Malayan, population), to conduct the mining ceremonies. Because they are the repositories of the most primitive religious traditions, these *pawang* are able to appease the guardian gods of the ore and to treat circumspectly the spirits haunting the mines.[1] Their help is especially indispensable in the matter of gold-bearing ores (which, like those of tin, constitute the main mineral wealth of Malaya). Mohammedan workmen must be very careful not to allow their religion to be recognized by outward signs or prayers. 'Gold is considered to be under the jurisdiction and in the possession of a *dewa* or god; to go in search of it is consequently an act of impiety, for the miners must win over the *dewa* by prayers and offerings, taking great care not to utter the name of God (Allah) or to practise rites of the Islamic cult. Any proclamation of the sovereignty of Allah offends against the *dewa*, who, forthwith, conceals the gold or renders it invisible.'[2] This tension between an imported creed and the local religion is a well-known phenomenon in the history of religions. As everywhere else in the world, the 'masters of the place' in Malaya make themselves felt in the cults connected with the earth. The treasures of the earth, its works, its 'children', belong to the aboriginals, and their religion alone authorizes access to them.

In Africa, among the Bayeka, when a new gallery of a

[1] Id., p. 253.
[2] W. W. Skeat, *Malay Magic*, pp. 271–2.

mine is opened, the chief, surrounded by a priest and workmen, recites a prayer to his ancestral 'copper-spirits' who rule
over the mine. It is always the chief who has to decide where
to begin to drill so as not to disturb or irritate the spirits of the
mountain. Similarly, the Bakitara miners have to appease the
'master spirits of the place' and during their labours they are
required to observe numerous taboos, especially sexual ones.[1]
Ritual purity plays a considerable part. The aborigines of
Haiti hold that in order to find gold one must be chaste, and
they do not begin the search for the ore until they have undergone prolonged fasting and several days of sexual abstinence.
They are convinced that if their searches remain fruitless it is
entirely due to their uncleanliness.[2] The importance of sexual
taboos observed during smelting operations will be discussed
in a later chapter.

It has been established that among miners, rites calling for
a state of cleanliness, fasting, meditation, prayers and acts of
worship were strictly observed. All these things were ordained
by the very nature of the operation to be conducted because
the area to be entered is sacred and inviolable; subterranean
life and the spirits reigning there are about to be disturbed;
contact is to be made with something sacred which has no
part in the usual religious sphere—a sacredness more profound
and more dangerous. There is the feeling of venturing into a
domain which by rights does not belong to man—the subterranean world with its mysteries of mineral gestation which
has been slowly taking its course in the bowels of the Earth-
Mother. There is above all the feeling that one is meddling
with the natural order of things ruled by some higher law and
intervening in a secret and sacred process. Consequently, every
precaution is taken that is considered indispensable to the '*rites
de passage*'. There is the obscure feeling that some mystery is

[1] Cline, *Mining and Metallurgy in Negro Africa*, pp. 119, 117.
[2] P. Sébillot, *op. cit.*, p. 421.

at stake involving human existence, for the discovery of metals has indeed left its mark on man. Mining and metallurgy have altered his entire mode of existence. All the myths surrounding mines and mountains, all those innumerable fairies, elves, genies, phantoms and spirits, are the multiple manifestations of the *sacred presence* which is affronted by those who penetrate into the geological strata of life.

Still charged with this dread holiness the ores are conveyed to the furnace. It is then that the most difficult and hazardous operations begin. The artisan takes the place of the Earth-Mother and it is his task to accelerate and perfect the growth of the ore. The furnaces are, as it were, a new matrix, an artificial uterus where the ore completes its gestation. Hence the infinite number of precautions, taboos and ritual acts which accompany the smelting. Camps (or camping-grounds) are set up in the vicinity of the mines and there the workers live, to all intents and purposes in a state of purity, throughout the season (in Africa for several months between May and November).[1] The *Achewa* smelters observe the most rigorous continence throughout this period (Cline, *op. cit.*, p. 119). The Bayeke do not allow women in the vicinity of the furnaces (*ibid.*, p. 120). The Baila, who live in a state of isolation throughout the metallurgical season, are even more rigorous; any workman who has had a wet dream must be cleansed (*ibid.*, p. 121). The same sexual taboos exist among the Bakitara: if the bellows-maker has had sexual relations during the course of his work, the bellows will be constantly filling up with water and refuse to function.[2] The Pangwe abstain from sexual

---

[1] Cline, *op. cit.*, p. 41.

[2] Among the Bakitara, however, 'the smith who makes his own bellows must cohabit with his wife as soon as he has completed them in order to make them solid and to secure their correct functioning'; Cline, *op. cit.*, p. 117. Among the Pa Nyankole, the smith cohabits with his wife as soon as a new hammer has been brought into his shop (*ibid.*, p. 118). We are here dealing with another kind of symbolism: the tool is rendered 'living' by its sexualization and by making its function parallel with the human generative act.

PHILOSOPHORVM.
CONCEPTIO SEV PVTRE
factio

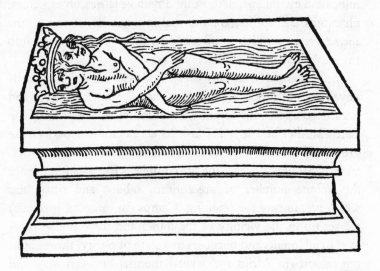

Hye ligen könig vnd köningin dot/
Die sele scheydt sich mit grosser not.

ARISTOTELES REX ET
Philosophus.

Nunquam vidi aliquod animatum crescere
sine putrefactione, nisi autem fiat putri-
dum inuanum erit opus alchimicum.

Rosarium philosophorum (Frankfurt, 1550)

'Here lie the King and Queen
Their souls have left them with great sorrow'

ROSARIVM
ANIMÆ EXTRACTIO VEL
imprægnatio

Hye teylen sich die vier element/
Aus dem leyb scheydt sich die sele behendt.

Rosarium philosophorum

'Here is the separation of the four elements
When the soul separates gently from the body'

relations for two months prior to the smelting operations and throughout their entire duration (Cline, p. 125). The belief that the sexual act can, in some way, compromise the success of the work is general throughout black Africa. The prohibition against such relationships even features in the ritual songs sung during the work. The Baila's song goes: 'Kongwe [clitoris] and Malaba the Black [labiae feminae] fill me with horror! I found Kongwe as I fanned the flames of the fire. Kongwe fills me with horror. Pass far from me, pass far, thou with whom we have repeated relations, pass from me!' (Cline, p. 121).

These songs still retain perhaps the obscure traces of the comparison of the fire and fusion with the sex act. In this case certain metallurgical taboos relating to sex may well be explained by the fact that smelting represents a sacred sexual union, a sacred marriage (cf. the mixture of 'male' and 'female' ores), and consequently all the sexual energies of the workman must be kept in reserve to ensure the magical success of the union, which is proceeding in the furnaces. For all these traditions are extremely complex and lie at the confluence of different symbolisms. To the idea of embryo-ores completing their gestation in the furnaces was added the idea that smelting, being a form of creation, necessarily implies the prior union of male and female elements. A similar symbolism found in China will be discussed in a later chapter.

To the same order of ideas belong certain elements of nuptial symbolism present in the metallurgical ceremonies of the Africans. The Bakitara smith treats the anvil like a bride. When men bring it into the house they sing as though for a nuptial procession. In accepting it, the smith sprinkles it with water 'in order that it may beget many children', and tells his wife that he has brought a second wife into the house (Cline, p. 118). Among the Baila, while the furnace is being constructed, a youth and girl go inside and crush beans (the crackling noise thus produced symbolizes the noise of the fire). The young people who have played this important role must later marry one another (*ibid.*, p. 120).

With the availability of more precise and elaborate information, a clearer picture is obtained of the ritual character of metallurgy in Africa. R. P. Wyckaert, who has made a close study of the smiths of Tanganyika, has some significant details. Before repairing to the camping-ground, the master-smith invokes the protection of the divinities. 'You, grandparents, who have taught us these works, precede us' (meaning: 'Be in front of us so that you may instruct us how to proceed'). 'Thou, Merciful One, whose habitation is unknown to us, forgive us. Thou, O Sun, my light, keep watch over me. I offer up thanks to you all.'[1] On the eve of the departure for the blast-furnaces everyone must practise continence. In the morning the master-smith takes out his box of remedies, worships before it and then all file in front of it, kneel down and receive on the forehead a light layer of white earth. When the procession is marching towards the furnaces, one child bears the remedy-box, another a couple of chickens. At the camp the most important operation is the introduction of the remedies into the furnace and the accompanying sacrifice. The children bring the chickens, slaughter them in front of the master-smith and sprinkle with blood the fire, the ore and the coal. Then 'one of them penetrate[s] into the interior of the oven while the other remains outside. They continue to sprinkle while repeating several times the following words (addressed, no doubt, to the divinity): "Do thou kindle the fire so that it may burn well!" ' (*op. cit.*, p. 375).

On the instructions of the chief, the child who is inside places the remedies in the basin hollowed into the base of the furnace, deposits the heads of the two hens and covers the

---

[1] R. P. Wyckaert, *Forgerons païens et forgerons chrétiens au Tanganyka*, p. 373.

whole with earth. The smithy is likewise sanctified by the sacrifice of a cock. The smith penetrates into the interior, immolates the victim and scatters its blood over the stone anvil, saying: 'May this forge not blemish my iron! May it bring me wealth and fortune!' (*ibid.*, p. 378).

The ritual role of the two children and the sacrifice offered up to the furnaces should be noted. The heads of the hens buried under the base of the furnace may represent a substition sacrifice. Chinese traditions are most illuminating on this point. We may recall that Yu the Great, the happy miner, is reputed to have achieved the casting of the nine cauldrons of the Hia which ensured the union of the High and the Low.[1] The cauldrons or boilers performed miracles; they moved of themselves, could boil without being heated and could recognize Virtue (one of the great tortures consisted in boiling the guilty person; Granet, p. 491, n. 2). Five of Yu's cauldrons were in correspondence with *yang*, four with *yin* (*ibid.*, p. 496). They therefore constituted a pair, a union of opposites (Heaven-Earth, Male-Female, etc.), and at the same time they represented the image of cosmic totality. As we have seen, ores and metals were also classified into male and female. At the time of smelting, youths and virgins played a part; they it was who sprinkled the water over red metal (*ibid.*, p.497). Now, if the tempering of a sword was looked upon as a union of fire and water, if the action of alloying is a marriage-rite, the same symbolism was necessarily implicit in the smelting of the metal.

Directly related to this sexual and marital symbolism is the blood sacrifice. 'Mo-ye and Kan-tsiang, male and female, are a pair of swords. They are also husband and wife, a "ménage" of smiths. Kan-tsiang, the husband, having received the order to forge *two* swords, set to work and was unable,

[1] Marcel Granet, *Danses et Légendes de la Chine ancienne*, pp. 489–90.

after three months of exertion, to get the metal to fuse. To his wife, Mo-ye, who demanded to know the reason for his failure, he at first gave an evasive reply. She insisted, reminding him that the transformation of holy matter (which is what metal is) demands for its accomplishment the sacrifice of a human being. Kan-tsiang then told her that his master had succeeded in bringing about this fusion only by throwing *themselves, him and his wife*, into the fiery furnace. Mo-ye declared herself prepared to give her body if her husband would allow his own to be melted down' (Granet, p. 500). They cut their hair and clipped their nails. 'Together they cast into the furnace hair and nail-parings. They gave the part in order to give all' (*ibid.*, p. 501). According to another version: 'Mo-ye, having asked her husband why the metal did not fuse successfully, received the reply: 'Ngeou the smelter, my deceased master (or Ancient Master), desiring to cast a sword and not succeeding, took a girl in order to marry her to the presiding spirit of the Furnace. Mo-ye, at these words, threw herself into the furnace and the casting then took place' (*ibid.*, p. 501, n. 3). The *Wou Yue tch'ouen ts'ieou* (Chap. 4), describing the making of two 'hooks or sickle-shaped cut-lasses', points out that the artisan consecrated them with the blood of his two sons (*ibid.*, p. 502, n. 2). 'When Keou-tsien, King of Yue, caused eight wondrous swords to be cast, before collecting the metal, he sacrificed oxen and white horses to the genius of Kouen-wou. Kouen-wou is the name of a sword' (*ibid.*, p. 493).[1]

The theme of sacrifice (or of personal sacrifice) at the time of smelting, which is a mythico-ritual motif more or less related to the idea of mystic union between a human

[1] See other variants of the legend of Mo-ye and Kan-tsiang in Lionello Lanciotti, 'Sword casting and related legends in China' (*East and West*, VI, 1955, 106–14), especially pages 110 sq. and 'The Transformation of Ch'ih Pi's Legend' (*ibid.*, pp. 316–22). On Chinese metallurgical myth and ritual see Max Kaltenmark, *Le Lie-sien tchouan*, pp. 45 sq., 170 sq.

being (or a couple) and metals, is especially important. Morphologically, this theme should belong with the great class of sacrifices of creation whose primal model in the cosmogomic myth I have already described. To ensure the 'marriage of metals' in the smelting process, a living being must 'animate' the operation and the best means of achieving this is by the sacrifice, the transfer of a life. The soul of the victim changes its fleshly envelope: it changes its human body for a new 'body'—a building, an object, even an operation—which it makes alive, or animates. The Chinese evidence which we have just cited seems to suggest that a human sacrifice was necessary for the success of the metallurgical process. Let us carry this enquiry into other cultural areas. We shall see to what extent the sacrifice offered up to the furnaces constitutes an application of the cosmogonic myth and the new values which develop from it.

6

Human Sacrifices to the Furnace

A GROUP of myths associated with certain aboriginal
tribes of central India tells us the story of the Asur smiths.
According to the Birhor, the Asur were the first people on
earth to smelt iron. But the smoke coming from their furnaces
incommoded the Supreme Being, Sing-bonga, who dis-
patched messenger-birds to enjoin them to cease their labours.
The Asur replied that metallurgy was their favourite occupation
and mutilated the messengers. Sing-bonga himself then came
down to earth. He approached the Asur without being recognized and, having persuaded them to enter the furnaces, burned
them. As a sequel, their widows become spirits of Nature.[1]

This myth is found in more complete form among the
Munda. In the beginning, the men worked for Sing-bonga
in the heavens. But the reflection of their faces in the water
revealed that they were similar, and therefore equal, to God,
and they refused to serve him. Sing-bonga then hurled them
down to earth. They came down upon a spot containing
deposits of iron-ore and the men proceeded to build seven
furnaces. The smoke displeased Sing-bonga and after vainly
pleading with them through his messengers, the birds, he
himself descended to earth disguised as a sick old man. It
was not long before the furnaces disintegrated and the smiths,
not having recognized Sing-bonga, asked his advice. His
reply was: 'You have but to offer up a human sacrifice.' And

[1] Sarat Chandra Roy, *The Birhors* (Ranchi, 1925), pp. 402 sq.

as no voluntary victim was forthcoming, Sing-bonga offered himself. He penetrated to the interior of the furnace, which was at white heat, and three days later emerged with gold, silver and precious stones. At the instigation of the god the smiths did likewise. Their wives operated the bellows and the smiths, burning alive, howled inside the furnaces. Sing-bonga reassured the wives; their husbands' cries, he said, were due to the fact that they were dividing out the treasure. The wives continued their task until the smiths had been completely reduced to ashes. And as they then asked what was to become of them, Sing-bonga changed them into *bhut*, spirits of the hills and rocks.[1]

Finally, a similar myth is found among the Oraons. The twelve Asur brothers, and the three Lodha brothers, all famous smiths, irritate Bhagwan (i.e. God) with the smoke of their furnaces. Disguised as a sick old man, Bhagwan comes down to earth, where he is given shelter by a widow, and the smiths, having consulted him for advice regarding the repair of their furnaces, end up, as in the Munda myth, by being burnt alive.[2]

The Asur are a tribe of smiths who probably lived in the northern Punjab, from which they were expelled by Aryan invaders to their present home in the mountains of Chota Nagpur. Walter Ruben has shown the probable links between the Asur and the Asuras of the Vedic hymns, those enemies of the gods (*deva*) with whom they engaged in innumerable combats.[3] The interest attaching to the mythological traditions concerning the Asur smiths will be readily appreciated; these traditions have been preserved by the neighbouring Munda and Dravidian (Oraon) peoples. In this matter we have to emphasize

[1] E. T. Dalton, *Descriptive Ethnology of Bengal* (Calcutta, 1872), pp. 186 sq.
[2] Rev. P. Dehon, 'Religion and Customs of the Uraons' (*Memoirs of the Asiatic Society of Bengal*, Calcutta, 1906, pp. 121–81), pp. 128–31; Cf. also R. Rahmann, 'Gottheiten der Primitivstämme im Nordöstlichen Vorderindien' (*Anthropos*, 31, 1936, pp. 37–96), pp. 52 sq. On the twelve Asur and the thirteen Lodha, see Walter Reuben, Eisenschmiede und Dämonen in Indien (Leiden, 1939), pp. 102 sq.
[3] Cf. Eisenschmiede und Dämonen, pp. 302–3 and *passim*.

above all the motif of human sacrifice associated with metallurgy, a motif barely concealed in the myths we have been examining.

In their present form, these myths are emphatic in their *hatred of iron* and metallurgy. In the eyes of the neighbouring populations the Asur smiths found in the burning coals of their furnaces a death well merited because they had affronted and irritated the supreme God. In this hatred of the work of the smith can be read the same negative and pessimistic attitude which is present, for example, in the theory concerning the ages of the world, where the Iron Age is regarded as at once the most tragic and most debased. We are not precluded from supposing that this attitude has a historical foundation. The Iron Age was characterized by an uninterrupted succession of wars and massacres, by mass slavery and by almost universal impoverishment.[1] In India, as elsewhere, a whole mythology classes iron-workers among the various categories of giants and demons. All are enemies of the gods who represent other ages and other traditions.

But in addition to this hatred of iron, the mythology of the Asur lays down the necessity for offering up sacrifices to the furnaces, for it may be that in the myths we have cited, human sacrifices underline the demoniac character of metallurgical work. The smelting of metal is regarded as a sinister operation requiring the sacrificing of a human life.[2]

Evidence that human sacrifices were made for metallurgical purposes is to be found in Africa. Among the Achewa of Nyasaland, the man who wishes to construct a furnace applies to a magician (*sing-anga*). The latter prepares 'medicines', places them in a stripped maize cob and instructs a small boy how to throw it at a pregnant woman, so causing her to

[1] Walter Ruben, *op. cit.*, pp. 153 sq.
[2] To the same sphere of belief belongs the idea that by killing a human being with smelted metal one becomes master of one's soul, one acquires a sort of 'slave-soul', a 'spiritual robot'; see the example of Batak sorcerers in Eliade, '*Le Chamanisme*', p. 313.

miscarry. The magician then looks for the foetus and burns it, with other medicines, in a hole in the ground.[1] The furnace is then built over the hole. The Atonga have a custom of throwing into the furnace a portion of the placenta to ensure the success of the smelting.[2] Leaving aside for the moment the symbolism of abortion, these two African examples represent an intermediary form between the actual or symbolic human sacrifice (as with nails and hair, for example) and the substitution sacrifice (for example, the sacrifice of hens among the smiths of Tanganyika, see above, p. 61). The idea of mystic links between the human body and metal ores coincides with other customs. Thus, after an accident, the Mandigo of Senegambia abandon the gold-mine for several years: they consider that the body, when decomposing, will determine the position of a rich gold-bearing deposit (Cline, *op. cit.*, p. 12).

These myths, rites and customs presuppose a body of primitive myth which precedes and justifies them[3]: metals derive from the body of a god or from an immolated supernatural being. And these rites are but the more or less symbolic reiteration of the event which, *in illo tempore*, inaugurated a mode of conduct or revealed phases of work—the work of metallurgy demands the imitation of the primordial sacrifice. Following all we have said about the cosmogonic myth (the world, man or plants, which take their birth from the body of a primordial giant), the theme of metals born from the limbs of a divine being appears as a variant of the same

[1] A. G. O. Hodgson, 'Notes on the Achewa and Angoni of the Dowa District of the Nyasaland Protectorate' (*Journ. Roy. Anthr. Inst.*, 63, 1933, 123–64), p. 163.

[2] Cline, *op. cit.*, p. 119.

[3] It is not always a matter of chronological antecedence but rather of an ideal one, implicit in each 'variant' of the central mythical theme. It is possible that a given tradition may never have had the 'consciousness' of the mythic totality from which it derives, all the more so because ideologies move through, and are transmitted, by history and usually a people receives or preserves only fragments of a 'system'. Which is why the meaning of a symbol only emerges clearly after a great number of 'variants' have been examined. These, moreover, are often devoid of historical sequence and thus are extremely difficult to interpret.

central motif. Just as sacrifices to promote harvests reiterate symbolically the self-sacrifice of the supreme being, who, *ab origine*, had rendered possible the appearance of grain, so the sacrifice (actual or symbolic) of a human being during metallurgical operations is intended to imitate a mythical model.

There are indeed several mythical traditions concerning the origin of metals, according to which the metals 'grow' from the body of a god or semi-divine being.[1] In the myth of the dismemberment of Indra, we are told that, intoxicated by an excess of *soma*, the body of the god began to 'flow out', giving birth to every kind of creature, plant and metal. 'From his navel, his life-breath flowed out and became lead, not iron, not silver; from his seed his form flowed out and became gold.' (*Shatapatha Brahmana*, xii, 7, 1, 7). A similar myth is found among the Iranians. When Gayomart, the Primordial Man, was assassinated by the corruptor, 'he allowed his seed to flow to earth. . . . As the body of Gayomart was made of metals, the seven kinds of metal appeared from his body.'[2]

According to the *Zath-sparam*, x, 2, 'when he died, the eight kinds of mineral of metallic nature came forth from his different members, namely, gold, silver, iron, brass, tin, lead, quicksilver, and diamond; and gold, in virtue of its perfection, issued from actual life and from the seed'.[3] We may note

[1] For our purpose, the fact that myths on the origin of metals are attested in cultural areas other than those where human sacrifices for smelting purposes are to be found does not constitute any special difficulty. At this stage of the enquiry we are mainly concerned to bring out the structure of the spiritual universe which is largely lost, submerged or disrupted. We do not intend to reconstruct any particular mythico-ritual pattern. This, in any case, could not be undertaken in the space of a few pages or without a technical erudition which we have been anxious to avoid in the present essay.

[2] The *Great Bundahishn*, trans. A. Christensen, *Le premier homme et le premier roi dans l'histoire légendaire des Iraniens* (Uppsala, 1918), I, p. 22. Cf. also H. H. Schaeder, in R. Reitzenstein and H. H. Schaeder, *Studien zum antiken Synkretismus aus Iran und Griechenland* (Leipzig–Berlin, 1926), pp. 225–9, and especially the note to pages 228–9, where the author discusses the somato-metallic parallels in Iranian traditions.

[3] A. Christensen, *ibid.*, p. 25. Diamond, not being a metal, does not belong to the original series of the seven metals (which no doubt represents a Babylonian influence. Cf. Christensen, p. 52).

here that it is from the seed of Gayomart, previously purified by the rotation of the heavens, that will later be born the first human couple in the form of a rîvâs plant, a theme which sets this Iranian tradition in a complex of myths which is extremely widespread and of great antiquity.

A similar myth was probably shared by the Greeks. P. Roussel had already drawn attention to a Greek proverb, handed down by Zenobius, which would point to the existence of a legend concerning the origin of iron. 'Two brothers put their third brother to death; they bury him beneath a mountain; his body changes to iron.'[1]

Morphologically, all these traditions are branches of the cosmogonic myth which is their original model. But we must not forget that at certain religious levels this cosmogony seems to be identifiable with an embryological symbolism. The creation of the world from the body of a primordial being is sometimes conceived and described in terms of the shaping of a 'foetus'. The cosmos takes shape from a primary matter, 'embryonic' (because formless), and 'chaotic'. We arrive therefore at a series of equivalent or complementary images in which the sacrificed body is compared to primary matter and hence to the germinal mass and the foetus. A like state of affairs seems to be well attested in certain Mesopotamian traditions. The facts we are now about to examine will perhaps allow us to grasp the relationships between the ores regarded as embryos and the sacrifices offered up to the furnaces.

---

[1] P. Roussel, κελμις ἐν σιδμρω, *Revue de Philologie*, 1905, p. 294. Concerning human sacrifices necessary to metallurgy, cf. Plutarch, Parall., 5, 306 sq. The connection between metals and the body of God may likewise be detected in Egyptian traditions. Plutarch and Diodorus tell us that the Egyptians hate iron which they call 'the bones of Seth'. In *De Iside*, ch. 62, Plutarch speaks of 'iron which has come out of Seth'. Haematite was 'the bones of Horus'; cf. Forbes, *Metallurgy in Antiquity*, p. 427. The Egyptians, on the other hand, considered the flesh of the gods as being of gold. But this is another sort of symbolism, the symbolism of Immortality. Gold is the perfect metal, the equivalent of Immortality. That is why, after the model of he Gods, Pharaoh is also assigned a flesh of gold.

7

Babylonian Symbolisms and
Metallurgical Rituals

I N 1925, after the publication by R. Campbell Thompson
of Assyrian chemical texts, R. Eisler produced his hypothesis
concerning the existence of a Babylonian alchemy. He based
it on the term *ku-bu* ('embryo', 'foetus'), which he understood
to refer to the ores arranged in the furnace, symbolically
compared to the matrix. As we have seen, this conception
finds support in a number of traditions. But in Eisler's view
something more was involved. In this Babylonian belief
Eisler thought he had put his finger on the first historical
document concerning the idea of the maturation and perfecting
of metals, and consequently he thought himself in a position
to establish the Mesopotamian origins of alchemy. This
hypothesis seems to have been accepted by Abel Rey but was
rejected by the assyriologist H. Zimmern and the historians of
chemistry Ernst Darmstaedter and Julius Ruska. The doyen
of the historians of alchemy, E. von Lipmann, took up a
neutral position.[1]

I give now the main text (from the library of Assurbanipal)
which follows the English translation made by R. Campbell
Thompson, and after comparison with the German of Zimmern and the French of Eisler.

[1] See the bibliography of the controversy in Note H.

71

'When thou settest out the [ground] plan of a furnace for "minerals" [ku-bu], thou shalt seek out a favourable day in a fortunate month, and thou shalt set out the [ground] plan of the furnace. While they are making the furnace, thou shalt watch [them] and thou shalt work thyself [?] [in the house of the furnace]: thou shalt bring in embryos [born before time . . ,][1], another [?], a stranger, shall not enter, nor shall one that is unclean tread before them; thou shalt offer the due libations before them: the day when thou puttest the mineral into the furnace, thou shalt make a sacrifice before the embryos[2]; thou shalt set a censer with incense of pine, thou shalt pour *kurunnu*-beer before them.

Thou shalt kindle a fire underneath the furnace and thou shalt put the "mineral" into the furnace. The men whom thou shalt bring to be over the furnace shall cleanse themselves and [then] thou shalt set them to be over the furnace. The wood which thou shalt burn underneath the furnace shall be of styrax [*sarbatu*], thick, decorticated billets which have not lain [exposed] in bundles, [but] have been kept in leather coverings, cut in the month of Ab. This wood shall go underneath thy furnace.'

Despite any subsequent variants and emendations, the ritual nature of the text seems to be beyond doubt. As was to be expected, in Mesopotamia too, metallurgical operations consisted of a series of liturgical acts. A propitious month and day were selected, the furnace area was consecrated, the uninitiated were barred from entering, the workmen were

---

[1] The text is obscure. I have followed Thompson's translation. Meissner translates the passage with question marks: 'While one looks at (?) the furnace and while one makes it, you must count (?) the (divine) embryos'. In his French version, Eisler seems to have avoided the difficulties: 'As soon as one has placed the oven in proper direction and you have commenced the work, place the divine "embryos" in the vault of the oven.'

[2] 'An ordinary sacrifice' (Eisler); 'sacrifice' (Meissner).

cleansed, libations were offered up to the ores and these were followed by sacrifices. A special wood was found for the fire (wood stripped of bark and kept in an envelope of skin— which might well betray a 'magic sympathy' with the 'embryos'). One has only to think of the African smiths (see pp. 55, 56 sq.) to appreciate to what extent metallurgical operations are steeped in an atmosphere of sanctity. There are even African parallels with the Mesopotamian text which we have just quoted. The Ushi smiths sacrifice hens[1] to the furnaces; the Bakitara immolate a sheep and a hen on the anvil (Cline, *op. cit.*, p. 118). The custom of placing 'medicines' in the furnace is widespread. Libations of beer are likewise common; among the Baila, the first ritual performed in the smelting process consists of pouring beer mixed with 'remedies' in the four holes made under the furnace.

There has been some controversy over the meaning of the term *ku-bu*, 'embryo'. Another text, published and trans-lated by Campbell Thompson, prescribes the following recipe: 'Take out the embryos, offer up a sacrifice, make sacrifices [for the dead], for the workmen; gather up the rest [?] in a mould, place [it] in a furnace.' Robert Eisler translates *ku-bu* as 'divine embryos', Thureau-Dangin as 'a sort of demon',[2] Zimmern as 'abortion'.[3] Julius Ruska thinks that the term has to do, not with 'embryos', but with 'fetishes' or 'protectors of the work of smelting'. The problem is therefore one of knowing whether *ku-bu* refers to the ores placed in the furnaces, or whether it designates certain spirits or even abortions which, by virtue of their magical qualities, are indispensable to the metal-work. We do not have to take sides in this controversy on Mesopotamian philology. We think,

[1] Cline, *op. cit.*, p. 119.
[2] Thureau-Dangin 'Notes assyriologiques', XXX (*Revue d'Assyriologie*, 19, 1922), p. 81.
[3] H. Zimmern, 'Assyrische chemish-technische Rezepte', p. 180: *Fehlgeburt, Missgeburt*.

however, that whatever the rendering suggested for *ku-bu*, it will always have an implied 'embryological significance'. Thureau-Dangin recalls that in the account of the creation (*Enuma elish*, IV, 136, line 3), '*ku-bu* designates the monstrous body of Tiamat likened to a foetus, whose demiurge is preparing to shape the world' (*op. cit.*, p. 82). In texts dealing with metallurgy *ku-bu* may therefore mean ores, the primal 'embryonic' material which will take shape in the furnaces. The palaeo-oriental parallels, mentioned above, between the mine and the uterus, would confirm this interpretation. If Eisler is correct in translating *ku-bu* as 'ores' in the sense of 'embryos', the furnace was felt to be a matrix, a substitute for the Earth-Mother, where the ores completed their process of maturation. The sacrifices performed on these occasions would then be comparable to obstetric sacrifices.

The other interpretation (*ku-bu* referring to human embryos) also finds a counterpart in metallurgical rituals. We have seen that in black Africa of today, the sorcerer brings on an abortion in order to make use of the foetus for the success of fusion.[1] This behaviour also suggests the, as it were, magical comparison of ores with embryos. For this savage rite could have only two 'theoretical justifications': (1) either the foetus transfers its entire reserves of life to the metallurgical operation in order thereby to ensure its successful outcome or (2) it precipitates the 'birth' of the metal in the furnaces, bringing it to birth before its due time and in its own image. In the first case, the choice of an 'embryo' rather than an adult (or in its place, an animal victim) suggests that the Achewa smiths felt obscurely that there was a parallel between the crude ore and the foetus. In the second case, the obstetric function of metallurgy is obvious: the fusion (smelting)—

---

[1] J. Ruska, 'Kritisches zu R. Eisler's chemie-geschichtlicher Methode', p. 275: *Fetische oder Schutzpatrone der Schmelzarbeit.*

hence the 'maturation' of the metal—is a birth before its time, and hence the magical role of the 'embryos'.

In both hypotheses, it is clear that the metallurgists were more or less aware that their art expedited the growth of metals. This idea, as we have seen, was widespread. Metals 'grow' in the belly of the earth. And, as the peasants of Tonkin still hold today, if bronze were to remain buried for the required time, it would become gold. To sum up: in the symbols and rites accompanying metallurgical operations there comes into being the idea of an active collaboration of man and nature, perhaps even the belief that man, by his own work, is capable of superseding the processes of nature.

The act, *par excellence,* of the cosmogony, starting from a living primal material, was sometimes thought of as a cosmic embryology: the body of Tiamat was, in the hands of Marduk, a foetus. And as all creation and all construction reproduced the cosmogonic model, man, in constructing or creating, imitated the work of the demiurge.

But where cosmogonic symbols were presented in an embryological context, the creation of objects was equivalent to a childbirth. All creation starting from chthonian living matter (in our example—ores) acquired an obstetric significance. It was an intervention in the process of growth, an attempt to expedite maturation or to induce the expulsion of the embryo. That is why the work of the metallurgist could be looked upon as an obstetric operation, performed before its due time, an abortion, in fact.

It was from such ritual experiences, taken in conjunction with metallurgical and agricultural techniques, that gradually there clearly emerged the idea that man can intervene in the cosmic rhythm, that he can anticipate a natural outcome, precipitate a birth.

These ideas were not, of course, clearly formulated, but

Accipe ovum & igneo percute gladio.

EPIGRAMMA VIII.

Est avis in mundo sublimior omnibus, Ovum
Cujus ut inquiras, cura sit una tibi.
Albumen luteum circumdat molle vitellum,
Ignito (ceu mos) cautus id ense petas:
Vulcano Mars addat opem: pullaster & inde
Exortus, ferri victor & ignis erit.

Michaël Maier, *Scrutinium chymicum* (Frankfurt 1867)

The Philosopher's Egg under the test of fire

Hic est Draco caudam suam devorans.

EPIGRAMMA XIV.

Dira fames Polypos docuit sua rodere crura,
   Humanaque homines se nutriisse dape.
Dente Draco caudam dum mordet & ingerit alvo,
   Magnâ parte sui fit cibus ipse sibi.
Ille domandus erit ferro, fame, carcere, donec
   Se voret & revomat, se necet & pariat.

Michaël Maier, *Scrutinium chymicum*

'The Dragon devouring his tail'

were more in the nature of presentiments, divinations. Nevertheless, that was the point of departure for the great discovery that man can take upon himself the work of Time, an idea which we have seen clearly expressed in later Western texts (see p. 47 sq.). Here, too, if we may repeat ourselves, lies the basis and justification of the alchemical operation, the *opus alchymicum* which haunted the philosophic imagination for more than two thousand years: the idea of the transmutation of man and the Cosmos by means of the Philosopher's Stone. On the mineral level of existence, the Stone was realizing this miracle: it eliminated the interval of time which separated the present condition of an 'imperfect' (crude) metal from its final condition (when it would become gold). The Stone achieved transmutation almost instantaneously: it superseded Time.

8

'Masters of Fire'

THE alchemist, like the smith, and like the potter before him, is a 'master of fire'. It is with fire that he controls the passage of matter from one state to another. The first potter who, with the aid of live embers, was successful in hardening those shapes which he had given to his clay, must have felt the intoxication of the demiurge: he had discovered a transmuting agent. That which natural heat—from the sun or the bowels of the earth—took so long to ripen, was transformed by fire at a speed hitherto undreamed of. This demiurgic enthusiasm springs from that obscure presentiment that the great secret lay in discovering how to 'perform' faster than Nature, in other words (since it is always necessary to talk in terms of the spiritual experience of primitive man) how, without peril, to interfere in the processes of the cosmic forces. Fire turned out to be the means by which man could 'execute' faster, but it could also do something other than what already existed in Nature. It was therefore the manifestation of a magico-religious power which could modify the world and which, consequently, did not belong to this world. This is why the most primitive cultures look upon the specialist in the sacred—the shaman, the medicine-man, the magician— as a 'master of fire'. Primitive magic and shamanism both carry the notion of 'mastery over fire', whether it is a question of involving the power to touch live coals with impunity or of

79

producing that 'inner heat' which permitted resistance to extreme cold.

Here we can only touch on a rather complex problem which we have investigated elsewhere.[1] We may note, however, that to produce fire in one's own body is a sign that one has transcended the human condition. According to the myths of certain primitive peoples, the aged women* of the tribe 'naturally' possessed fire in their genital organs and made use of it to do their cooking but kept it hidden from men, who were able to get possession of it only by trickery.[2] These myths reflect the ideology of a matriarchal society and remind us, also, of the fact that fire, being produced by the friction of two pieces of wood (that is, by their 'sexual union'), was regarded as existing naturally in the piece which represented the female. In this sort of culture woman symbolizes the natural sorceress. But men finally achieved 'mastery' over fire and in the end the sorcerers became more powerful and more numerous than their female counterparts. In Dobu the aboriginals believe that both male and female magicians fly by night and traces of the fire which they leave behind them can be seen.[3]

Primitive peoples are universally known to have conceived the magico-religious power as something 'burning' and express it in terms signifying 'heat', 'very hot', 'burns', etc. This is why magicians and sorcerers drink salt or peppered water and eat exceedingly piquant plants; in this way they seek to increase their 'inner heat'.

[1] See Eliade, *Le Chamanisme et las techniques archaiques de L'extase*, from which most of the following examples are taken.

* A woman of an older generation (Goga). See Sir James Frazer, *Myths on the Origin of Fire*, Macmillan, 1930, p. 43 (Translator's note).

[2] Cf. Sir James Frazer, *Myths of the Origin of Fire* (London, 1930), pp. 5 sq. (Australia), 25 sq. (New Guinea), 48 sq. (Trobriand), 83 (Marquesas Islands), 123 sq. (South America), etc.

[3] *Le Chamanisme*, p. 327, after R. F. Fortune, *Sorcerers of Dobu* (London, 1932), pp. 150 sq.

As 'masters of fire', shamans and sorcerers swallow burning coal, handle red-hot iron and walk on fire. On the other hand, they have great resistance to cold; shamans in the Arctic regions as well as the ascetics in the Himalayas, thanks to their magic heat, show an incredible resistance.[1] The true significance of this magic heat and of the 'mastery over fire' is not difficult to divine. These powers indicate access to a certain ecstatic state or, on another cultural plane (in India, for example), to an unconditioned state of perfect spiritual freedom. The mastery over fire and insensibility both to extreme cold and to the temperature of burning coals, translated into ordinary terms, signify that the shaman or yogi have gone beyond the human condition and have achieved the level of spirits.

Like the shamans, the smiths were reputed to be 'masters of fire'. And so in certain cultures, the smith is considered equal, if not superior, to the shaman. 'Smiths and shamans come from the same nest', says a Yakut proverb. 'The wife of a shaman is worthy of respect, the wife of a smith worthy of veneration', says another.[2] And a third: 'The first smith, the first shaman and the first potter were blood brothers. The smith was the eldest and the shaman came in between. This explains why the shaman cannot bring about the death of a smith.'[3] According to the Dolganes, the shaman cannot 'swallow' the soul of a smith because the latter protects it with fire; but on the other hand, it is possible for the smith to get possession of the soul of a shaman and to burn it in fire.[4] According to the myths of the Yakut, the smith received his trade from the 'evil' deity, K'daai Maqsin, the

---

[1] *Le Chamanisme*, pp. 233, 327, 386 sq., 412 sq.
[2] Id., p. 408.
[3] A. Popov, 'Consecration ritual for a blacksmith novice among the Yakuts (*Journal of American Folklore*, 46, 1933, pp. 257–71), p. 257.
[4] A. Popov, *ibid.*, p. 258., Eliade, *Le Chamanisme*, p. 409.

Master-Smith of Hell. He dwells in a house made of iron, surrounded by splinters of fire. K'daai Maqsin is a master of great renown; it is he who mends the broken or amputated limbs of heroes; sometimes he participates in the initiation of celebrated shamans from the next world: he tempers their souls as he tempers iron.[1]

According to another tradition, the ancestor of the Yakut, Elliei, was the first smith. Another mythical smith, Chyky, was the counsellor of warriors: he forged their arms and also gave them sage advice. The Yakut attribute to the smiths the power to heal by natural means and, unlike the shamans, without the assistance of spirits. Down to the ninth generation, a smith has supernatural powers at his command; he has no fear of spirits, which is why he dares to forge the objects of iron which adorn the shaman's costume (for the noise of iron keeps away evil spirits).[2]

Among all Siberian populations the smith has quite a high social standing; his craft is not looked upon as a commercial one; his is a vocation, something handed down from father to son and implying the possession of initiatory secrets. The smiths are under the protection of special spirits. In Shignan and other regions of Pamir the smith's art is regarded as a gift from 'the prophet David', which is why the smith receives greater respect than the *mullah*. But he must be clean, both physically and spiritually. The smithy is venerated as a place of worship, and where there is no special house for prayers or assemblies, people foregather at the smithy.[3]

The 'prophet David' obviously came to be substituted for some celestial god or primitive civilizing hero. This emerges clearly from the Buriat beliefs. According to the Buriat, in early times when men had not learnt the use of

[1] A. Popov, pp. 260–1, Eliade, *op. cit.*, p. 409.

[2] W. Jochelson, *The Yakut* (1931), pp. 172 sq.

[3] Jochelson, *ibid.*, after J. Sarubin.

iron, they slaughtered their beasts with stones, ate the meat, by tearing it with their teeth, dressed as best they could with animals' skins and so on. Then the white Tängri (the good gods) sent down to earth Boshintoj, the heavenly smith, together with his daughter and nine sons, so that they might teach human beings the benefits of metallurgy. Another legend has it that the sons of Boshintoj married earthly maidens and thereby became ancestors of smiths. Nobody can become a smith unless he is descended from one of these families. The Buriates likewise know of 'black smiths', in the same way as they divide their pantheon into 'white' and 'black' gods. Their shamans, too, are divided into black and white (good and bad). The 'black' smiths, who are under the protection of evil spirits, are held in special dread by the people; they are capable of 'eating' men's souls. During ceremonials they smear their faces with soot.

Gods and guardian spirits of the Buriate smiths are not content merely to assist them in their work but defend them against evil spirits. The smiths have special rites. They sacrifice a horse, open its belly, and tear out its heart—a specifically shamanic rite. The soul of the horse will later rejoin the celestial smith, Boshintoj. Nine young men play the role of Boshintoj's nine sons, and one man, incarnating the heavenly smith himself, falls into a state of ecstasy and recites a lengthy monologue in which he reveals how he *in illo tempore* sent his sons down to earth to civilize its human inhabitants. Then he touches the fire with his tongue. In the ancient custom the person representing Boshintoj would take in his hands a piece of iron that was being smelted[1]—as do today the shamans of Siberia and North America.

The identification of shamanism with the art of the smith likewise appears in the ceremonial spectacles of certain

[1] Eliade, *op. cit.*, pp. 409–10, after Sandschejew.

shamanic initiations. In their dreams or initiatory hallucinations
the future shamans watch themselves being torn to pieces by
the 'demon'-masters of the initiation. Now these traditional
spectacles entail, directly or otherwise, gestures, tools and
symbols belonging to the sphere of the smith. During his
initiatory sickness, a Yakut shaman has looked on as his own
limbs have been detached and separated with an iron hook by
demons; after all kinds of operations (cleansing of bones,
scraping of flesh, etc.), the demons have reassembled the bones
and joined them with iron. Another shaman has had his body
cut into small pieces by the Mother Bird of Prey who possessed
an iron beak, hooked claws and iron feathers. Another, also
during his initiatory hallucinations, has been rocked in an
iron cradle. And finally, from a long autobiographical account
by an Ava-Samoyede shaman, we extract this episode. The
future shaman, during his initiation sickness, saw himself
penetrate to the interior of a mountain where he beheld a
naked man operating a bellows. On the fire was a cauldron.
The naked man seized the shaman with an enormous pair of
tongs, cut off his head, sliced his body into small fragments
and threw the whole lot into the cauldron, where it was left
to cook for three years. In the cave there were also three
anvils and the naked man forged his head on the third anvil,
the one reserved for the best shamans. Finally he rescued his
bones, reassembled them and covered them with flesh. According to another source, a Tungus shaman, during initiation,
had his head cut off and forged with metal pieces.[1] It is also
worth remembering that the shamanic costume is loaded with
iron objects, some of them being imitations of bones and
tending to give him the appearance of a skeleton (see my
Chamanisme, pp. 143 sq., 152 sq.).

From all that has been said, it would appear that the

---

[1] Eliade, *op. cit.*, pp. 48 sq., after G. W. Ksenofontov and A. Popov.

presence of iron in the body of the shaman plays a role which is to a certain extent similar to that of the crystals or other 'magic' stones among the medicine-men in Australia, Oceania and South America. It is known that the rock crystals with which he is fed, allow the Australian or Oceanian shaman to see spirits and souls, to fly in the air, etc., for he has assimilated in himself the celestial sacredness of the crystals which have fallen from the heavenly vault (see above, pp. 19 sq.). A similar identification, this time with iron, can be discerned in certain Siberian shamanisms.[1] This is not without significance; since iron is the preserve of the smith he thereby increases his magico-religious prestige. We have seen that the common origins of the sacredness of shamans and smiths is shown in their 'mastery over fire'. In theoretical terms, this 'mastery' signifies the attainment of a state superior to the human condition. What is more, it is the smith who creates weapons for heroes. It is not their material creation that matters but the magic with which they are invested; the smith's mysterious art transforms them into magic tools. Hence the relationship, described in the epic writings, between smiths and heroes. F. Altheim observes that in the epic songs of almost all Mongolian tribes (and among the Turks too) the word for 'smith' (*darkhan*) signifies both 'hero' and 'free-horseman'.[2] The same writer stresses the military importance of the shamanic costume and drum, the former being a kind of metal breastplate. Smiths sometimes rise to the level of royalty. According to certain accounts, Gengiz Khan was originally a simple smith; and the tribal legends of the Mongols link the smith's craft with the royal household.[3] In the Iranian tradition the Kavi smith was the ancestor of the Kavya

---

[1] It is not necessarily primitive relationships that are involved here, for in other cases of shamanism (American, Oceanian), iron does not play an important part.

[2] F. Altheim, *Attila* (French trans., Paris, 1952), p. 33.

[3] F. Altheim, *ibid.*, p. 128, after d'Ohsson and Sandschejew.

dynasty; one day he 'had fixed his leather apron to the end of a lance and in this way had raised the standard of revolt against the dragon-king. The simple skin apron became the royal banner of Iran.'[1]

Let us bear in mind this group of identifications: 'masters of fire', shamans, smiths, heroes, mythical kings (founders of dynasties). We shall return later to certain relationships between 'magic heat', heroic and military initiation and the smith. For the moment let us examine the religious and social status of the smith in other cultural areas.

[1] Altheim, *ibid.* The word *kavay* also means 'wise', *ibid.*, p. 126. Snorri relates that King Inge owed his origin to a 'smith's hut'; cf. H. Ohlhaver, *Der Germanische Schmied* (Leipzig, 1939), p. 13.

9

Divine Smiths and Civilizing Heroes

Nowadays the smith in Java is a poor and humble man but there are indications that he still enjoys a privileged position. He is called *pande* (expert) if he is a smith, and *empu* or *kyai* (lord, master) when he is an armourer. But in ancient Java metal smelting was a mysterious operation and a whole literature was woven around the figure of the *kris*-smith who was often honoured like a prince. It is not long since they occupied positions of honour at the court, and under certain circumstances could represent the entire community. In ancient Java the relationship between prince and smith was comparable to that existing between brothers. Their genealogy, like that of princes, goes back to the gods. Even nowadays when a *kris* is to be forged by the armourer, the workshop is decorated like a *kayon* or sacred enclosure. The offerings brought before the commencement of the work are comparable to those presented at circumcision or marriage ceremonies.[1] In Bali there are initiation rites for apprentice smiths and during their work *mantra* are uttered before each tool is used. The *pande-wesi* of Bali possess a written tradition which tells of their creation through the intercession of Brahma, who endowed them with the *shakti*, the mystic force necessary to their trade.[2]

[1] R. J. Forbes, *Metallurgy in Antiquity*, pp. 79–80, after W. H. Rassers.
[2] Forbes, *op. cit.*, p. 65, after R. Goris and P. de Kat Angelino. The majority of the Bali smiths came from Java in the fifteenth century.

By ruling out recent Hindu influences (*mantra*, Brahman, *shakti*) it is possible to sort out the complicated background of the Indonesian smith—the myth of divine descent, the traditional or written transmission of genealogies (the beginnings, as it were, of epic poems), the sacred nature of their craft and the initiation rites, their mystic fraternity with kings and their privileged social status. Most of these specific points have attracted our attention to the mythico-ritual complex of the Siberian and central-Asiatic smith. This information concerning the written genealogies should be noted, for these presuppose the existence of a long oral tradition. To know and to be able to recite these genealogies would be the work of both the poet and the shaman-priest. This relationship between shamans, heroes and smiths is strongly supported in the epic poetry of central Asia. Karl Meuli, after showing the shamanic structure of certain Greek epic themes, has very aptly thrown light on the identification of the smith with the shaman-heroes of the Finnish *Kalewala*.[1] Certain aspects of this kinship between the craft of the smith and epic poetry are perceptible even today in the Near East and Eastern Europe where smiths and Tzigane tinkers are usually bards, singers or genealogists.[2] We cannot dwell at this point on this complex and fascinating problem, which would indeed require quite a lengthy exposition. It is, however, important to point out that the smith, in virtue of the sacred character of his craft, the mythologies and genealogies of which he is the keeper, and his association with the shaman and the warrior, has come to play a significant part in the creation and diffusion of epic poetry.

As early as the year 1880 or thereabouts, Richard Andrée,

---

[1] Karl Meuli, 'Scythica' (*Hermes*, 70, 1935, 121–76), p. 175. On the link between smiths, sorcerers and poets, cf. too H. Ohlhaver, *Der germanische schmied und seine Werkzeug*, pp. 95 sq.

[2] Cf. R. Eisler, *Das Qainzeichen*, p. 111.

with the documents which were available to him at the time, had succeeded in showing that metal workers, almost everywhere, form groups apart; they are mysterious beings who must be isolated from the rest of the community.[1] Hardly anything is known about the social position or the magico-religious function of the smith in pre-Columbian America (cf. Forbes, *op. cit.*, p. 68). Among the tribes of north-west America he enjoys a privileged position and the secret traditions of his trade are passed on solely to members of the family.[2] In Africa, however, the situation is much clearer, thanks to the work of Walter Cline and the Griaule Mission.[3] In 1936 Cline drew from his researches the following conclusions:

(1) on the grassy plains of eastern North Africa, smiths are a lowly caste and their work has no clearly marked ritual;

(2) in West Africa, on the other hand, the smiths are closely associated with secret societies, enjoy the prestige normally accorded to magicians and form separate clans;

(3) in the Congo and surrounding regions the smiths are grouped in guilds, are in close association with priests and chiefs (sometimes being one and the same person) and the work of the smithy is a ritual backed by all the paraphernalia of spirits and remedies. Still following Cline, we must add to this picture the fact that the whole of the black continent is acquainted with the magico-ritual complex of the smith— his initiation secrets, sexual taboos, the personification of the hammer and anvil and the whole hereditary pattern of the profession.

Outside of these guilds of non-mobile smiths there are also the itinerant smiths who have a reputation as potent

[1] R. Andrée, *Ethnographische Parallelen und Vergleiche*, p. 153; id., *Die Metalle bei den Naturvölkern*, pp. 42 sq.

[2] R. Andrée, *Die Metalle bei Naturvölkern*, pp. 136 sq.

[3] See the works mentioned below, notes 14–17. Cf. too M. D. W. Jeffries, 'Stone Age Smiths' (*Archiv f. Völkerkunde*, III, 1948, pp. 1–8).

magicians (cf. Forbes, p. 64). And although the Baris of the White Nile regard the itinerant smiths as pariahs,[1] the Balolo of the Congo pay them great respect and even credit them with royal or aristocratic ancestry.[2]

The explanation for this ambivalence in the profession of the coloured smith is to be found, partly at least, in the cultural history of Africa. As Herman Baumann has shown,[3] the palaeo-nigritian civilization (embracing the northern Congo, the upper Nile as far as Abyssinia, the south and centre of East Africa) represents the true iron civilization of Africa and it is in the heart of this region that the smith is held in the highest esteem and plays an important role. The mythical smith is believed to have brought with him the tools necessary for the cultivation of the soil and thereby became a 'civilizing hero', a collaborator in the divine work of creation. The smith is tied to the sacred earth, as are potters and the women who dig the earth in search of gold; and in more than one place (for example, in the area of the upper Niger) the wives of smiths are the potters of the tribe (Baumann, *op. cit.*, p. 498).

By contrast, in the pastoral Hamitic civilization and that of the steppe hunters, the smiths are despised and form a caste apart. The iron and tools forged by him do not have the civilizing role accorded to them in palaeo-nigritian cultures. This applies, among others, to the Abyssinians, the Somalis (where the Toumal smiths constitute a caste of untouchables), and the Teda (north of the Tchad, mainly in central Sahara), among whom the smiths were disdained and form a caste of endogamous pariahs (Baumann, pp. 283, 431). The Wa-Ndorobos (Hamitic inhabitants of the Nile Valley, hunters) likewise hold the smith in disdain; he has no legal rights in the

---

[1] R. Andrée, *Die Metalle*, pp. 9, 42.

[2] Cline, *op. cit.*, p. 22.

[3] H. Baumann and D. Westermann, *Les peuples et les civilisations de l'Afrique* (trans. by L. Homburger, Paris, 1948).

community and may be put to death by his superiors (Cline, p. 114). Their neighbours, the Massaïs (Hamitic inhabitants of the Nile Valley nomads, cattle-raisers), leave the work of iron-smelting and operations in the smithy to the Il-Konnonos, a caste held in great contempt (Baumann, p. 259). In the creed of the Massaï, 'the vicinity of the smith's *kraal* may bring death, disease or various other misfortunes to other kraals. Cohabitation with a woman belonging to a smith caste will cause a man to lose his reason, to beget infirm children, or may result in his death in a future raid. *Ol kononi* ("smith") is a term of abuse when applied to a non-smith; to utter this name after sunset is to invite the nocturnal attacks of lions or human enemies. The craft of the smith is an unclean one' (Cline, p. 114).

Let us now glance at the African populations where the smith is held in high honour. Among the Wa Tchaggas (Hamitic Bantu, agricultural workers), the smith is both feared and respected. But as far as marriage is concerned, however, the picture has its dark side. 'One does not willingly give one's daughter in marriage to a smith, for in case of divorce she exposes herself to great peril. If divorce is unavoidable, the smith can immunize his wife by rubbing her body with butter in the presence of his mother or other female witness—recalling the method used by the Massaï to remove contamination from the smith by a new iron object—and by handing her a stick before pronouncing the divorce.'[1] A very special power resides in the hammer. Before beginning to forge one, the smith receives from his client a goat and a certain quantity of beer. It is primarily thanks to his hammer that he can magically strike a thief or a personal enemy.[2] Generally speaking, the smiths do not place their powers at

[1] Cline, *op. cit.*, p. 115; B. Guttmann, 'Der Schmied und seine Kunst im animistischen Denken' (*Zeitsch. f. Ethnologie*, 44, 1912, pp. 81–93), p. 89.

[2] B. Guttmann, *op. cit.*, pp. 83 sq.

the service of black magic and many are even renowned as beneficent shamans. Iron makes amulets effective and is, in addition, an excellent medicament. Women of the western Wa tchaggas wear iron rings around their necks and arms, for these objects are held to confer fertility and to cure sick children.

Among the people of the Katanga (southern Congo) those who work in metals constitute a secret religious society (*bwanga*), having specific rites of worship and initiation (Cline, p. 119). The master-smelter among the BaYeke (a Nyamwezi tribe in the southern Congo) works with a shaman. Among the Balla (agricultural workers, Zambesi) the 'iron doctor' supervises smelting operations (Cline, *ibid.*, p. 120). In the southern Congo the smiths form a hereditary guild 'whose members enjoy a social status equal to that of the shamans and are under the control of masters who bear the name *ocim banda* [witch-doctor] or *ocivinda* [smith]' (Cline, p. 122). Among the Mosengere and BaSakata (southern Congo) the master-smith is generally the founder of the village and his craft is hereditary (*ibid.*, p. 124). This plurality of functions—smith and tribal head—is well attested among a number of other groups in the Congo region: in the upper Ogowe, where the smiths are always sorcerers and often chiefs; in the Loango, where the sacred national fire is in the care of a smith-priest; among the BaSongués, where the smiths come immediately below the chiefs in the hierarchy; among the Baholoholo, where they come immediately after the chiefs and hunters and above the lieutenants of the chief and the shamans', etc. (Cline, p. 125). The Tiv of northern Nigeria attribute to iron the power of ensuring communication between the quick and the dead; they believe, too, that iron tools contribute the magical power, which permeates the smithy and manifests itself in the thunderbolt (*ibid.*, p. 126).

The privileged status of the African smith and his religious function are chiefly explained in the cosmogonic myths and the myths on origins. Thanks to Marcel Griaule and his collaborators, there is now available an ample documentation concerning the mythology of the First Smith among the Dogons (Volta area) and the Bambara (upper Niger). Among the Dogons, the profession of smith is highly esteemed and his tools have an important place in the cult. The First Smith occupies an essential place in mythology. From the supreme deity, Amma, he received specimens of the main cultivable grains which he placed inside his sledge-hammer; then he suspended himself to the end of an iron chain and God sent him down to earth. According to another variant, the smiths at first dwelt in the sky and worked for Amma.[1] But one of them, having stolen the millet from God and concealed it in his sledgehammer, Amma sent him down to earth. When he made contact with the earth he became unclean and consequently unworthy of reascending to heaven. A third variant, the most complete one, tells us that the Ancestor Smith built in heaven a granary divided into eight compartments representing the principal organs of man: in each one he placed one of the eight cultivable grains. This granary, built of celestial earth, was afterwards brought down to earth by the First Smith, where, as it dispersed, it became the primordial pure field around which humanity later became organized.[2] It was also the celestial First Smith who invented fire and taught man agriculture and the domestication of animals.[3]

[1] The correspondence between the dogon myth and the Munda and Buriat myths relative to the first celestial smiths is to be noted; see above, pp. 65 sq., 83.

[2] For the different versions of the myth, see Marcel Griaule, *Masques Dogons* (Paris, 1938), p. 48; id., *Dieu d'eau* (1949), pp. 52 sq. id., 'Descente du troisième verbe' (*Psyche*, 13–14, 1947), pp. 13–36 sq. G. Dieterlen and S. de Ganay, 'Le Génie des Eaux chez les Dogons' (*Miscellanea Africana*, V. Paris, 1942), pp. 6 sq. Harry Tegnaeus, *Le Héros Civilisateur, Contribution à l'étude ethnologique de la religion et de la sociologie Africaines* (Uppsala, 1950), pp. 16 sq.

[3] Griaule, *Masques Dogons*, p. 49; id., Descente du troisieme verbe, pp. 13–35 sq. Dieterlen and de Ganay, *Le Génie des eaux*, p. 7; H. Tegnaeus, *op. cit.*, pp. 18 sq.

According to other myths, the Civilizing Hero of the Dogons, the Guardian-Counsellor Nommo, transformed himself into a smith and came down to earth to reveal civilization to mankind. In the heavens the activities of Nommo are visible during storms: like Däntsien Sân des T'oujen (see above, p. 30), he hurls thunderbolts and strikes the earth with stones of thunder.[1]

This linking of the celestial Smith with Civilizing Hero, with agriculture and with the Smith in his religious role, is not exclusive to the Dogons. It is found, more or less complete, among the Sawadogo (Tegnaeus, p. 35); among the Gourounsi (First Smith = Civilizing Hero; the smith performs the function of priest of fire and thunderbolt; *ibid.*, p. 40); among the Bolos, one of the most primitive populations in the Volta (according to the myths, the First Smith, son of the supreme God, came down to earth and revealed to humans the use of fire, the domestication of animals and agriculture; the smith plays an important part in religious and social life—he is the master-instructor in initiation ceremonies, he is prophet and divine, etc., Tegnaeus, pp. 42 sq.); and among the Somons, Bambara fishermen (a cosmogonic myth attributes to the primordial smith the role of collaborator in creation; 'the sacrificer in the worship of the guardian spirit of water must belong to a family whose ancestors were smiths descended from Heaven', Tegnaeus, p. 47). Among the Bambara the high priest is almost always a smith and secret societies are generally controlled by smiths. The same situation, according to Tauxier, exists among the other Mandés, Malinkés, Ouassoulonkés, etc.[2] According to an Achanti myth, the smith came down to earth enjoined by God to fashion two dozen men and animals (Tegnaeus, p. 55).

---

[1] Griaule, *op. cit.*, p. 157; id. *Dieu d'eau*, pp. 130 sq. H. Tegnaeus, pp. 20 sq.

[2] Tegnaeus, p. 47; L. Tauxier, *Histoire des Bambara* (Paris, 1942), pp. 276 sq. G. Dieterlen, *Essai sur la religion Bambara* (Paris, 1951), pp. 143 sq.

Among the Ewés the smith and his tools play a considerable part in religious life. The hammer and anvil are believed to have fallen from heaven and it is in their presence that the oath is taken. The smith is a rain-maker and can bring a war to a successful conclusion. According to the myths, the First Smith—sometimes regarded as the true Son of the Supreme God—was sent by God to complete the creation, and to impart the trade-secrets to men.[1] Among the Yoruba, it was Ogun, the First Smith, who forged the first weapons, taught hunting and founded the secret society of Ogboni (Tegnaeus, pp. 82 sq.). Nzeanzo, the Civilizing Hero of the Mboulas, was at once smith, doctor and counsellor. He taught all useful techniques and inaugurated the guilds of smiths (*ibid.*, p. 102). Among the Tchamba, the Daka, the Dourrou and other neighbouring tribes, the mythology of the Smith-Civilizing Hero is extremely rich. The First Smith revealed not only fire and the means of preparing food by cooking but also the art of building houses, the sexual behaviour necessary for procreation, the technique of giving birth, circumcision, forms of burial, etc., etc. (*ibid.*, p. 105). The mythology of the Kikuyu introduces three brothers, all Civilizing Heroes. The first one taught the domestication of cattle, the second agriculture, and the third the art of forging metals (*ibid.*, pp. 142 sq.). To conclude this brief survey, let us recall that the first King of Angola was, according to tradition, the Smith King (Tegnaeus, p. 172).

All the entire mass of palaeo-nigritian culture bears witness to a whole complex of religious activities concerning the smith, whose ideological foundations are to be found in the myth of the Celestial Smith and the Civilizing Hero. It would nevertheless be an error to explain this ritual significance of

---

[1] There are a multitude of myths including the inevitable variants, especially those concerning the traditions of the western and eastern Ewés. We have summed up the essential argument, following Tegnaeus, *Le Héros Civilisateur*, pp. 61–3.

the smith solely on the basis of his role in the making of agricultural tools. Neither iron itself nor the smith is necessarily exalted in agricultural civilizations. An agricultural civilization such as that of the Slavs, which is agricultural *par excellence*, uses iron for apotropaic purposes only. Despite the vicinity of two of the most ancient metallurgical centres of the earth (Tauric and Jenissian), the Slavs have a material culture in which metals play no part at all.[1]

In order, therefore, to understand the function of the smith, we must turn to the religious myths and ideologies. We have already seen that the Heavenly Smith is the son, the messenger or the collaborator of the supreme God. He completes his work and for the most part does this in his name. The 'civilization' imparted by the Heavenly Smith is not merely confined to the organization of the world (which is, one might say, almost a cosmology); it is also a spiritual one. The Smith-Counsellor continues and completes the work of God by making man capable of understanding mysteries. Hence the role of the smith in the initiations at puberty and in secret societies, and his importance in the religious life of the community. Even his relations with the chiefs and sovereigns, whom, in certain regions, he overlaps, are of a religious character.

As for the despised status of the smiths among the Massaï and other Hamitic populations, it should be noted that not only do these peoples *not* practise agriculture but that they have an ambivalent (magico-religious) attitude to iron; like every sacred object, metal is both dangerous and beneficent. This ambivalent attitude both towards smith and metals is fairly universal.

[1] Evel Gasparini, *L'Ergologia degli Slavi* (Venice, 1951), pp. 172 sq., 179.

10

Smiths, Warriors, Masters of Initiation

WE SHALL do no more than touch on another group of myths—one in which the relationship between the divine smith and God is on an entirely different plane. The mythological theme here is the celebrated one of the struggle between the celestial deity (more precisely the God of the Hurricane) and the Aquatic Dragon. At stake in this struggle is the sovereignty of the world, but there is more than a suggestion of cosmological significance about it. After overcoming the monster, the God pulls out the world from his body (the Marduk-Tiamat theme) or, in other versions, he organizes the world, establishes it on solid foundations by "tying up" the monster and hurling it down into a subterranean abyss. In the majority of versions, it is from a smith-god that the God of the Hurricane receives the wondrous weapons which give him victory. In the Canaanitish text, *the Poem of Baal*, the God Kôshar-wa-Hasis (literally, 'skilful' and 'astute') forges for Baal the two cudgels with which he later overthrows Yam, Lord of the seas and underground waters.[1]

In Ugaritic mythology Kôshar has the status of divine smith. According to the tradition handed down by Sanchoniaton, Chusôr was the first to discover iron (Gaster, Thespis, p. 154 commentary). In an Egyptian version, *Ptah* (the

[1] See the text, translated and abundantly commented in Theodore H. Gaster, *Thespis, Ritual, Myth and Drama in the Ancient Near East* (New York, 1950), pp. 154 sq.

97

Potter-God) forges arms which permit Horus to conquer Set. Similarly, the divine smith Tvashtri creates the weapons of Indra for his struggle with the Dragon Vritra; Hephaistos forges the thunderbolt with which Zeus will vanquish Typhon; Thor crushes the serpent Midhgardhsormr with his hammer Mjölnir, forged by dwarfs which are the Scandinavian counterparts of the Cyclops.

The collaboration of the divine smith with the Gods is not confined to his co-operation in the great struggle for the sovereignty of the world. The smith is also the architect and artisan of the Gods. Kôshar fashions the bows of the Gods, supervises the building of Baal's palace and equips the sanctuaries of other deities. Gaster observes that this smith-god is also associated with music and song. Sanchoniaton says that Chusôr likewise invented the art of 'good speech' and that of composing chants and incantations. In the Ugaritic texts the chanters are called Kôtarât. The identification of smith-craft with song is clearly indicated in the semitic vocabulary: the Arab *q-y-n*, 'to forge', 'to be a smith', is related to the Hebrew, Syriac and Ethiopian terms denoting the act of 'singing', 'intoning a funeral lament'.[1] There is, too, the well-known etymological connection between poet and the Greek *poietes*, meaning 'creator', 'maker', and also the semantic resemblance between 'artisan' and 'artist'. The Sanskrit *taksh*, meaning 'to create', is employed to express the composition of the Rig Veda songs (I, 62, 13, V, 2, 11). The Old-Scandinavian *lotha-smithr*, meaning 'smith-song', and the Rhenish term *reimschmied*, meaning 'poetaster', or 'rhymster', underline even more clearly the close connections between the profession of smith and the art of the poet and musician (Gaster, *ibid.*). According to Snorri, Odin and his priests were called 'forgers of songs' (Ohlaver, *Die Germanische Schmiede*,

---

[1] Ginsburg, quoted by Th. L. Gaster, *Thespis*, p. 155.

p. 11). The same associations are to be found among the Turco-Tartars and Mongols, where the smith is linked with heroes, singers and poets (see above, p. 85). Also to be noted are the Tzigane nomads who are a combination of smith, tinker, musician, healer and fortune-teller. The name given by the Tziganes to themselves is in Europe, Rom, in Armenia, Lom, in Persia, Dom and in Syria, Dom or Dum. 'It is interesting,' writes Jules Bloch, 'that *dom* in India is the name of a tribe, or rather a conglomeration of tribes very widespread and well known in former times.'[1] In the Sanskrit texts they are associated with musicians and untouchables, but they are primarily known as smiths and musicians. It is not without interest to note that there are links between the Asur smelters and smiths—to whom we have already referred (p. 65 sq.) —and the *dom*; before the present dynasty a Dom dynasty, which had originated in the north, ruled over the Asur.[2]

There would appear to have existed therefore, at several different cultural levels (which is a mark of very great antiquity), a close connection between the art of the smith, the occult sciences (shamanism, magic, healing, etc.) and the art of song, dance and poetry. These overlapping techniques, moreover, appear to have been handed down in an aura of sacred mystery comprising initiations, specific rituals and 'trade secrets'. We are far from understanding all the arrangements and aspects of this complex ritual and some will probably remain for ever a mystery. The few groups of myths and metallurgical rituals which we have reviewed are enough to give us some idea of their extreme complexity and an inkling of the various underlying conceptions of the world. One element nevertheless is constant—that is the sacredness of

---

[1] Jules Bloch, *Les Tsiganes* (Paris, 1953), p. 28.
[2] W. Ruben, *Eisenschmiede und Dämonen in Indien*, p. 9; Jules Bloch, *op. cit.*, p. 30.

metal and consequently the ambivalent, eccentric and mysterious character of all mining and metallurgical operations. As we have mentioned earlier (pp. 29 sq.), certain mythological themes of the earlier stone ages were integrated in the mythology of the age of metals. What is especially significant is the fact that the symbolism of the 'thunderstone', in which projectiles and stone missiles are compared with the thunderbolt, underwent a great development in the mythologies of metallurgy. The weapons which the smith-gods or divine-smiths forge for the celestial gods are thunder and lightning. This was the case, for example, with the weapons presented by Tvashtri to Indra. The clubs or cudgels of Ninurta are called 'world-crusher' or 'world-grinder', and are compared with thunder and lightning. Just as thunder and lightning are the weapons of Zeus, so the hammer (*mjölnir*) of Thor is the thunderbolt. The clubs 'jump' from the hands of Baal, for Kôshar has forged arms for him which can be hurled to very distant points (Gaster, *op. cit.*, p. 158). Zeus hurls his thunderbolt afar.

This concatenation of images is very significant: thunderbolt, 'thunderstone' (mythological souvenir of the Stone Age), and the magical weapon with a long-distance strike (sometimes returning like a boomerang to its master's hand; cf. Thor's hammer). It is possible to detect here certain traces of the mythology of *homo faber*, to divine the magic aura of the manufactured tool, the exceptional prestige of the artisan and workman and, above all, in the Metal Age, of the smith. It is in any case significant that, in contrast to pre-agricultural and pre-metallurgical mythologies, where, as a natural prerogative, God is the possessor of the thunderbolt and all the other meteorological epiphanies, in the myths of historic peoples, on the other hand (Egypt, the Near East and the Indo-Europeans), the God of the hurricane *receives* these weapons—lightning and thunder—from a divine smith. It is difficult to avoid seeing in this the mythologized victory of *homo faber*, a victory which presages his supremacy in the industrial ages to come. What clearly emerges from all these myths concerning smiths who assist the gods to secure their supremacy is the extraordinary importance accorded to the *fabrication of a tool*. Naturally, such a creation retains for a long time a magical or divine character, for all 'creation' or 'construction' can only be the work of a superhuman being. One final aspect of this mythology concerning the maker of tools must be mentioned: the workman strives to imitate divine models. The smith of the gods forges weapons similar to lightning and the thunderbolt ('weapons', naturally possessed by the celestial gods of pre-metallurgical mythologies). In their turn, human smiths imitate the work of their super-human patrons. On the mythological level, however, it has to be emphasized that the imitation of divine models is superseded by a new theme: the importance of the work of manufacture, the demiurgical capabilities of the workman; and finally the apotheosis of the *faber*, he who 'creates' objects.

We are tempted to find in this category of primordial experiences the source of all mythico-ritual complexes, in which the smith and divine or semi-divine artisan are at once architects, dancers, musicians and medicine-sorcerers. Each one of these highlights a different aspect of the great mythology of 'savoir faire', that is to say, the possession of the occult secret of 'fabrication', of 'construction'. The words of a song have considerable creative force; objects are created by 'singing' the requisite words. Väinämöinen 'sings' a boat, i.e. he builds it by modulating a chant composed of magic words; and when he lacks the three final words he goes to consult an illustrious magician, Antero Vipunen. 'To make' something means knowing the magic formula which will allow it to be invented

or to 'make it appear' spontaneously. In virtue of this, the
artisan is a connoisseur of secrets, a magician; thus all crafts
include some kind of initiation and are handed down by an
occult tradition. He who 'makes' real things is he who *knows*
the secrets of making them. In the same way we may look for
an explanation of the function of the mythical African smith
in his capacity of civilizing hero. He has been enjoined by
God to complete creation, to organize the world and to
educate men, that is, to reveal to them the arts. It is
especially important to underline the role of the African
smith in the initiations at puberty and in the secret societies.
In both cases we are dealing with a revelation of mysteries or
the knowledge of ultimate realities. In this religious role of the
smith there is a foreshadowing of the celestial smith's mission
as civilizing hero; he collaborates in the spiritual 'formation'
of young men; he is a sort of guide, the earthly counterpart
of the First Counsellor who came down from heaven *in illo
tempore*.

It has been noted[1] that in early Greece, certain groups of
mythical personages—Telchines, Cabiri, Kuretes, Dactyls—
were both secret guilds associated with mysteries *and* cor-
porations of metal-workers. According to various traditions,
the Telchines were the first people to work in iron and bronze,
the Idaean Dactyls discovered iron-smelting and the Kuretes
bronze work. The latter, too, were reputed for their special
dance which they performed with a clash of arms. The Cabiri,
like the Kuretes, are given the title of 'masters of the furnace'
and were called 'mighty in fire'; their worship spread all
over the eastern Mediterranean.[2] The Dactyls were the priests
of Cybele, the goddess of mountains as well as of mines and

---

[1] L. Gernet and A. Boulanger, *Le génie grec dans la religion* (Paris, 1932), pp. 78 sq.
[2] J. de Morgan, *La Préhistoire orientale* (Paris, 1927), III, pp. 173 sq. For all
this, see the relevant articles in the *Real-Enzyklopädie* by Pauly and Wissowa. Exhaustive summary of textual and epigraphic sources in Bengt Hemberg's volume,
Die Kabiren (Uppsala, 1950).

caves and having her dwelling inside the mountains.[1] 'According to some, the Dactyls split up into two groups—twenty male persons on the right and thirty-two female persons on the left. Or again: the Dactyls on the left were sorcerers whose work was destroyed by those on the right. The 'semi-choirs' encircling the hearth . . . and of opposite sex always evoke some rite of sacred marriage . . . or sacred struggle which bear a curious resemblance to the Chinese hierogamies and victims.'[2] According to a tradition handed down by Clement of Alexandria (*Protreptic*, II, 20), the Corybantes, who are also given the name of Cabiri, were three brothers, one of whom was slain by the two others who buried his head at the foot of Mount Olympus. This legend, relating to the origins of the mysteries, is linked, as we have already seen (p. 69), with the myth concerning the origin of metals.

Now, these groups of mythical metallurgists deal in magic (the Dactyls, Telchines, etc.), the dance (the Corybantes, the Kuretes), the mysteries (Cabiri, etc.) and the initiation of young boys (Kuretes).[3] And so we have here the mythological relics of an ancient order of things, where the guilds of smiths had a part to play in mysteries and initiations. H. Jeanmaire has rightly emphasized the function of 'counsellors' in the initiation ceremonies of the Kuretes in connection with the age-grades of the initiates. As educators and masters of initiation, the Kuretes remind us, in certain respects, of the function of the African civilizing smith-heroes. It is indeed significant that at a subse-

[1] Cf. Radet, *La Lydie et le monde grec an temps des Mermnades* (Paris, 1892), p. 269, etc. Hugo Gressmann, *Die Orientalischen Religionen in hellenristisch-römischer Zeit* (Berlin, 1930), p. 59. Bengt Hemberg; 'Die idaiischen Daktylen' (*Eranos*, 50, 1952, pp. 41–59). On the connection between the Dactyls and the Mediterranean goddess, see U. Pestalozza, *Religione Mediterranea* (Milan, 1951), pp. 188 sq., 202 sq. On the obstetric functions of the Dactyls, *ibid.*, p. 204.

[2] Gabriel Germain, *Genèse de l'Odysée* (Paris, 1954), p. 164.

[3] Cf. H. Jeanmaire, *Couroï et Courètes* (Lille, 1939); R. Pettazzoni, *I. Misteri* (Bologna, 1924), pp. 71 sq. K. Kerényi, 'Mysterien der Kabiren' (*Eranos-Jahrbuch* XI, 1944, pp. 11–60).

quent, and infinitely more complex, stage of culture the initiatory function of the smith and blacksmith still survives very markedly. The blacksmith shares both the prestige of the smith and takes part in the symbolisms crystallized around the horse.

It was not a draught horse used for the war-chariot but the riding horse, a discovery of the nomadic horsemen of Central Asia. It was in this last cultural context that the horse inspired the greatest number of myths. The horse and its rider have held a considerable place in the ideologies and rituals of the 'male societies' (Männerbünde); it is in this connection that we shall meet the blacksmith. The phantom-horse would come into his workshop, sometimes with Odin or the troop of the 'furious army' or 'savage hunt' (*Wilde Heer*), to be shod.[1] In certain parts of Germany and Scandinavia the blacksmith until quite recently participated in initiatory scenarios of the Männerbünde type. In Styria he shoes the 'war-horse' or 'charger' (i.e. the Hobby-Horse) by 'killing' him in order to 'revive' him afterwards (Höfler, p. 54). In Scandinavia and north Germany, shoeing is an initiatory rite of entry into the secret society as well as a marriage rite (*ibid.*, pp. 54–5). As Otto Höfler has shown (p. 54), the ritual of shoeing and that of the death and resurrection of the 'horse' (with or without rider) on the occasion of a marriage marks both the fiancé's break with bachelordom and his entry into the class of married men.

Smith and blacksmith play a similar role in the rituals of Japanese 'male-societies'.[2] The smith-god is called *Ame no ma-hitotsu no kami*, 'the one-eyed god of the sky'. Japanese

---

[1] Otto Höfler, *Geheimbünde der Germanen* (Frankfurt A.M., 1934), pp. 53 sq. Cf. too H. Ohlhaver, *Der germanische Schmied*, pp. 95 sq.

[2] Alexander Slawick, 'Kultische Geheimbünde der Japaner und Germanen' (*Wiener Beiträge zur Kallurgerchichte*, IV Salzburg-Leipzig, 1936, pp. 675–764), pp. 697 sq.

mythology presents a certain number of one-eyed and one-legged divinities, inseparable from the Männerbünde; they are the gods of the thunderbolt and the mountains or of anthropophagous demons (Slawik, p. 698). It is known that Odin was also represented as an old one-eyed man, short-sighted or even blind.[1] The phantom-horse which came into the blacksmith's shop was one-eyed. Here we come up against an intricate mythico-ritual motif which we cannot investigate at this stage. What is important for us is that it deals with a scenario of the Männerbünde in which the infirmities of the characters (one-eyed or one-legged, etc.) recall the initiatory mutilations or describe the appearance of the masters of initiation (short, dwarfish, etc.). The divinities who bore some infirmity were put into contact with 'strangers', the 'men of the mountains', the 'underground dwarfs', that is to say, with mountain populations surrounded by mystery, generally dreaded metal-workers. In Nordic mythologies the dwarfs were renowned for their admirable smithcraft. Certain fairies enjoyed the same prestige.[2] The tradition of a people of small build, dedicated wholly to metallurgy and living in the depths of the earth, is also found elsewhere. To the Dogons, the first mythic inhabitants of the region were the Negrillos, who have since disappeared underground: but, being indefatigable smiths, the resounding clang of their hammers is still to be heard.[3] The warrior 'male-societies' both in Europe and in central Asia and in the Far East (Japan), performed initiatory rituals in which the smith and blacksmith had their place. It is known that after the conversion to Christianity of northern Europe, Odin and the 'Savage Hunt' were compared with the devil and the hordes of the damned. This was already

[1] Otto Höfler, *op. cit.*, p. 181, Note 56.
[2] Cf. the references grouped by Stith Thompson, *Subject-Index of Folk-Literature* (Helsinki, 1932), vol. III, p. 87 (dwarf smiths), III, 39 (fairy metallurgists).
[3] H. Tegnaeus, *Le Héros Civilisateur*, p. 16.

a great step towards the identification of the smith and blacksmith with the devil.[1]

The 'mastery of fire', common both to magician, shaman
and smith, was, in Christian folklore, looked upon as the
work of the devil: one of the most frequently recurring
popular images shows the devil spitting flames. Perhaps we
have here the final mythological transformation of the archetypal image of the 'master of fire'. Odin-Wotan was the master
of the *wut*, the *furor religiosus* (*Wotan, id est furor*, wrote
Adam von Bremen). Now the *wut*, like other terms in the
Indo-European religious vocabulary (furor, ferg, ménos),
signifies the anger and extreme heat provoked by an excessive
ingestion of sacred power. The warrior becomes heated during
his initiation fight; he produces a 'heat' which is not un-
reminiscent of the 'magic heat' produced by the shamans and
yogi (see p. 81). On this plane the warrior resembles other
'masters of fire': magicians, shamans, yogi or smiths. The
exact relationship mentioned above between the fighting
Gods (Baal, Indra, etc.) and the divine smiths (Kôshar,
Tvashtr, etc.) may be given a new interpretation: the divine
smith works with fire while the warrior god, by his *furor*,
magically produces fire in his own body. It is this intimacy,
this sympathy with fire, which unites such differing magico-
religious experiences and identifies such disparate vocations
as that of the shaman, the smith, the warrior and the mystic.

It remains for us to point out yet another theme in European folklore, one which embraces the motif of rejuvenation
through the furnace fire.[2] Jesus Christ (or St. Peter, St.
Nicholas or St. Eloi) plays the role of a blacksmith who heals
the sick and rejuvenates the old by putting them in a heated

---

[1] Cf. Bachtold-Staubli, *Handwörterbuch des deutschen Aberglaubens*, under *Schmied*,
Teufel; Hedwig von Beit, *Symbolik des Märchens* (Berne, 1952), pp. 118 sq.

[2] The theme has been exhaustively studied by C. Manstrander, in 1912, and
Carl-Martin Edsman in 1949 (*Ignis Divinus*, pp. 30 sq.).

oven or forging them on an anvil. A soldier, a priest (or St. Peter, etc.) or a smith, endeavour to repeat the miracle on an old woman (mother-in-law, etc.): they fail lamentably. But Jesus Christ saves the imprudent smith by resurrecting the victim from his bones or ashes. In a number of tales, Jesus Christ arrives at a smithy bearing the sign: 'Here dwells the master of masters'. There enters a man with a horse to be shod and Jesus obtains the smith's leave to perform the task. One after the other he removes the horse's hooves, places them on the anvil, heats the shoe, fits it on the hoof and nails it on. Next he throws into the furnace fire an old woman (wife or mother-in-law of the smith) and, by forging her on the anvil, transforms her into a beautiful maiden. The smith tries to do the same with results that are known (Edsman, *Ignis Divinus* pp. 40, 82 sq.).

These popular tales recall the mythico-ritual scenario in which fire was the initiation test and represented both the agent of purification and transmutation (baptism by fire in primitive Christianity and Gnosticism is one of the most elaborate examples of such a spectacle).[1] In these folkloric creations Jesus is presented as the 'master of fire' *par excellence*, and the blacksmith is endowed with magical qualities. This is an indirect demonstration of the persistence of beliefs of undeniable antiquity. The 'master of fire', like fire itself, can be endowed with a significance of various kinds: he may be divine or demoniac. There exists, too, a celestial fire which flows before the throne of God, and a hell-fire which, in Gehenna, burns constantly. In the religious and lay folklore of the Middle Ages, Jesus, as well as the devil, are 'masters of fire'. For our purpose, it is well to bear in mind that the mythical images of the smith and blacksmith have for long

---

[1] See C. M. Edsman, *Le baptême de feu* (Uppsala, 1940), especially pp. 93 sq., 134 sq., 185 sq.

retained their hold on the popular imagination and that these stories continued to have initiatory significance. (Certainly the obvious or consciously accessible significance can be a matter for discussion, but to limit the problem in this way is to sin through an excess of rationalism. A folktale does not address itself to the awakened secularized consciousness: it exerts its power in the deep recesses of the psyche, and nourishes and stimulates the imagination. The initiation symbolisms of fire and forge, death and resurrection by fire, forging on the anvil, etc., are clearly borne out in myths and shamanic rituals; cf. above pp. 83, 84. Similar images, inspired by tales, act directly on the psyche of the audience even when, *consciously*, the latter does not realize the primal significance of any particular symbol.)

11

Chinese Alchemy

To a certain extent it would be true to say that in China there was no break between mystical metallurgy and alchemy. Marcel Granet had already noted that 'Taoism goes back to the days of the guilds of smiths, custodians of the most wondrous of the magic arts and the secrets of the primal forces'.[1] It was in Taoist and neo-Taoist circles that alchemical techniques were propagated. As is known, what has been generally termed 'Taoism' has from time immemorial received, and in turn given, a new significance to a large number of spiritual traditions. To cite only one example: primitive methods of reintegrating the spontaneity and state of bliss of the 'Animal Life' were adopted and carefully preserved by the Taoist masters; now, such practices are in direct descent from a proto-shamanism of hunting peoples, which, of course, is already a mark of their great antiquity (cf. my *Chamanisme*, pp. 402 sq.).

We must not, of course, confuse continuity with identity. The position of the Chinese alchemist could not be that of the smith or primitive mystic. 'Among the Taoists, whose alchemical furnace is successor to the ancient forge, immortality is no longer (at any rate since the second Han dynasty) the result of the casting of a magic utensil (which would require a sacrifice to the forge) but is acquired from him who

[1] Marcel Granet, *Danses et Légendes*, p. 161.

has succeeded in producing the "divine cinnabar". From that moment there was a new means of self-deification; it was sufficient to absorb drinkable gold or cinnabar in order to become like the gods.'[1] The alchemist, especially in the Neo-Taoist period, strove to recover an 'ancient wisdom', adulterated or mutilated by the very transformation of Chinese society. The alchemist was a cultured man: his predecessors—hunters, potters, smiths, dancers, agriculturists, ecstatics—lived in the very heart of traditions orally transmitted by initiations and 'trade-secrets'. From the very first Taoism had turned with sympathy, even with fervour, to the representatives of these traditions. This has been described as the Taoists' infatuation for 'popular superstitions', which included techniques of various kinds—dietetic, gymnastic, choreographic, respiratory, magic, shamanist, ecstatic and spiritualist, etc. Everything points to the notion that on the 'popular' level on which they were sought, some of the traditional practices had already undergone numerous changes; we have only to recall the aberrant varieties of certain shamanist techniques of ecstasy (cf. my *Chamanisme*, pp. 398 sq.). The Taoists somehow could sense beneath the crust of such superstitions authentic fragments of an ancient wisdom which they strove to recapture and make their own.

It was in this rather vague area, in which primitive intuitions and traditions of great antiquity lingered on, unaffected by the vicissitudes of cultural history, that Taoism collected its crop of precepts, secrets and recipes. (These traditions derived from spiritual situations long past, situations connected with the magic of the hunt, the discovery of pottery, agriculture and metallurgy, and the experiences and ecstasies that went with them.) One may say, therefore, that the Taoist alchemists, despite inevitable innovations, continued

[1] Max Kaltenmark, *Le Lie-Sien Tchouan*, p. 18.

and prolonged an ageless tradition. Their ideas of longevity and immortality belong to the sphere of mythologies and folklore which is virtually universal. The notions of the 'herb of immortality', of animal or vegetable substances charged with 'vitality' and containing the elixir of eternal youth, as well as the myths concerning inaccessible regions inhabited by immortals, are part of a primitive ideology going far beyond the confines of China. It is not our purpose to examine them here (see a few examples in Note J). Let us simply point out in what sense those rudimentary intuitions in the myths and rites of smelters and smiths were taken up and interpreted by the alchemists. It will be especially edifying to highlight the subsequent development of a few fundamental ideas concerning the growth of ores, the natural transformation of metals into gold and the mystic value of gold. As for the ritual complex, comprising brotherhoods of smiths and initiatory trade-secrets, something of its structure was transmitted to the Chinese alchemist, and not *only* to him. Initiation by a master, and the initiatory communication of secrets, for long continued to be the norm in alchemical teaching.

Specialists are not all agreed about the origins of Chinese alchemy; the *dates of the earliest texts* which mention alchemical operations are still under discussion. According to H. Dubs, the first document dates from the year 144 B.C. That year an imperial edict threatens with public execution all those caught in the act of counterfeiting gold.[1] According to W. H. Barnes, the first mention of alchemy may date from the fourth or third century B.C. Dub's view (*op. cit.*, p. 77) is that the founder of Chinese alchemy was Tsou Yen, a contemporary of Mencius (fourth century). Whether this opinion is well founded or not, it is important to distinguish the *historical*

---

[1] The text is reproduced by H. Dubs, *Beginnings of Alchemy*, p. 63. For a bibliography of Chinese alchemy see Note I.

beginning and development of a *pre-chemistry* from alchemy as a soteriological technique. As we have already said, this latter was identifiable with the methods and mythologies, mainly Taoist, whose aim was quite other than that of 'making gold' (it remained so up to the end of the eighteenth century).

Indeed, Chinese alchemy was built up, in so far as it is an autonomous discipline, by utilizing

(1) traditional cosmological principles;

(2) myths connected with the elixir of immortality and the immortal saints;

(3) techniques pursuing the prolongation of life, beatitude and spiritual spontaneity.[1]

These three elements—principles, myths and techniques —belonged to the cultural heritage of protohistory. It would be an error to believe that the date of the first documents which gives evidence of them also establishes their age. There is a very obvious and close connection between the 'preparation of gold', the 'drug of immortality' and the 'evocation' of the Immortals. Luan Tai presents himself to the Emperor Wu and assures him that he can perform these three miracles but he only succeeds in 'materializing' the Immortals.[2]

The magician Li Chao Kuin advises the Emperor Wu Ti of the Han dynasty as follows: 'Sacrifice to the furnace (*tsao*) and you will be able to summon (supernatural) beings; when you have called forth these beings, the powder of cinnabar can be transformed into yellow gold; when the yellow gold is produced you will be able to make of it utensils for drinking and eating and in so doing you will have a prolonged longevity. When your longevity is prolonged you will be able to see the blessed (*hsien*) of the island of P'eng Lai which is in the midst of the seas. When you have seen them and have made

[1] See Eliade, *Le Yoga, Immortalité et Liberté*, pp. 283 sq.

[2] Edouard Chavannes, *Les Mémoires historiques de Se-Ma-Ts'ien* (Paris, 1897 sq.), III, p. 479.

the *feng* and *chan* sacrifices, then you will not die' (Ssŭ-ma Chien, vol. III, p. 465). Another celebrated personage, Liu Hsiang (79–8 B.C.), claimed to be able 'to make gold' but failed (texts in Dubs, p. 74). A few centuries later, the most celebrated Chinese alchemist, Pao Pu'tzu (pseudonym of Ko Hung, 254–334), attempts to explain Liu Hsiang's failure by telling us that he was not in possession of 'true medicine' (the philosopher's stone) and that he was not spiritually prepared (for the alchemist must fast a hundred days and purify himself with perfumes, etc.). This transmutation cannot be brought about in a palace, adds Pao Pu'tzu: one must live in solitude apart from ordinary people. Books are not enough; what one finds in books is only for beginners, the rest is secret and communicable only by oral teaching, etc.[1]

The quest for the elixir was thus bound up with the search for distant mysterious islands where the 'Immortals' lived: to encounter these Immortals was to transcend the human condition and share in an existence of timeless bliss. This search for the Immortals in distant islands exercised the minds of the early emperors of the Tsin dynasty (219 B.C.; Ssŭ-ma Chien, *Memoirs*, II, 143, 152; III, 437) and the Emperor Wu of the Han dynasty (110 B.C.; *ibid.*, III, 499; Dubs, p. 66).

The search for gold was also a spiritual quest. Gold was imperial; it was to be found in the 'Centre' of the earth and was mystically connected with the *chüe* (realgar or sulphur), yellow mercury and life in the hereafter (the 'yellow sources'). This is how it was presented in a text dated 122 B.C., *Huai Nan T͡zu*, where we likewise find evidence for the belief in an *accelerated metamorphois of metals* (fragment translated by Dubs, pp. 71–3). It is possible that this text may derive from

[1] See summary given by Dubs, pp. 79–80, and supplementary bibliography in Eliade, *Le Yoga*, p. 287, n. i.

the school of Tsou Yen, if not from the Master himself
(*ibid.*, p. 74). As we have seen (above, p. 50), belief in the
natural metamorphosis of metals was common in China.
The alchemist only accelerates the growth of metals. Like his
Western colleague, the Chinese alchemist contributes to
Nature's work by precipitating the tempo. But we should not
forget that the transmutation of metals into gold also has a
spiritual aspect; gold being the imperial metal, 'perfect', freed
from impurities, the alchemical operation must seek to imitate
the perfection of nature which is, in the final instance, its
absolution and its liberty. The gestation of metals in the
bowels of the earth obeys the same temporal rhythms as
those which bind man to his carnal and fallen condition;
to hasten the growth of metals by the operation of
alchemy is tantamount to absolving them from the laws of
Time.

Gold and jade, since they take part in the *yang* cosmological principle, preserve bodies from corruption. 'If there
is gold and jade in the nine apertures of the corpse, it will
preserve the body from putrefaction,' writes the alchemist
Ko Hung. And T'ao Hung Ching (fifth century) gives the
following details: 'When on opening an ancient grave, the
corpse seems alive, then there is inside and outside the body a
large quantity of gold and jade. According to the regulations
of the Han dynasty, princes and lords were buried in clothes
adorned with pearls and boxes of jade for the purpose of
preserving the body from decay.'[1] For the same reason, vases
of alchemical gold have a specific virtue; they prolong life
indefinitely. Ko Hung writes: 'If with this alchemical gold
you make dishes and bowls and if you eat and drink out of

[1] B. Laufer, *Jade, a study in Chinese Archaeology and Religion* (Chicago, 1912),
p. 299. Tch'e-song tseu consumed liquid jade: he could walk through fire without
getting burnt and attained immortalité; cf. M. Kaltenmark, *Le Lie-sien Tchouan*,
pp. 35 sq., *ibid.*, p. 37, n. 2, other references to the absorption of jade. Cf., too, Eliade,
Le Yoga, p. 284, n. 1.

them you shall live long'.[1] The same author on another occasion says: 'As to the true man, he makes gold because he wishes, by the medicinal use of it (that is, by assimilating it as a food), to become an immortal.'[2] But to be effective, gold had to be 'prepared', 'fabricated'. Gold produced by the processes of alchemical sublimation and transmutation possessed a higher vitality by means of which one could achieve immortality.

If even the herb *chü-sheng* can make one live longer,
Why not try putting the Elixir into the mouth?
Gold by nature does not rot or decay;
Therefore it is of all things most precious.
When the artist (i.e. alchemist) includes it in his diet,
The duration of his life becomes everlasting.
When the golden powder enters the five-entrails,
A fog is dispelled, like rain-clouds scattered by the wind.
Fragrant exhalations pervade the four limbs;
The countenance beams with joy and well-being.
Hairs that were white all turn to black;
Teeth that had fallen grow in their former place.
The old dotard is again a lusty youth.
The decrepit crone is a young girl once more.
He whose form is changed and has escaped the perils of life,
Has for his title the Name of True Man.[3]

According to a tradition preserved in *Lieh Hsien Ch'uan* (The Complete Biographies of the Immortals), Wei Po-yang, the author of this poem in praise of the Elixir, had successfully prepared the 'pills of immortality'. He swallowed a few of these pills and gave some to one of his disciples and his dog.

---

[1] Translation by A. Waley, *Notes on Chinese Alchemy*, p. 4.
[2] Translation by Johnson, *A Study of Chinese Alchemy*, p. 71.
[3] Ts'an T'ung Ch'i, ch. XXVII, trans. by Waley, *Notes on Chinese Alchemy*, p. 11. This treatise, the first to be entirely devoted to alchemy, was written in A.D. 142 by Wei Po-yang. It has been translated into English by Lu-Ch'iang Wu, with introduction by Tenney L. Davis, see Note I and Eliade, *Le Yoga*, p. 285, n. 1.

Whereupon they left the earth in their mortal flesh and went to join the other immortals (cf. Lionel Giles, *Chinese Immortals*, pp. 67 sq.).

The alchemist accepts the traditional identity of microcosm and macrocosm, so familiar to Chinese thought. The universal quintet, *wu-hsing* (water, fire, wood, gold, earth), is regarded as intimately allied with the organs of the human body: the heart with the essence of fire, the liver with the essence of wood, the lungs with the essence of metal, the kidneys with the essence of water, the stomach with the essence of earth (texts in Johnson, p. 102). The microcosm which the human body is, is likewise interpreted in alchemical terms. 'The fire of the heart is red like cinnabar and the water of the kidneys is dark, as lead,' writes a biographer of the famous alchemist Lü Tsu (eighth century A.D.).[1] Closely allied with the macrocosm, man possesses all the elements which constitute the cosmos and all the vital energies which secure his periodic renovation. All that is necessary is to reinforce certain essences. Hence the importance of cinnabar is due not so much to its red colour (the colour of blood, the vital principle) as to the fact that when put into fire cinnabar produces mercury. It therefore conceals the mysteries of regeneration by death (for combustion symbolizes death). It follows from this that it can ensure the perpetual regeneration of the human body and ultimately achieve immortality. Pao Pu'tzu writes that if one mixes three pounds of cinnabar with one pound of honey and if one dries the whole in the sun in order to obtain pills of the size of a grain of hemp, ten of such pills taken in the course of one year will restore the blackness to white hair and make decayed teeth grow again. And if one continues beyond one year, one becomes immortal (text in Johnson, p. 63).

[1] Quoted by W. A. Martin, *The Lore of Cathay*, p. 60.

The collection of the legendary biographies of the Taoist Immortals, *Lieh Hsien Ch'uan*—attributed to Liu An (77–76 B.C.), but certainly revised in the first century of our era—is one of the oldest texts which mention cinnabar as a longevity drug. 'Under the first Han emperors, alchemists used cinnabar to obtain gold (which was not put to further use but changed into magic dishes—an intermediate stage). But from the first centuries of our era it was believed that the absorption of cinnabar could make the whole body red' (Max Kaltenmark, *Le Lie-sien tchouan*, pp. 18–19). According to the *Lieh Hsien Ch'uan*, a governor 'fed himself with cinnabar for three years, then obtained light snow from the divine cinnabar. After having consumed it for five years he was able to fly about.' (Kaltenmark, pp. 146–7). Tche'fou 'could make mercury and purify the cinnabar which he absorbed with saltpetre; after thirty years of this diet he had become like an adolescent; his hair (including his body-hair) had all become red' (*ibid.*, p. 271).

But cinnabar can also be made inside the human body, mainly by means of the distillation of sperm. 'The Taoist, imitating animals and vegetables, hangs himself upside down, causing the essence of his sperm to flow up to his brain.'[1] The *tan-t'ien*, the 'famous fields of cinnabar', are to be found in the most secret recesses of the brain and belly: there it is that the embryo of immortality is alchemically prepared. Another name for these 'cinnabar fields' is *K'un Lun*, meaning both 'mountain of the western sea'—a sojourn of the immortals—and a secret region of the brain, comprising the 'chamber similar to a cave' (*tong-fang*, which also signifies 'nuptial chamber') and the 'nirvana' (*ni-wan*). 'In order to enter therein by mystic meditation, one falls into a 'chaotic' state (*houen*) resembling the primordial, paradisal, 'uncon-

[1] Rolf Stein, *Jardins en miniature d'Extrême-Orient*, p. 86.

scious' condition of the uncreated world' (R. Stein, *op. cit.*, p. 54).

Two elements especially call for attention:

(1) the parallelism of the mythical mountain, K'un Lun, with the secret regions of the brain and belly;

(2) the role given to the 'chaotic state' which, once attained by means of meditation, allows one to penetrate to those secret recesses of the 'cinnabar fields', thus making possible the alchemical preparation of the embryo of immortality.

The identification of the *K'un Lun* in the human body confirms what we have several times emphasized: that the Taoist alchemist takes up and carries on a time-old tradition, embracing recipes for longevity and techniques of mystic physiology. Indeed the Mountain of the Western Sea, sojourn of the Immortals, is a traditional and very ancient image of the 'world in little', of a universe in miniature. The Mountain of *K'un Lun* has two tiers: an upright circular cone surmounted by an inverted one,[1] similar to the alchemist's furnace. But the calabash too consists of two superposed spheres. The calabash, of course, plays a considerable part in Taoist ideology and folklore and is regarded as representing the cosmos in miniature. In this gourd-shaped microcosm resides the source of Life and Youth. This theme—the universe having the shape of a calabash—is of undeniable antiquity.[2] It is therefore significant that an alchemical text should declare:

---

[1] Concerning the protohistory of this symbolism, cf. Carl Hentze, *Tod, Auferstehung, Weltordnung* (Zürich, 1955), pp. 33 sq., 160 sq., *et passim*.

[2] Cf. R. Stein *Jardins en miniature*, pp. 45 sq. The theme of the paradisal dwelling of perfect bliss and magic efficiency has from very ancient times been associated with the theme of the calabash or narrow-necked vase; *ib.*, p. 55. Magicians and alchemists withdrew into a calabash each evening. The primal model for this is the grotto, the secret retreat of the Immortals, in the obscurity of which the adept is initiated into the mysteries. 'Initiation themes are so closely linked with the grotto that *tong* ("grotto") finally came to signify "mysterious, profound, transcendent"' (R. Stein, p. 44). These grottoes (a paradise world on its own) are difficult to enter. They are closed vases, narrow-necked and gourd-shaped' (p. 45).

'He who cultivates cinnabar (that is, the pill of immortality) takes Heaven as his model and fashions Earth. He seeks them by turning in on himself and then finds that a Heaven shaped like a gourd has come into spontaneous existence in his body.'[1] Indeed, when the alchemist achieves the 'chaotic' state of unconsciousness, he penetrates 'to the innermost recesses of the being, the space of the size of a thumb, round and square' (R. Stein, p. 59). This inner space is in the form of a gourd.

As for this 'chaotic' state, attained through meditation and indispensable to the operations of alchemy, it is, for several reasons, of interest to our investigation. And this is primarily because of the resemblance between this 'unconscious' state (comparable to that of the embryo or the egg) and the *materia prima*, the *massa confusa* of Western alchemy, to which we shall return later (pp. 153 sq.). The *materia prima* should not be understood merely as a primordial condition of the substance but also as an inner experience of the alchemist. The reduction of matter to its original condition of absolute indifferentiation, corresponds, on the plane of inner experience, to the regression to the pre-natal, embryonic state. The theme of rejuvenation and longevity by means of the *regressus ad uterum* is a leitmotif of Taoism. The most usual method is 'embryonic respiration' (*t'ai-si*). But the alchemist also achieves this state by the smelting of various ingredients in his furnace. A text of modern syncretist Taoism expresses itself thus: 'that is why the (Buddha) Jou-lai (= Tathâgata), in his great mercy, has revealed to man the (alchemical) method of work with fire and has taught him to *penetrate anew to the matrix* in order to refashion its (true) nature and (the plenitude of) his lot in life' (quoted by R. Stein, p. 97).

We may add that this 'return to the matrix', exalted both

[1] Commentary quoted by the *P'ei-wen yun fou*, translated by R. Stein, p. 59.

by Taoist writers and Western alchemists (pp. 154 sq.) is simply the development of a more ancient, more widespread conception already attested at primitive levels of culture: recovery from disease by a symbolic return to the origins of the world, that is, by a re-enactment of the cosmogony.[1] Many primitive therapies include a ritual reiteration of the creation of the world, permitting the sick man to be born anew and thus to recommence existence with an intact reserve of the vital forces. The Taoist and Chinese alchemists have taken up and perfected this traditional method. Instead of reserving it for the healing of particular maladies, they have applied it, above all, to cure man of the illness resulting from the ravages of time, that is from old age and death.

From a certain date onward writers begin to distinguish between an esoteric (*nei tan*) and an exoteric (*wai tan*) alchemy. Peng Hsiao, who lived towards the end of the ninth and the first half of the tenth centuries, in his commentary on the treatise *Ts'an T'ung Ch'i*, made a clear distinction between exoteric alchemy, which is concerned with concrete substances, and the esoteric variety, which uses only the 'souls' of those substances (Waley, *op. cit.*, p. 15). The distinction had been made a long while previously by Hui-ssu (A.D. 515–577). A clear exposition of 'esoteric' alchemy is given in the *Treatise on the Dragon and the Tiger* by Su Tung P'o, written in A.D. 1110. The 'pure', transcendental metals are identified with different parts of the body, and the alchemical processes, instead of being realized in the laboratory, take place in the body and in the consciousness of the experimenter. In the words of Su Tung P'o: 'The dragon is mercury. It is the semen and blood. He issues from the kidney and is stored in the liver. The tiger is lead. He is breath and bodily strength.

[1] Cf. M. Eliade, 'Kosmogonische Mythen und Magische Heilung' (*Paideuma*, 1956).

He issues from the mind and the lungs bear him. When the mind is moved, breath and strength act with it. When the kidneys are flushed, then semen and blood flow with them.'[1]

It was in the thirteenth century, when the Zen schools flourished, that alchemy became a fully-fledged ascetic and contemplative technique. The principal representative of Taoist-Zen alchemy is Ko Ch'ang Keng, also known as Po Yu Chuan. Here is how he describes the three methods of esoteric alchemy (Waley, Notes, p. 16 sq.). In the first, the body plays the part of the element lead, and the heart that of mercury; 'meditation' (*dhyana*) provides the necessary fluid and the sparks of intelligence the necessary fire. Ko Ch'ang Keng adds: 'By this method a gestation which normally requires ten months can be achieved in the twinkling of an eye.' The detail is revealing; as Waley points out, Chinese alchemy estimates that the process by which a child is engendered is capable of producing the Philosopher's Stone. This analogy is implicit in the writings of Western alchemists (they say, for example, that the fire under the receptacle or container must burn continuously for forty weeks—the period necessary for the gestation of the human embryo).

The method advocated by Ko Ch'ang Keng is the focus of several traditional conceptions, some of which are of great antiquity. In particular there is the parallelism of ores and metals with organisms that 'grow' inside the earth, like an embryo inside the womb. There is, too, the idea that the Elixir (that is, the Philosopher's Stone) has the characteristics both of a metal and of an embryo. Finally there is the notion that the respective processes of growth (of both metal and embryo) can be accelerated miraculously by achieving the state of maturity and perfection at the mineral level of existence (i.e.

[1] Quoted by Waley, *Notes on Chinese Alchemy*, p. 15; cf. too Lu Ch'iang Wu and T. L. Davies, *An Ancient Chinese treatise on alchemy*, p. 255 (ch. LIX of Ts'an T'ung Ch'i).

Naturam natura docet, debellet ut ignem.

EPIGRAMMA XX.

Flamma, vorat quæ cuncta, velut Draco, gnaviter ursit
  Virginis eximium vi superare decus:
Hinc lachrymis suffusa viro dum fortè videtur,
  Ille fuit miseræ ferre paratus opem.
Protinus hanc clypeo velans contendit in hostem,
  Et docuit tantas spernere mente minas.

Michaël Maier, *Scrutinium chymicum*

'Nature instructs Nature to vanquish Fire'

Fac ex mare & fœmina circulum, inde quadran-
gulum, hinc triangulum, fac circulum & ha-
bebis lap. Philosophorum.

EPIGRAMMA XXI.

Fœmina masque unus fiant tibi circulus, ex quo
Surgat, habens æquum forma quadrata latus.
Hinc Trigonum ducas, omni qui parte rotundam
In sphæram redeat: Tum Lapis ortus erit.
Si res tanta tuæ non mox venit obvia menti,
Dogma Geometræ si capis, omne scies,

Michaël Maier, *Scrutinium chymicum*

'From a man and woman make a circle, then a square, then a triangle,
finally a circle, and you will obtain the Philosopher's Stone'

by producing gold) and also—more particularly—on the human level, by producing the Elixir of Immortality. For as we have seen, thanks to the unity of microcosm-macrocosm, both levels correspond with one another. Since alchemical processes play out their part in the very body of the adept, the perfectibility and transmutation of metals correspond to the perfection and transmutation of men. This practical application of esoteric alchemy was indeed hinted at in the Chinese traditional system of the man-universe unity: by operating at a given level, results for all corresponding levels were obtained.

The two other methods of esoteric alchemy recommended by Ko Ch'ang Keng were variations of an analogous process. In the first method the body was compared to lead and the heart to mercury, the principal alchemical elements being aroused and activated at the *physical* and *anatomical* levels of the human being. In the second, they are at the *physiological* and *psychic* levels; indeed it is now the breath which takes the place of lead and the soul that of mercury. This amounts to saying that the alchemical operation is achieved when the respiration and psychic states are worked upon, that is, by practising a kind of Yoga (holding the breath, control and immobilization of the psycho-mental process). Finally, in the third method, the sperm corresponds to the element lead, and the blood to mercury, while the kidneys take the place of the element water and the mind that of fire.

It is not difficult to see in these last methods of esoteric Chinese alchemy certain striking resemblances to the Indian yoga-tantric techniques. Ko Ch'ang himself recognizes it implicitly: 'To the above it may be objected that this is practically the same as the method of the Zen Buddhists. To this I reply that under Heaven there are no two ways and that the wise are ever of the same heart' (Waley, p. 16). The sexual element, particularly, may be suspected to be of Indian origin. Let us add that the mutual influences operating between the alchemical methods and yoga-tantric techniques (including both the retention of the breath and the 'immobility of the semen') work both ways: if the Chinese alchemists borrow specific, near-tantric methods from the Taoist schools, the latter in their turn employ alchemical symbolism (comparing, for example, woman to the crucible of the alchemists, etc.).[1]

As for the exercises in rhythm-control culminating in the stoppage of breathing, these had for many centuries been part of the discipline of Chinese alchemy. Pao Pu'tzu writes that rejuvenation is obtained by halting respiration for a thousand heart-beats. 'When an old man has reached that stage then he will be transformed into a young man.'[2] Under Indian influence, certain neo-Taoist sects, like the Tantrics of the *'left hand'*, considered the stopping of respiration a means of immobilizing the semen and the psycho-mental flow. In the view of the Chinese, the retention both of breath and semen ensured longevity.[3] But since both Lao Tseu and Chuang were already acquainted with 'methodic' respiration, and since embryonic respiration is exalted by other Taoist

[1] Cf. Eliade, *Le Yoga*, p. 396. Jong Tch'eng Kong was fully conversant with the method of 'repairing and leading' (an expression frequently employed to indicate taoist sexual techniques, 'practices of the sleeping-chamber'). 'He drew the essence from the mysterious Female; his principle was that the vital Spirits residing in the Valley do not die for it is through them that life and breath are maintained and nourished. His hair which was white became black again; his teeth which had fallen out grew once more. His practices were identical with those of Lao-tseu' (Max Kaltenmark, *Le Lie-sien tchouan*, pp. 55–6). The mysterious female was the Valley from which the world has emerged; cf. R. Stein, *op. cit.*, p. 98. But in the text just quoted, this expression refers to the microcosm and has a precise physiological connotation (M. Kaltenmark, p. 56, n. 3). The practice was to absorb the vital energy of the women with whom one had intercourse: 'this energy, being at the source of life itself, helps to achieve a considerable longevity' (*ibid.*, p. 57). 'Ko Hung affirms that there were more than ten writers who dealt with Taoist sexual practices, the principle of all their methods being 'to bring back the essence in order to repair the brain' (*ibid.*). Cf. too *ibid.*, p. 84, 181–2.

[2] Trans. Johnson, *A Study of Chinese Alchemy*, p. 48.

[3] See Eliade, *Le Yoga*, pp. 395 sq.

writers,[1] we are entitled to assume that these respiratory techniques originated in China. Like so many other Chinese spiritual techniques, they derived from the proto-historic tradition to which we have referred (p. 110) and which included, inter alia, recipes and exercises for the purpose of achieving perfect spontaneity and vital beatitude.

The aim of 'embryonic respiration' was to imitate the breathing of the foetus in the womb. 'By returning to the base, the origin, we drive away old age, we return to the condition of the foetus', says the preface to *T'ai-hsi K'eou Kiue* (Oral Formulae for Embryonic Respiration).[2] Now this 'return to the beginning', as we have just seen, was what the alchemist also sought by other means.

---

[1] See the texts in Eliade, *Le Yoga*, pp. 71 sq. The antiquity of respiratory techniques in China has been recently confirmed by the discovery of an inscription of the Chou epoch; cf. Hellmut Wilhelm, 'Eine Chou-Inschrift über Atemtechnik' (*Monumenta Serica*, 12, 1948, pp. 385–8).

[2] Trans. H. Maspéro, 'Les procédés de "Nourir le Principe vital" dans la religion taöiste ancienne' (*Journal asiatique*, 1937, pp. 177–252; 353–430), p. 198.

12

Indian Alchemy

In INDIA, too, there is an abundance of evidence for the existence of alchemy as a spiritual technique. We have studied elsewhere its numerous affinities with Hatha-yoga and tantrism.[1] We shall here mention only the more important ones. First there is the 'popular' tradition, recorded both by Arab and European travellers, concerning the yogi-alchemists. These latter, by means of the rhythmic control of the breathing (prânâyâma) and the use of vegetable and mineral remedies, are said to have succeeded in prolonging their youth indefinitely and in transmuting ordinary metals into gold. Many legends speak of the yogi-fakir miracles performed by alchemists. They fly, make themselves invisible, etc. (see *Le Yoga*, p. 176). Let us note in passing that these miracles are yogic powers *par excellence* (*siddhi*).

The symbiosis of tantric yoga and alchemy is also well attested in the literary tradition of the Sanskrit and vernacular texts. Nâgârjuna, the famous mâdhyamika philosopher, is regarded as the author of a large number of alchemistical treatises. Among the *siddhi* achieved by the yogi appears the transmutation of metals into gold: the most celebrated tantric *siddha* (Capari, Kamari, Vyali, etc.) are also reputed alchemists. The *somarasa*, a technique peculiar to the school of the Nâtha Siddha, has an alchemical significance. Finally, in his *Sarva-*

[1] *Le Yoga, Immortalité et Liberté*, pp. 274 sq.

darshana-samgraha, Mādhava shows alchemy (*raseshvara darshana*, lit., 'the science of mercury') to be a branch of Hatha-yoga: 'the mercurial system (rasāyana) must not be looked upon as a simple eulogy of metal, for it is an immediate means—by preserving the body—of attaining the supreme goal, which is deliverance'. And the alchemical treatise *Rasas-iddhanta*, quoted by Mādhava, says: 'The deliverance of the living soul [*jīva*] is set forth in the mercurial system.'[1]

Certain overlaps between yoga, especially tantric Hatha-yoga, and alchemy, occur naturally to the mind. There is, first, the obvious analogy between the yogi who works on his own body and his psycho-mental life, on the one hand, and the alchemist who works on substances, on the other. The one, like the other, aims at 'purifying' these impure materials, at 'perfecting' them and, finally, transmuting them into 'gold'. For, as we have seen (p. 51), 'gold is immortality': it is the perfect metal, and its symbolism rejoins the symbolism of the pure spirit, free and immortal, which the yogi endeavours, by asceticism, to 'extract' from the 'unclean' and 'enslaved' psycho-mental life. In other words the alchemist hopes to achieve the same results as the yogi by 'projecting' his asceticism *on* to matter. Instead of submitting his body and his psycho-mental life to the rigours of yoga, in order to separate the Spirit (*purusha*) from all experience belonging to the sphere of the substance (*prakṛti*), the alchemist subjects metals to chemical operations which correspond to 'purifications' and ascetic 'tortures'. For there is a complete solidarity between physical matter and the psycho-somatic body of the man: both are products of the primordial substance (*prakṛti*). Between the 'basest' metal and the most refined psycho-mental experience there is no break of continuity. And since with the post-Vedic epoch, results important to man's spiritual

[1] See the texts in Eliade, *Le Yoga*, pp. 281–2.

condition were expected from the 'interiorisation' of rites and physiological operations (alimentation, sexuality, etc.), it was logical to expect analogous results from the 'interiorisation' of the operations performed on matter. Asceticism projected by the alchemist on to matter was equivalent, in fact, to an 'interiorisation' of the operations performed in the laboratory.

This analogy between the two methods is substantiated in all forms of yoga, even the classical yoga of Patañjali. As to the different kinds of tantric yoga, their resemblance to alchemy is even clearer. Indeed the Hatha-yogis and the Tantrists aim to transmute their bodies into incorruptible ones, which they call 'divine body' (*divya-deha*), 'body of gnosis' (*jñāna-deha*), 'perfect body' (*siddha-deha*) or, in other contexts, the body of 'the one delivered in life' (*jīvan-mukta*). For his part, the alchemist pursues the transmutation of the body and dreams of indefinitely prolonging its youth, strength and suppleness. In both cases—tantra-yoga and alchemy—the process of the transmutation of the body comprises an experience of initiatory death and resurrection (cf. my *Le Yoga*, pp. 272 sq.). In addition, both Tantrist and alchemist strive to dominate 'matter'. They do not withdraw from the world as do the ascetic and metaphysician, but dream of conquering it and changing its ontological régime. In short, there is good ground for seeing in the tantric *sādhana*, and in the work of the alchemist, parallel efforts to free themselves from the laws of Time, to 'decondition' their existence and gain absolute freedom.

The transmutation of metals may be ranged among those 'freedoms' which the alchemist succeeds in enjoying: he intervenes actively in the processes of Nature (*prakṛti*) and in a sense it could even be said that he collaborates in its 'redemption'.[1] In the perspective of the Sâmkhya-Yoga, every spirit

---

[1] This term has not, of course, the same significance as it has in Christian theology.

(*purusha*) which has attained its autonomy, liberates thereby a fragment of the *prakṛti*, for it allows the matter which constitutes his body, his physiological and his psycho-mental life, to reabsorb itself, to reintegrate the primordial mode of nature, in other words, absolute repose. Thus the transmutation operated by the alchemist precipitates the tempo of the leisurely changes of Nature (*prakṛti*), and in so doing helps him to free himself from his own destiny just as the yogi, by forging a 'divine body', delivers Nature from its own laws: indeed, he succeeds in modifying its ontological status, in transmuting the indefatigable 'becoming' of Nature into a paradoxical and unthinkable stasis (for stasis belongs to the mode of being of the mind and not to the modalities of life and living matter).

All this is more easily understood if one studies the ideology, symbolism and techniques of alchemy in their yogi-tantric context, and if one takes account of a certain Indian spiritual prehistory embracing the belief in men-gods, magicians and immortals. Tantric yoga and alchemy have integrated, and given a new significance to these myths and yearnings as, in China, Taoism and alchemy have done with a number of immemorial traditions. We have discussed in a previous study the intimate connection between the different Indian 'mystical' techniques (cf. *Le Yoga*, pp. 292 sq., *et passim*), so there is no need to go into it again here.

The problem of the historical origins of Indian alchemy has not received a definitive solution. According to certain orientalists (A. B. Keith, Lüders) and most historians of science (J. Ruska, Stapleton, Renhardt Müller, E. von Lippmann), alchemy was introduced to India by the Arabs. They stress in particular the importance of mercury in alchemy and its late appearance in texts.[1] But there are other writers (e.g.

[1] See bibliography in Eliade, *Le Yoga*, pp. 278 sq., 398 sq. See also Note K.

Hoernle) who maintain that mercury is already mentioned in the 'Bower Manuscript', dating from the fourth century of the present era. On the other hand, several Buddhist texts, at intervals between the second and fifth centuries, draw attention to the transmutation of metals and ores into gold. *Avataṁska Sûtra* (second–fourth century) says: 'There exists a Hataka juice or essence. One *liang* of this solution can transform one thousand *liangs* of bronze into pure gold.' *Mahâprajñâpâramitopadesha* (translated into Chinese in 402–5) gives further details. 'By means of drugs and incantations one can change bronze into gold. By a skilful use of drugs, silver may be transformed into gold and gold into silver. By spiritual strength man can change clay or stone into gold.' Finally, the *Mahâprajñâpâramitâshâstra* of Nâgârjuna, translated into Chinese by Kumārajīva (344–13 B.C.), and thus three full centuries before the heyday of Arab alchemy which begins with Jâbir ibn Hayyân (*circa* A.D. 760), counts among the *siddhi* ('miraculous powers') the transmutation of 'stone into gold and gold into stone'. Nâgârjuna explains that the transformation of substances can be achieved both by herbs (*osadhi*) and by 'the force of the *samādhi*', that is, by yoga (Eliade, *Le Yoga*, pp. 278–9).

In short, belief in transmutation, like faith in the indefinite prolongation of human life, preceded, in India, the influence of the Arab alchemists. The treatise of Nâgârjuna says so clearly enough: transmutation can be effected either by drugs or by yoga: alchemy, as we have seen, takes its natural place among the most authentic of the 'mystical' techniques. The dependence of Indian alchemy on Arabian culture does not command conviction. Alchemical ideology and practices are to be found in the milieux of ascetics and yogi who were left untouched by Islamic influence when the Muslims invaded India. Alchemical tantras are especially found in those regions where Islam has barely penetrated—in Nepal and the Tamil country. Even supposing that mercury was introduced into India by Muslim alchemists, it was not at the roots of Indian alchemy. As a technique and ideology parallel with tantric yoga, it had been in existence for several centuries. Mercury was added to the list of substances already known to, and used by, Indian alchemists. Experiments with mercury must, however, have led to a rudimentary pre-chemistry which gradually developed side by side with the traditional Indian alchemy.

Let us look at some alchemical texts proper. Apparently less obscure than the works of Western alchemists, they nevertheless do not reveal the true secrets of their operations. But it is sufficient for us that they illuminate the plane on which these alchemical experiments are situated and allow us to deduce the ends which they pursued. *Rasaratnâkara*, a treatise attributed to Nâgârjuna, thus describes the adept: 'intelligent, devoted to his work, without sin and master of his passions'.[1] The *Rasaratnasamuccaya* (VII, 30) is even more precise: 'Those who are truthful, free from temptation, love the Gods and are self-controlled and used to live upon proper diet and regimen—such are to be engaged in performing chemical operations' (P. C. Ray, I, p. 117). The laboratory must be set up in the forest, far away from all unclean presence (*Rasaratnasamuccaya*, in Ray, I, p. 115). The same text (Book VI) teaches that the disciple must respect his master and venerate Shiva, for alchemy was revealed by the God Shiva himself; in addition, he must make a phallus of mercury for Shiva and participate in certain erotic rituals (Ray, I, pp. 115–16), which clearly demonstrates the alchemico-tantric symbioses.

[1] Praphula Chandra Ray, *A History of Hindu Chemistry*, II, p. 8. In the following pages the references are to the texts grouped and published by P. C. Ray. It should be borne in mind that P. C. Ray, who was himself a celebrated chemist and disciple of Marcelin Berthelot, gave preference to those works which seemed to have affinities with pre-chemistry.

The *Rudrayamâlâ Tantra* calls Shiva the 'god of mercury' (Ray, II, p. 19). In the *Kubjika Tantra*, Shiva speaks of mercury as his generating principle and lauds its efficiency when it has been 'fixed' (i.e. dead) six times. The lexicon of *Maheshvara* (twelfth century) gives a similar connotation to mercury by using the term Harabîja (lit. semen of Shiva). Moreover, in certain tantras, mercury is regarded as the 'generating principle' for all creatures. As for the phallus of mercury for Shiva, several tantras prescribe the manner of its making.[1]

Side by side with the chemical significance of the 'fixation' (or 'death') of mercury, there is a purely alchemical (yogi-tantric) meaning. To reduce the fluidity of mercury is equivalent to the paradoxical transmutation of the psycho-mental flow in a 'static consciousness', without any modification and hence without 'becoming'. In alchemical terms, to 'fix' or to 'kill' mercury is tantamount to attaining to the *citta-vṛttinirodha* (suppression of conscious states), which is the ultimate aim of yoga. Hence the limitless efficiency of 'fixed' mercury. The *Survarna Tantra* affirms that by eating 'killed mercury' (*nasta-pista*), man becomes immortal; a small quantity of this 'killed mercury' can change to gold a quantity of mercury 100,000 times as large. Even the alchemists' urine and faeces are capable of transmuting copper into gold.[2] The *Kâkacandesvarimata Tantra* asserts that 'killed' mercury produces a thousand times its quantity of gold; copper treated with a certain preparation of mercury turns into gold (text reproduced by Ray, II, p. 13). The *Rudra-yamâlâ* (I, 40) describes the *nasta-pista* as being without brilliance or fluidity, lighter than quicksilver, coloured, etc.

[1] P. C. Ray, I, p. 79 of Introd. On the 'purification' and 'fixation' of mercury. Cf. *ibid.*, I, pp. 130 sq., on the means of 'killing' metals generally, see *ibid.*, I, pp. 246 sq.

[2] Ray, II, pp. 28–9. *Yogatattva Upanisad* (73 sq.) quotes among the yogic *siddhi* the faculty of 'transmuting' iron or other metals to gold by smearing it with excrement; cf. Eliade, *Le Yoga*, p. 138. On *Nasta-pista*, cf. too *Rasârnava*, XI, 24, 197–8 (Ray, I, pp. 74–5), and Rasendracintâmani (*ibid.*, II, p. 16).

The same work declares that the alchemical process of 'killing' mercury was revealed by Shiva and secretly transmitted from one generation of adepts to another.[1] According to the *Rasaratnasamuccaya*, I, 26, man, by assimilating mercury, can avoid diseases arising out of the sins of former existences (Ray, I, p. 78). The *Rasaratnākara*, III, 30–2, mentions an elixir obtained from mercury which achieves the transformation of a human body into a divine one (Ray, II, p. 6). In the same text Nâgârjuna claims he can provide remedies against 'wrinkles, and white hair and other signs of old age' (Ray, II, p. 7). 'Mineral preparations act with equal efficiency on metals as on the human body' (*ibid.*). This favourite metaphor of Indian alchemists illustrates one of their fundamental conceptions. Like the human body, metals can be 'purified' and 'made divine' by mercuric preparations which communicate the healing virtues of Shiva, for Shiva, to the whole tantric world, is the God of deliverance. The *Rasârnava* recommends that mercury should be applied first on metals and then on the human body.[2] If we are to believe the *Rasahṛdaya Tantra*, alchemy may even cure leprosy and restore to old men their pristine youth (text in Ray, II, p. 12).

These few quotations, which it would be easy to multiply, have sufficiently illuminated the character of Indian alchemy: it is not a pre-chemistry but a technique of the same order as the other methods of 'subtile physiology' elaborated by Hatha-yoga and tantrism and pursuing a similar goal—the transmutation of the body and the conquest of liberty. This emerges clearly from a treatise such as the *Rasendracintāmaṇi* which gives the greatest number of indications as to the preparation and use of 'killèd mercury'. Here is the essential

---

[1] See Ray, II, p. 21. Cf. the myth of the 'doctrinal transmission' among the tantric *siddha* in Eliade, *Le Yoga*, pp. 305 sq.

[2] Text quoted by Madhava in his *Sarva-darsana-sam graha* (Anandâshrama Series), p. 80.

passage: 'When quicksilver is killed with an equal weight of purified sulphur it becomes one hundred times more efficacious; when it is killed with twice its weight of sulphur it cures leprosy; when killed with thrice its weight of sulphur it cures mental langour; when it is killed with four times its weight of sulphur it removes grey hair and wrinkles; when it is killed by five times its weight of sulphur it cures consumption; when it is killed with six times its weight of sulphur it becomes a panacea for all the ills that flesh is heir to' (text published by Ray, II, pp. 55–6). One appreciates the 'mystical' value of all these operations. Their scientific or chemical value is nil; it is known that in the combination of mercury with sulphur the maximum proportion is 25 parts to 4 respectively; over and above this proportion the excess of sulphur is sublimated without combining. In the passage quoted, the author of the *Rasendracintāmaṇi* uses the language of chemical experiments for what are merely commonplaces of magic medicine and Hatha-yoga concerning the universal panacea and rejuvenation.

This does not mean, of course, that the Hindus were incapable of scientific discoveries. Like his Western colleague, the Indian alchemist drew up the elements of a pre-chemistry the moment he abandoned the strictly traditional plane of reference and applied himself to the objective study of phenomena and experimentation with the aim of completing his knowledge of the properties of matter. Hindu scholars were capable of exact observation and scientific thought and several of their discoveries were in advance of those of the West. To cite only a few examples, they recognized, as far back as the twelfth century, the importance of the colour of flame in the analysis of metals.[1] According to P. C. Ray,

---

[1] Cf. the fragments from the *Rasārnava* in P. C. Ray, *op. cit.*, I, p. 68. The entire text of the *Rasārnava* has been edited by Ray in the *Biblioteca Indiea* (Calcutta).

metallurgical processes were described with greater accuracy by Hindu writers three centuries before Agrippa and Paracelsus. In the pharmacopoeia, the Hindus achieved impressive results: long before the Europeans, they had urged the internal use of calcinated metals. Paracelsus was the first to try to impose the internal use of sulphide of mercury; this remedy had already been used in India in the tenth century.[1] As for the internal use of gold and other metals, there is ample evidence for this in Indian medicine from the time of Vâgbhata[2]

According to P. C. Ray, Vrinda and Cakrāpani usher in the transitional period of Indian medicine during which the use of mineral substances gained the ascendancy over the vegetable substances of the previous epoch. Tantric influences nevertheless persist in the work of these two writers. They recommend gestures and formulae peculiar to the tantric cult (Ray, I, p. lvi). It was in the era following the tantric period, which Ray calls the iatro-chemical era, that preoccupations which can be more properly described as scientific or empirical come into play. The quest for the elixir and similar mystical activities disappears to give way to laboratory techniques (Ray, I, p. xci). The *Rasaratnasamuccaya* (thirteenth–fourteenth centuries) is a typical production of this period. It is therefore all the more significant to meet traces of traditional alchemy in a work of this kind. *Rasaratnasamuccaya* begins with a salutation to God who rescues human beings from illness, old age and death (Ray, I, p. 76). Then follows a list of alchemists, including the illustrious names of the tantric masters (*ibid.*, p. 77). The treatise communicates the mystic formulae by means of which metals may be purified,[3]

---

[1] Cf. Ray,'*op. cit.*, vol. I, p. 59, text of the *Siddha Yoga* of the doctor Vrinda.

[2] Cf. Ray, I, p. 55.

[3] The recitation of these formulae is an alchemical operation in itself which the *Rasaratnasmuccaya*, *inter alia*, expounds.

speaks of the diamond,[1] which conquers death and of the
internal use of gold, etc. (Ray, I, p. 105). All this proves the
persistence of the spiritual function of alchemy even in a work
as late as this and which nevertheless includes a number of
precise indications and scientifically exact descriptions.[2]

From time to time, assertions of the following character
are to be found in alchemical texts. 'I shall give publicity only
to such processes as I have been able to verify by my own
experiments.'[3] One is justified in wondering whether these
experiments are purely chemical operations or merely concerned with tantrico-alchemical ones. For a complete ascetic
and mystical tradition derives its authority from *experiment*.
In contrast to what we may call the metaphysical and abstract
path, the important spiritual current which embraces yoga,
tantrism and more particularly the hatha-yogic schools,
accord considerable weight to *experiment*: it is by acting and
working on the various planes of his physiological and psycho-
mental life that the yogi achieves concrete results which lead
him gradually to the threshold of deliverance. From times of
the greatest antiquity an important section of the Indian
spiritual élite applied itself to 'experimentation'—the direct,
experimental knowledge of all that constitutes the bases and
processes of the human body and the psycho-mental life.
There is no need to recall here the considerable results
obtained by the yogi in the control of the vegetative system
and the mastery of the psycho-mental flow.

As we have already noted, alchemy takes its place in the
framework of the pan-Indian experimental tradition. It would

----

[1] The diamond (*vajra*), identifiable with the 'thunderbolt' and the essence of
Buddha, plays a considerable role in tantric symbolism; cf. Eliade, *Le Yoga*, pp. 254
sq., *et passim*.
[2] A good description of salammoniac to be found widely circulated by Iranian
alchemy; adopted by the great Jâbir ibn Hâyyan, it became very popular in Arab
alchemy. See Note L.
[3] Cf. Rasendracintâmani, in Ray, II, p. lxiv; other texts *ibid*.

Hermaphroditus mortuo similis, in tenebris jacens, igne indiget.

EPIGRAMMA XXXIII.

Ille biceps gemini sexus, en funeris instar
 Apparet, postquam est humiditatis inops:
Nocte tenebrosâ si conditur, indiget igne,
 Hunc illi præstes, & modò vita redit.
Omnis in igne latet lapidis vis, omnis in auro
 Sulfuris, argento Mercurii vigor est.

Michaël Maier, *Scrutinium chymicum*

'The Hermaphrodite, like a dead man, lying in darkness has need of fire'

Draco mulierem, & hæc illum interimit, simulque sanguine perfunduntur.

EPIGRAMMA L.

ALta venenoso fodiatur tumba Draconi,
    Cui mulier nexu sit bene vincta suo:
Ille maritalis dum carpit gaudia lecti,
    Hæc moritur cum qua sit Draco tectus humo.
Illius hinc corpus morti datur, atque cruore
    Tingitur: Hæc operis semita vera tui est.

Michaël Maier, *Scrutinium chymicum*

'The Dragon and the Woman destroy one another and cover themselves
with blood'

follow from this that the alchemist who proclaims the importance of *experiment* is not thereby necessarily showing that he has a scientific mind in the modern sense of the term. He is simply proclaiming his part in a great Indian tradition as opposed to others, notably the scholastic or speculative tradition. There is no possible doubt about the *reality* of the alchemical operations; they are not speculations but concrete experiments, carried out in laboratories, on various mineral and vegetable substances. But to understand the nature of these experiments, we take into account not only the alchemist's aim and his behaviour, we also have to understand what, in the eyes of the Indians, these 'substances' could be. They were not inert, they represented stages in the inexhaustible manifestations of primordial matter (*prakrti*). We have already observed that plants, stones, metals, as well as the bodies of men, their physiological and psycho-mental life, were but different moments of a same cosmic process. It was therefore possible to pass from one stage to another, to transmute one form into another.

Furthermore, the operational contact with the 'substances' was not without spiritual consequences—as was the case in the West from the time when scientific chemistry came into its own. To work actively on ores and metals was to touch *prakrti*, to modify its forms, to intervene in its processes. Now, in the ideological universe in which the alchemist works, and which is that of tantrism, *prakrti* is not only the cosmological principle of classical Sāṅkhya and yoga; *prakrti* is the primordial mode of the Goddess, of the Shakti. Thanks to the symbolism and techniques elaborated by tantrism, *prakrti* becomes accessible to immediate experience; for the tantric, every naked woman incarnates *prakrti* and reveals it. It is not a question, of course, of an erotic or aesthetic experience. India had long possessed a whole literature dealing with similar experiences. But tantrism estimates that with an appropriate psycho-somatic and spiritual training, man can have the revelation of the primordial mode of nature by contemplating the nude body of a woman.

All this is equivalent to saying that, as far as the Indian alchemist is concerned, operations on mineral substances were not, and *could not be*, simple chemical experiments. On the contrary, they involved his karmic situation; in other words, they had decisive spiritual consequences. It is only when mineral substances have been emptied of their cosmological virtues and have become inanimate objects that chemical science proper becomes possible. Such a radical change of perspective would permit the constitution of a new scale of values and would render possible the appearance (that is, observation and recording) of chemical phenomena. For, in the words of the axiom dear to modern scientists, *it is the scale of values which creates phenomena*.

13

Alchemy and Initiation

WE DO NOT intend here to embark on a study of the principles and methods of Alexandrian, Arabian and Western alchemy. The subject is immense. The reader will refer to the classic works of Marcelin Berthelot and Edmund von Lippmann and to the investigations of Julius Ruska, J. R. Partington, W. Gundel, F. Sherwood Taylor, John Read, W. Ganzenmüller, etc., bearing in mind, however, that these writers regard alchemy as an embryonic stage of chemistry. On the other hand, there is no shortage of works in which alchemy is looked upon as both an operational and spiritual technique. The reader curious to know more about the traditional view would do well to read the works of Fulcanelli, Eugène Canseliet, J. Evola, Alexander von Bernus and René Alleau, to mention only the publications of the last quarter of the century and dealing with the traditional alchemical doctrine. As for C. G. Jung's psychological interpretation, it forms a chapter apart in the historiography of alchemy.[1]

It is sufficient for our purpose to single out very briefly certain alchemistic symbolisms and operations and to demonstrate their solidarity with the primitive symbolisms and techniques linked with the processes of matter. In our view, one of the principal sources of alchemy is to be sought in those conceptions dealing with the Earth-Mother, with ores and metals, and, above all, with the *experience* of primitive man

[1] See Note M for essential bibliography concerning the history of alchemy.

142

engaged in mining, fusion and smithcraft. The 'conquest of matter' began very early, perhaps in the palaeolithic age, that is, as soon as man had succeeded in making tools from silex and using fire to change the states of matter. In any case certain techniques—mainly agriculture and pottery—were fully developed during the neolithic age. Now these techniques were at the same time mysteries, for, on the one hand, they implied the sacredness of the cosmos and, on the other, were transmitted by initiation (the 'craft-secrets'). Tilling, or the firing of clay, like, somewhat later, mining and metallurgy, put primitive man into a universe steeped in sacredness. It would be vain to wish to reconstitute his experiences; too much time has elapsed since the cosmos has been desanctified as a result of the triumph of the experimental sciences. Modern man is incapable of experiencing the sacred in his dealings with matter; at most he can achieve an aesthetic experience. He is capable of knowing matter as a 'natural phenomenon'. But we have only to imagine a communion, no longer limited to the eucharistic elements of bread or wine, but extending to every kind of 'substance', in order to measure the distance separating a primitive religious experience from the modern experience of 'natural phenomena'.

Not that man in primitive society was still 'buried in Nature', powerless to free himself from the innumerable 'mystic' participations in Nature, totally incapable of logical thought or utilitarian labour in the modern sense of the word. Everything we know of our contemporary 'primitives' shows up the weakness of these arbitrary judgements. But it is clear that a thinking dominated by cosmological symbolism created an experience of the world vastly different from that accessible to modern man. To symbolic thinking the world is not only 'alive' but also 'open': an object is never simply itself (as is the case with modern consciousness), it is also a sign of, or a repository for, something else. To take one example, the tilled field is something more than a patch of earth, it is also the body of the Earth-Mother: the spade is a phallus while still remaining an agricultural tool; ploughing is at once a 'mechanical' labour (carried out with man-made tools) and a sexual union prescribed for the hierogamous fertilization of the Earth-Mother.

Although it is impossible for us to relive such experiences, we can at any rate imagine their effect on the lives of those who did experience them. The cosmos being a hierophany and human existence sacred, work possessed a liturgical value which still survives, albeit obscurely, among the rural populations of contemporary Europe. What is especially important to emphasize is the possibility given to primitive man to immerse himself in the sacred by his own work as a *homo faber* and as a creator and manipulator of tools. These primordial experiences have been preserved and handed down through numerous generations thanks to the 'craft-secrets'. When the general experience of the world had been modified as a result of technical and cultural innovations following in the wake of an urbanized civilization (that is, 'history' in the full sense of the word[1]), the primordial experiences linked with a sacred cosmos were periodically given a new life by means

[1] From a certain point of view, man, even the most primitive, has always been a 'historic being' by reason of the fact that he was conditioned by the ideology, sociology and economy peculiar to his tradition. But I do not wish to speak of this historicity of man as a man, or as a being conditioned by temporality and culture, but of a more recent and infinitely more complex phenomenon, namely, the enforced involvement of entire humanity in events taking place in a few restricted regions of the globe. This is what happened after the discovery of agriculture and especially after the crystallization of the earliest urban civilizations in the ancient Near East. From that moment all human culture, however strange and remote, was doomed to undergo the consequences of the historic events which were taking place at the 'centre'. These consequences sometimes became manifest thousands of years later but they could not in any way be avoided; they were part of the historic fatality. With the discovery of husbandry it is possible to say that man was destined to become an agricultural being or at any rate to suffer the influences of all subsequent discoveries and innovations which agriculture made possible: domestication of animals, urban civilization, military organization, empire, imperialism, mass wars, etc. In other words all mankind became involved in the activities of some of its members.

of craft-rites and initiations. We have come across examples of initiatory transmission rites among miners, smelters and smiths; in the West, they preserved, right up to the Middle Ages (and in other parts of the world, up to the present time), their primitive attitude *vis-à-vis* minerals and metals.

There is an abundance of testimony in the works on metallurgy and the craft of the goldsmith in the ancient Orient to show that men of primitive cultures were able to gain knowledge of, and mastery over, matter. A number of technical prescriptions have come down to us, some of which date from the sixteenth century B.C. (e.g. the Ebers Papyrus). They deal with alloyage, dyeing and gold copying (e.g. the Leyden and Stockholm Papyri dating from the third century B.C.). Historians of science have rightly emphasized that the authors of these prescriptions make use of *quantities* and *numbers* which would prove, in their view, the scientific character of these operations. It is certain that the smelters, smiths and master-goldsmiths of oriental antiquity could calculate quantities and control physico-chemical processes of smelting and alloyage. For all that, we must recognize that for them it was not solely a metallurgical or chemical operation, a technique or science in the strict sense of the word. African and Asiatic smiths who used analogous prescriptions with the known practical results, were not concerned with the mere practical aspect of the operations: they also had a ritual aspect. It would therefore be unwise to single out in those early beginnings of Graeco-Egyptian alchemy the prescriptions for the 'colouring of metals'; no craft, even in late antiquity, was a simple technique. However advanced the desacralisation of the cosmos was at that time, the trades still retained

Thus, from this time on—parallel with the rise of the first urban civilizations in the Near East—it is possible to speak of *history* in the full sense of the term, that is, of universal modifications effected by the creative will of certain societies (more precisely, of privileged elements in those societies). On this problem, see *Paradis et Histoire* (in preparation).

their ritual character, though the hierurgical context is not necessarily indicated in the prescriptions.[1]

The fact remains that historical documents allow us to distinguish three periods in the beginnings of Graeco-Egyptian alchemy:

(1) the period of technical prescriptions;

(2) the philosophical period, probably ushered in by Bolos de Mendes (second century B.C.), and manifesting itself in the *Physika Kai Mystika* attributed to Democritus; and, finally,

(3) the period of alchemistic writings proper, that of the apocryphas, of Zosimos (third–fourth centuries A.D.) and the commentators (fourth to seventh centuries).[2]

Although the problem of the *historical origins* of Alexandrian alchemy is still unsolved, one could explain the sudden appearance of *alchemical texts* at the beginning of the Christian era as the result of the encounter of differing currents. On the one hand, there were the esoteric currents, represented by the Mysteries, neo-Pythagorism, neo-Orphism, astrology, the 'revealed wisdom of the East', gnosticism, etc.—currents arising from the work of cultivated people, the 'intelligentsia', and, on the other hand, those arising from popular traditions which acted as the custodians of the trade-secrets and the very ancient magical techniques. A similar phenomenon may be noted in China with the advent of Taoism and neo-Taoism, and in India with tantrism and Hatha-yoga. In the Mediterranean world up to the Alexandrian epoch these popular traditions carried on this primitive spiritual behaviour. The growing interest in 'oriental wisdom' and traditional science

---

[1] The communication of 'trade-secrets' by writing is an illusion of modern historiography. If indeed there is a literature which claimed 'to reveal the secrets' it is tantric literature. But in this mass of writings we never find any practical indications indispensable to the *sādhana*: at the crucial moments a master must be to hand if only to confirm the authenticity of the experiment.

[2] State of research on this subject, with choice of texts, will be found in the clear exposé given by R. P. Festugière, in *La Révélation Trismégiste*, I, pp. 217 sq.

and the technology of substances, precious stones and plants, characterizes all this period of antiquity, so brilliantly investigated by Franz Cumont and R. P. Festugière.

To what historical causes are we to attribute the birth of practical alchemy? We shall probably never know. But it is doubtful whether prescriptions for counterfeiting or imitating gold were the starting point for alchemy as an autonomous discipline. The Hellenist Orient had inherited its metallurgical techniques from Mesopotamia and Egypt and it is well known that, starting with the fourteenth century of the present era, the Mesopotamians had perfected the assaying of gold. To attempt to link up a discipline, which dominated the Western world for 2000 years, with attempts to counterfeit gold is to forget the extraordinary knowledge of metals and alloys possessed by the Ancients. It is also to underestimate their intellectual and spiritual capacity. Transmutation, which was the principal aim of Alexandrian alchemy, was not, in the state of science as it then was, an absurdity, for the unity of matter had for long been a tenet of Greek philosophy. But it is difficult to believe that alchemy emerged from experiments undertaken to validate this tenet and to demonstrate experimentally the unity of matter. It is difficult to conceive of a spiritual technique and a soteriology rising out of a philosophical theory.

On the other hand, when the Greek mind applies itself to science it evinces an extraordinary sense of observation and argument. What strikes us when we read the texts of the Greek alchemists is their lack of interest as far as physico-chemical phenomena are concerned, in other words, the absence of the scientific spirit. As Sherwood Taylor remarks: 'No one who had used sulphur, for example, could fail to remark the curious phenomena which attend its fusion and the subsequent heating of the liquid. Now while sulphur is mentioned hundreds of times, there is no allusion to any of its characteristic properties except its action on metals. This is in such strong contrast to the spirit of the Greek science of classical times that we must conclude that the alchemists were not interested in natural phenomena other than those which might help them to attain their object. Nevertheless, we should err were we to regard them as mere gold-seekers, for the semi-religious and mystical tone, especially of the later works, consorts ill with the spirit of the seeker of riches. . . . We shall not find in alchemy any beginnings of a science. . . . At no time does the alchemist employ a scientific procedure.'[1] The texts of the ancient alchemists show 'that these men were not really interested in making gold and were not in fact talking about real gold at all. The practical chemist examining these works feels like a builder who should try to get practical information from a work on Freemasonry' (Sherwood Taylor, *ibid.*, p. 138).

If, therefore, alchemy could not be born from the desire to counterfeit gold (gold assay had been known for at least twelve centuries), nor from a Greek scientific technique (we have just seen the alchemists' lack of interest in physico-chemical phenomena as such), we are compelled to look else-where for the origins of this discipline *sui generis*. Much more than the philosophic theory of the unity of matter, it was probably the old conception of the Earth-Mother, bearer of embryo-ores, which crystallized faith in artificial transmuta-tion (that is, operated in a laboratory). It was the encounter with the symbolisms, myths and techniques of the miners, smelters and smiths which probably gave rise to the first alchemical operations. But above all it was the experimental discovery of the *living* Substance, such as it was felt by the artisans, which must have played the decisive role. Indeed, it

---

[1] F. Sherwood Taylor, *A Survey of Greek Alchemy*, p. 110. Cf. too F. S. Taylor, *Origins of Greek Alchemy*, pp. 42 sq.

is the conception of a *complex and dramatic Life of Matter* which constitutes the originality of alchemy as opposed to classical Greek science. One is entitled to suppose that the *experience* of *dramatic life* was made possible by the knowledge of Graeco-oriental mysteries.

It is known that the essence of initiation into the Mysteries consisted of participation in the passion, death and resurrection of a God. We are ignorant of the modalities of this participation but one can conjecture that the sufferings, death and resurrection of the God, already known to the neophyte as a myth or as authentic history, were communicated to him during initiations, in an 'experimental' manner. The meaning and finality of the Mysteries were the transmutation of man. By experience of initiatory death and resurrection, the initiate changed his mode of being (he became 'immortal').

Now the dramatic spectacle of the 'sufferings,' 'death' and 'resurrection' of matter is very strongly borne out in the very beginnings of Graeco-Egyptian alchemistical literature. Transmutation, the *magnum opus* which culminated in the Philosopher's Stone, is achieved by causing matter to pass through four phases, named, from the colours taken on by the ingredients: *melansis* (black), *leukosis* (white), *xanthosis* (yellow) and *iosis* (red). Black (the *nigredo* of medieval writers) symbolizes death, and we shall return again to this alchemical mystery. But it is important to emphasize that the four phases of the *opus* are already mentioned in the pseudo-Democritean *Physika kai Mystika* (fragment preserved by Zosimos)— that is, in the first alchemical writing proper (second to first century B.C.). With innumerable variations, the four (or five) phases of the work (*nigredo, albedo, citrinitas, rubedo*, sometimes *viriditas*, sometimes *cauda pavonis*) are retained throughout the whole history of Arabian Western alchemy.

Furthermore, it is the mystical drama of the God—his

passion, death and resurrection—which is projected on to matter in order to transmute it. All in all, the alchemist treats his Matter as the God was treated in the mysteries; the mineral substances 'suffer', 'die' or 'are reborne' to another mode of being, that is, are transmuted. Jung has drawn attention to a text by Zosimos (*Treatise on Art*, III, 1, 2-3), in which the famous alchemist talks of a vision which he had in a dream. A personage named Ion reveals to him that he has been pierced by a sword, cut into pieces, decapitated, scorched, burned in fire, all of which he suffered 'in order to be able to change his body into Spirit'. On waking, Zosimos wonders whether what he has seen is not linked with the alchemical process of the combination of water; whether Ion is not the figure, the model image of water. As Jung has pointed out, this water is the *aqua permanens* of the alchemists, and his 'tortures' by fire correspond to the operation of *separatio*.[1]

Let us note that Zosimos's description recalls not only the dismemberment of Dionysius and other 'dying Gods' of the Mysteries (whose passion is, on a certain plane, closely allied with the different moments of the vegetal cycle, especially with the tortures, death and resurrection of the Spirit of Corn), but that it presents striking analogies with the initiation visions of the shamans and, in general, with the fundamental pattern of all primitive initiations. It is known that every initiation comprises a series of ritual tests symbolizing the death and resurrection of the neophyte. In the shamanic initiations, these ordeals, although undergone 'in the second state', are of an extreme cruelty. The future shaman is present, in a dream, at his own dismemberment, decapitation and

---

[1] C. G. Jung, 'Die Visionen des Zosimos' (in the volume *Von den Wurzeln des Bewusstseins*, pp. 137-216), pp. 153 sq. The text of the 'Vision' is to be found in M. Berthelot, *Collection des Alchmistes grecs* (Textes), pp. 107-12, 115-18. Cf. the new English translation by F. Sherwood Taylor, *Ambix*, I, pp. 88-92. The *separatio* is expressed in alchemical works as the dismemberment of a human body. Cf. Jung, *op. cit.*, p. 154, no. 127. On the 'torture' of elements, see *ibid.*, p. 211.

death.[1] If one takes account of the universality of the initiation pattern and the close parallelism between workers in metals, smiths and shamans; if one reflects that the ancient Mediterranean guilds of metallurgists and smiths very probably had at their disposal mysteries which were peculiar to them, one finally realizes that Zosimos's vision has its place in that spiritual universe which the preceding pages have attempted to interpret and define. And now one is in a position to measure the extent of the alchemists' innovation: *they projected on to Matter the initiatory function of suffering.* Thanks to the alchemical operations, corresponding to the tortures, death and resurrection of the initiate, the substance is transmuted, that is, attains a transcendental mode of being: it becomes gold. Gold, we repeat, is the symbol of immortality. In Egypt the flesh of the Gods was believed to be of gold. By becoming God, the flesh of Pharaoh also became gold. Alchemical transmutation is therefore equivalent to the perfecting of matter or, in Christian terminology, to its redemption.[2]

We have seen that ores and metals were regarded as living organisms: one spoke in terms of their gestation growth, birth and even marriage (cf. pp. 36 sq.). The alchemists adopted and gave a new significance to these primitive beliefs. The alchemical combination of sulphur and mercury is always expressed in terms of 'marriage'. But this marriage is also a mystical union between two cosmological principles. Herein lies the novelty of the alchemical perspective: the life of Matter

---

[1] Cf. Eliade, *Le Chamanisme*, pp. 52 sq., *et passim*. C. G. Jung has already shown the relationship between Shamanic initiations and alchemical symbolism. Cf. *Von den Wurzeln des Bewusstseins*, p. 157, n. 38.

[2] C. G. Jung, *Psychologie und Alchemie*, pp. 416 sq., speaks of the redemption by the alchemical operation; he talks of the *anima mundi*, captive in matter (see Note N). This conception, gnostic in origin and structure, was certainly held by certain alchemists: it fits in with the whole trend of eschatological thought which culminated in the conception of cosmic salvation. But, in its beginnings, at any rate, alchemy did not postulate the captivity of *anima mundi* in matter: obscurely perhaps, matter was conceived as the *Terra Mater*.

is no longer designated in terms of 'vital' hierophanies as it was in the outlook of primitive man; it has acquired a spiritual dimension; in other words, by taking on the initiatory significance of drama and suffering, matter also takes on the destiny of the spirit. The 'initiation tests' which, on the spiritual plane, culminate in freedom, illumination and immortality, culminate on the material plane, in transmutation, in the Philosopher's Stone.

The *Turba Philosophorum* expresses very clearly the spiritual significance of the 'torture' of metals: '*eo quod cruciata res, cum in corpore submergitur, vertit ipsum in naturam inalterabilem ac indelebilem*'.[1] Ruska considers that to the Greek alchemists, 'torture' did not yet correspond to an actual operation but was symbolic. It is only with the Arab writers that 'torture' has reference to chemical operations. In the *Testament of Ga'far Sadiq*, we read that dead bodies must be tortured by fire and by all the Arts of Suffering in order that they may revive; for without suffering or death one cannot achieve eternal life.[2] 'Torture' always brought 'death' with it —*mortificatio*, *putrefactio*, *nigredo*. There was no hope of 'resuscitating' to a transcendent mode of being (that is, no hope of attaining to transmutation), without prior 'death'. The alchemical symbolism of torture and death is sometimes equivocal; the operation can be taken to refer either to man or to a mineral substance. In the *Allegoriae super Librum Turbae* we read: 'Take a man, shave him and drag him on to the stone until his body dies' (*accipe hominem, tonde eum, et trahe super lapidem . . . donec corpus eius moriatur*).[3] This ambivalent symbolism permeates the whole *opus alchymicum*. It is important therefore to appreciate its significance.

[1] Julius Ruska, 'Turba Philosophorum', *Ein Beitrag zur Geschichte der Alchemie*, p. 168.

[2] Julius Ruska, *Arabische Alchemisten*, II, p. 77.

[3] *Artis Auriferae* (Basilae, 1593), vol. I, p. 139, quoted by Jung, *Psychologie und Alchemie*, p. 455, n. 3.

14

Arcana Artis

At the operational level, 'death' corresponds usually to the black colour (the *nigredo*) taken on by the various ingredients. It was the reduction of substances to the *materia prima*, to the *massa confusa*,[1] the fluid, shapeless mass corresponding—on the cosmological plane—to chaos. Death represents regression to the amorphous, the reintegration of chaos. This is why aquatic symbolism plays such an important part. One of the alchemists' maxims was: 'Perform no operation till all be made water.'[2] On the operational level, this corresponds to the solution of purified gold in *aqua regia*. Kirchweger, the supposed author of the *Aurea Catena Homeri* (1723)—a work which, incidentally, had a great influence on the young Goethe—writes: 'For this is certain, that all nature was in the beginning water, and through water all things were born and again through water all things must be destroyed.'[3] The alchemical regression to the fluid state of matter corresponds, in the cosmologies, to the primordial chaotic state, and in the initiation rituals, to the 'death' of the initiate.

The alchemist also obtained solutions by placing substances in the mercury bath. In the words of Starkey (Eirenaeus

[1] Cf. examples in Jung, *Psychologie und Alchemie*, pp. 442 sq.
[2] Cf. John Read, *Prelude to Chemistry*, p. 132. On *aqua permanens*, see texts quoted by Jung, *op. cit.*, pp. 320 sq.
[3] Text quoted by R. D. Gray, *Goethe the Alchemist* (Cambridge, 1952), p. 14.

Philalethes), 'the main ground for the possibility of transmutation is the possibility of the reduction of all metals, and such Minerals which are of metallick principles, into their first mercurial matter'.[1] A treatise attributed to 'Alphonso, King of Portugal', states: 'our dissolution is no other thing but that the body be turned again to moistness. . . . The first result of this work is the body reduced to water, that is to Mercury, that is what the Philosophers call solution, which is the foundation of the work'.[2] According to certain writers, dissolution is the first operation; according to others it is calcination, the reduction to the amorphous by Fire. However that may be, the result is the same: 'death'.

This alchemical reduction to the *prima materia* may be interpreted in a great variety of ways: notably it may be equated with a regression to the pre-natal state, a *regressus ad uterum*. There is support for this seminal symbolism in a codex studied by Carbonelli, in which it is written that before using gold in the *opus* 'it is necessary to reduce it to sperm'.[3] The *vas mirabile*, of which Mary the Prophetess proclaimed that the whole alchemical secret resided therein, is 'a kind of *matrix* or *uterus* from which will be born the *filius philosophorum*, the miraculous Stone' (Jung, *Psychologie und Alchemie*, p. 325). 'The vase is akin to the work of God in the vase of divine germination,' writes Dorn.[4] According to Paracelsus, 'he who would enter the Kingdom of God must first enter with his body into his mother and there die'. The whole world, according to the same writer, must 'enter into its mother', which is the *prima materia*, the *massa confusa*, the

---

[1] G. Starkey, Ripley Reviv'd (London, 1678), p. 3, quoted by Gray, *op. cit.*, p. 16.

[2] Cf. John Read, *op. cit.*, p. 137.

[3] *Et in che l'oro si vogli mettere in opra é necessario che si riduchi in sperma*; text reproduced by G. Carbonelli, *Sulle fonti storiche della chimicha e della alchimia in Italia* (Rome, 1925), p. 7.

[4] Dorn, 'Physica Trismegisti' (*Theatrum Chemicum*, vol. I, Ursellis, 1602, pp. 405–37), 430, quoted by Jung, *Psychologie und Alchemie*, p. 325, n. 1.

abyssus, in order to achieve eternity.[1] John Pordage has it that the *Bain Marie* is 'the place, the *matrix*, and the centre whence the divine tincture flows from its source and origin'.[2] In the verses published as an appendix to the *Opus Mago-Cabbalisticum et Theosophicum* (1735) by Georg von Welling, we may read: 'For I cannot otherwise reach the Kingdom of Heaven unless I am born a second time. Therefore I desire to return to the mother's womb, that I may be regenerated, and this I will do right soon.'[3] The *regressus ad uterum* is sometimes presented in the form of incest with the mother. Michael Maier tells us that 'Delphinas, an anonymous philosopher, in his treatise *Secretus Maximus*, speaks very clearly of the mother who must, of natural necessity, unite herself with her son' (*cum filio ex necessitate naturae conjugenda*).[4] But it is obvious that the 'mother' symbolizes, in these different contexts, nature in her primordial state, the *prima materia* of the alchemists, and that the 'return to the mother' translates a spiritual experience corresponding to any other 'projection' outside Time—in other words, to the reintegration of a primal situation. The dissolution to the *prima materia* is also symbolized by a sexual union which is completed by disappearance into the uterus. In the *Rosarium Philosophorum* we read: 'Beya mounted Gabricus and enclosed him in her womb in such a fashion that nothing of him remained visible.

---

[1] Quoted by Gray, *op. cit.*, p. 31.

[2] Cf. the letter written by John Pordage (1601–1681) concerning the *opus* and addressed to his *soror mystica* Jane Leade, reproduced by C. G. Jung in *Die Psychologie der Übertragung*.

[3] Quoted by Gray, *op. cit.*, pp. 32, 268. It was Fräulein von Klettenberg who, in 1768, had urged the young Goethe to read the *Opus Mago-Cabbalisticum*. Goethe found the book 'obscure and incomprehensible'; cf. Gray, p. 4. But he certainly read the appendix (cf. *ibid.*, p. 31); the alchemical symbolism of the 'return to the Mother' appears in Goethe's later poetic work; cf. Gray, pp. 202 sq. See also Alexander von Bernus, *Alchymie und Heilkunst*, pp. 165 sq. On the Goethean symbolism of the Gang zu den Müttern, see Eliade, *Mitul Reintegrarii* (Bucharest, 1942), pp. 16 sq.

[4] Maier, *Symbola aureae mensae duodecim nationum* (Frankfurt, 1617), p. 344, quoted by Jung, *Psychologie und Alchemie*, p. 453, n. 1. See, too, J. Evola, *La Tradizione ermetica*, pp. 78 sq. (*l'incesto filosofale*).

She embraced him with so much love that she absorbed him entirely into her own nature. . . .' (*Nam Beya ascendit super Gabricum, et includit eum in suo utero, quod nil penitus videri potest de eo. Tantoque amore amplexata est Gabricum, quod ipsum totum in sui naturam concepit* . . .)[1] Such a symbolism naturally lends itself to innumerable interpretations. The Bath of Mary is not only the 'matrix' of the divine tincture (see above, p. 155), it is also the symbolical representation of the womb in which Jesus was born. The incarnation of the Lord in the adept may therefore begin as soon as the alchemical ingredients of the Bain Marie enter into a state of fusion and reintegrate the primordial state of matter. This return to primal matter is associated with the *birth* of Christ as well as with his *death*.[2]

From different points of view, J. Evola and C. G. Jung have commented very pertinently on the symbolism of initiatory death as seen in the *nigredo*, the *putrefactio* and the *dissolutio*.[3] It is necessary to add that the dissolution and reintegration of chaos is an operation which, whatever the context, presents at least two interdependent significations: cosmological and initiatory. Every 'death' is at once a reintegration of cosmic night and pre-cosmological chaos. At many different levels, darkness expresses the dissolution of forms, the return to the seminal stage of existence. Every 'creation', every appearance of forms, or, in another context, any access to a transcendental level, is expressed by a cosmological symbol. As we have repeatedly pointed out—a birth, a construction, a spiritual creation, always has the same

---

[1] *Rosarium Philosophorum* (*Artis Auriferae*, I, pp. 204–384), p. 246, quoted by Jung, *op. cit.*, p. 459, n. 1. As Beya was the sister of Gabricus, his disappearance in the womb retains the symbolic value of the 'philosophic incest'. See also C. H. Josten, 'William Baekhouse of Swallowfield' (*Ambix*, IV, 1949, pp. 1–33), pp. 13–14.

[2] R. D. Gray, *op. cit.*, pp. 32–3.

[3] J. Evola, *La Tradizione ermetica*, pp. 116 sq. C. G. Jung, *Psychologie und Alchemie*, pp. 451 sq.; id., *The Psychology of the Transference*, pp. 256 sq.

exemplar, viz., the cosmogony. This accounts for the repeated recital, in so many different cultures, of the cosmogonic myth, not only on New Year's Day (when the world is symbolically created anew), or when a new king is enthroned, or on the occasion of a marriage, a war, etc., but also in the case of saving a threatened harvest or healing a sick man. The profound significance of all these rituals seems abundantly clear: to *do* something well, or to *remake* a living integrity menaced by sickness, it is first necessary to go back *ad originem*, then to repeat the cosmogony.[1] Initiatory death and mystic darkness thus also possess a cosmological significance: they signify the reintegration of the 'first state', the germinal state of matter, and the 'resurrection' corresponds to the cosmic creation. In modern terminology, initiatory death abolishes Creation and History and delivers us from all failures and 'sins'. It delivers us from the ravages inseparable from the human condition.

In this respect the alchemist was not an innovator. While seeking the *materia prima* he pursued the reduction of substances to their pre-cosmogonic state. He knew that he could not achieve transmutation if he used as his starting point 'forms' already worn by time. In the initiatory context, 'dissolution' meant that the initiate 'was dying' as far as his profane, worn, fallen existence was concerned. That cosmic night was compared to death (darkness) as well as to the regression *ad uterum* is something which emerges both from the history of religions and from the alchemical texts already quoted. Western alchemists integrated their symbolism into Christian theology. The 'death' of matter was sanctified by the death of Christ who assured its redemption. Jung has brilliantly expounded the Christ-Philosopher's Stone

[1] Cf. Eliade, *Mythe de l'Eternel Retour*, pp. 83 sq., *et passim*; see also Eliade, *Traité d'Histoire des Religions*, pp. 350 sq.

parallelism and the daring theology which it implies.[1]

It is essential that we understand the plane on which the alchemical operation unfolds. Without a shadow of doubt, the Alexandrian alchemists were from the very beginning aware that in pursuing the perfection of metals they were pursuing their own perfection.[2] The *Liber Platonis quartorum* (the original Arabic of which cannot be later than the tenth century) gives great importance to the parallelism between the *opus alchymicum* and the inner experience of the adept. 'Things are rendered perfect by their similars and that is why the operator must take part in the operation' (*opportet operatorem interesse operi*).[3] The same text recommends the use of an occiput as the vessel for transformation because the skull is the repository of thought and intellect (*os capitis . . . vas mansionis cogitationis et intellectus*; quoted by Jung, *op. cit.*, p. 365, n. 3). The adept must transform himself into a Philosopher's Stone. 'Transform yourself from dead stones into living philosophic stones', writes Dorn (*transmutemini de lapidibus mortuis in vivos lapides philosophicos*; quoted by

[1] See especially *Psychologie und Alchemie*, pp. 469 sq. Albert-Marie Schmidt has presented the Christ-Philosopher's Stone parallelism most felicitously: 'They profess the belief that, in order to consummate the "Magnum Opus" (the regeneration of matter), they must pursue the regeneration of their own souls. This gnosis attempts to assume a Christian aspect. Just as in their sealed vase matter dies and is reborn, perfect, so they wish their souls, after succumbing to a mystic death, to be reborn in order to lead, in God, a life of ecstasy. In all things they show a pride in conforming to Christ's example, for He, in order to overcome death, had to experience, or rather accept, death's touch. For them, therefore, the imitation of Christ is not only a method of spiritual life but a means of regulating the course of material operations, whence the Master will emanate: the well-known words of the parable "except the grain fall to the ground and die" applies both to matter and to soul. A similar occult vitalism stimulates, by God's grace, both the one and the other.' (*La Poésie Scientifique en France au XVIe siècle*, p. 319). Cf. also J. Evola, *La Tradizione ermetica*, pp. 168 sq.

[2] See Arthur John Hopkins, *Alchemy, child of Greek Philosophy*, pp. 214–15. According to Hopkins, the first Alexandrian alchemists believed themselves able to raise ordinary metals to the dignity of silver and gold by impressing upon the 'bodies' (of the metals) a 'volatile spirit' (*ibid.*, p. 69, etc.). Whatever may be thought of this hypothesis it is obvious that this effort (to impose a 'volatile spirit' on the 'bodies' of substances), presupposes a religious estimation of matter and, consequently, a soteriological signification of the *opus alchymicum*.

[3] Quoted by Jung, *Psychologie und Alchemie*, p. 363.

Jung, p. 367, n. 1). And Morienus addresses himself in the following terms to King Kallid: 'For this substance [that is, the one which conceals the divine secret], is extracted from you and you are its ore (that is, the crude matter); they [the adepts] find it in you and, to speak more accurately, from you they take it' (quoted by Jung, p. 426, n. 1). For his part, Gichtel writes concerning the operation *albedo* (which, in certain contexts, designates the first hermetic transmutation: that of lead or copper into silver): 'We receive not only a new Soul with this regeneration but also a new body. This body is extracted from the Divine Word or from the heavenly Sophia. ... It is more spiritual than the Air, akin to the rays of the Sun which penetrate all bodies, and as different from the old body as the resplendent Sun is from the dark earth; and although it remains in the old Body, this Body cannot conceive it even though it may sometimes feel it.'[1] In short, the Western alchemist, in his laboratory, like his Indian or Chinese colleague, worked upon himself—upon his psycho-physiological life as well as on his moral and spiritual experience. All texts agree in emphasizing the virtue and qualities of the alchemist.[2] He must be healthy, humble, patient, chaste; his mind must be free and in harmony with his work; he must be intelligent and scholarly, he must work, meditate, pray, etc. It is obvious therefore that it is not merely a question of experiments conducted in the laboratory. The alchemist must involve himself completely in his work. But these qualities and virtues must not be understood in a purely moral sense. In the alchemist they have the same function as patience, intelligence, equanimity, etc., have in the tantric *sādhana*, or in the novitiate period preceding initiation to the Mysteries. Which is to say that

[1] Gichtel, *Theosophia Practica*, III, 13, 5, quoted by Evola, *La Tradizione ermetica*, p. 164. Concerning the 'incorruptible and celestial' body, see C. Della Riviera, *Il Mondo Magico degli Heroi* (ristampa, Bari, 1932), pp. 123 sq.

[2] Cf. Jung, *op. cit.*, pp. 367 sq. Similar instructions have been noted in the case of Chinese and Hindu alchemists; see above, pp. 117, 135 sq.

no virtue or erudition could dispense with the initiation experience, which alone was capable of operating the break in level implicit in transmutation.

We are of course quite ignorant of the exact nature of the crucial experience which for the alchemist was equivalent to obtaining the Philosopher's Stone or the Elixir. Excessively prolix in all that concerns the preliminaries and various phases of the *opus*, alchemical literature makes only cryptic and, for the most part, incomprehensible allusions to the *mysterium magnum*. But if we are right in insisting on the interdependent relationships between mineralogical symbolism, metallurgical rites, the magic of fire and the beliefs in the artificial transmutation of metals into gold by operations which replace those of Nature and time; if we take into account the close connection between Chinese alchemy and neo-Taoist techniques, between Indian alchemy and tantrism; if, in short, the Alexandrian alchemists did, as seems probable, project on to mineral substances the initiatory spectacles of the Mysteries—it becomes possible to penetrate into the nature of alchemical experience. The Indian alchemist provides us with a point of comparison: he works on mineral substances in order to 'cleanse' and to 'awaken' himself, or, in other words, to enter into possession of those divine substances which were dormant in his body. The Western alchemist by endeavouring to 'kill' the ingredients, to reduce them to the *materia prima*, provokes a *sympatheia* between the 'pathetic situations' of the substance and his innermost being. In other words, he realizes, as it were, some initiatory experiences which, as the course of the *opus* proceeds, forge for him a new personality, comparable to the one which is achieved after successfully undergoing the ordeals of initiation. His participation in the phases of the *opus* is such that the *nigredo*, for example, procures for him experiences analogous to those of the neophyte in the initiation ceremonies when he feels 'swallowed up' in the belly of the monster, or 'buried', or symbolically 'slain by the masks and masters of initiation'.

It is not possible in the space of a few pages to give a detailed description of the *opus alchymicum*. Nor are writers always in agreement concerning the order of operations. But it is interesting to note that the *coniunctio* and the ensuing death is sometimes expressed in terms of *hieros gamos*: the two principles —the Sun and Moon, King and Queen, unite in the mercury bath and die (this is the *nigredo*): their 'soul' abandons them to return later and give birth to the *filius philosophorum*, the androgynous being (Rebis) which promises the imminent attainment of the Philosopher's Stone. This order of operations is suggested in the *Rosarium Philosophorum* by a series of engravings, to the interpretation of which Jung has devoted the bulk of his *Psychologie der Übertragung*. We must emphasize the importance accorded by the alchemists to the 'terrible' and 'sinister' experiences of 'blackness', of spiritual death, of descent into hell. Not only are they constantly referred to in texts, but they can be detected in the art and iconography inspired by alchemy, where this sort of experience is translated by saturnine symbolism, by melancholy, the contemplation of skulls, etc.[1]

The figure of Chronos—Saturn—symbolizes Time the Great Destroyer, death (*putrefactio*) and birth. Saturn, symbol of Time, is often represented holding a balance. The importance of the symbolism of the Balance in hermetism and alchemy is well known (see illustration, p. 34, Read, *Prelude to Chemistry*). The illustrious Geber (Jâbîr ibn Hayyân) is also the author of a *Book of Balances*.[2] Ought not one to see in

---

[1] Cf. G. F. Hartlaub, *Arcana Artis. Spuren alchemistischer Symbolik in der Kunst des 16 Jahrhunderts* (Zeit. f. Kunstgeschichte, VI, 1937, pp. 289–324), pp. 316 sq.

[2] On the symbolism of the Balance in Jâbîr, see Henri Corbin, 'Le Livre du Glorieux de Jâbîr ibn Hayyân (*Eranos-Jahrbuch*, 18, 1950), pp. 75 sq.

this 'mastery of the Balance' (which renders them omniscient and clairvoyant), in this familiarity with the work of Time (*putrefactio*, death, which destroys *omne genus et formam*), in this 'wisdom' reserved exclusively for those who have anticipated the experience of death at the height of life— ought one not to see in all this the explanation of the famous 'saturnine melancholy' of the magi and alchemists?[1] Be that as it may, we should not forget that the acrostic constructed by Basil Valentine with the term *vitriol* emphasizes the implacable necessity of the *descensus ad inferos*: *Visita Interiora Terrae Rectificando Invenies Occultum Lapidem* ('Visit the interior of the Earth, and by purification thou wilt find the secret Stone').

The phase which follows the *nigredo*, that is, the 'work in white', the *leukosis*, the *albedo*, probably corresponds, on the spiritual plane, to a resurrection expressed by the assumption of certain states of consciousness inaccessible to the uninitiated. (On the laboratory level, it is the phenomenon of 'coagulation' which follows the initial *putrefactio*.) The two subsequent phases, the *cinitritas* and the *rubedo*, which are the consummation of the alchemical operation and culminate in the Philosopher's Stone, further develop and fortify this new initiatic consciousness.[2]

We should like to stress the paradoxical character of the *beginning* and the *end* of the *opus alchymicum*. One starts with the *materia prima* in order ultimately to arrive at the Philosophic Stone, but both substances defy precise identification— a consequence not of the writers' brevity but rather of their

---

[1] This is apparently what Hartlaub believes, *op. cit.*, p. 352, following the exegesis of hermetic symbolism in Dürer's *Melancholia* (studied in detail by F. Saxl and Panowski).

[2] An exposition of the '*albedo*' and '*rubedo*', from the traditional viewpoint, will be found in J. Evola, *La Tradizione ermetica*, pp. 156 sq. The psychological interpretation will be found in Jung's *Psychologie der Übertragung* (American edn., pp. 271 sq.). See also Albert-Marie Schmidt, *La Poésie Scientifique en France au XVIe siècle*, pp. 133 sq.

prolixity. Indeed, the synonyms employed for *materia prima* are numerous: the *Lexicon Alchemiae* of Martin Ruland (Frankfurt, 1612) records more than fifty, and even this list is far from exhaustive. As for the precise character of the *materia prima*, it, too, defies all definition. Zacharia wrote that though it is not an error to call 'our matter' spiritual, it is not untrue to declare it corporeal. To call it 'celestial' would be to give it its true name, though 'terrestrial' would be equally exact. As J. Evola justly observes in connection with this text, we are not dealing with a philosophic concept but a symbol; the implication is that the alchemist takes on the garb of Nature *sub specie interioritatis* (*op. cit.*, p. 32). Hence the great number of synonyms for *materia prima*. Some alchemists identify it with sulphur, mercury or lead; others with the Water of Youth, heaven, mother, moon, dragon, Venus, chaos, or even with the Philosopher's Stone or God.[1]

This ubiquity of the *materia prima* corresponds in every way with that of the Philosopher's Stone. For if the Stone represents the end point of a fabulous operation ('know that this is a very long path', *longissima via*, the *Rosarium* warns us), it is also extremely accessible: indeed, it is to be found everywhere. Ripley (*c.* 1415–90) writes: 'The philosophers say that the birds and fishes bring the Stone to us, each man possesses it, it is everywhere, in you, in me, in all things, in time and in space. It presents itself in base guise (*vili figura*). And from it springs our *aqua permanens*.'[2]

According to a text dated 1526, in the *Gloria Mundi*, the Stone 'is familiar to all men, both young and old; it is found in the country, in the village and in the town, in all things created by God; yet it is despised by all. Rich and poor handle it every day. It is cast into the street by servant maids.

[1] For the identification of the *prima materia* with God and the Aristotelian origin of this paradox, cf. Jung, *op. cit.*, American edn., p. 314, n. 23.

[2] Quoted by Jung, *Psychologie und Alchemie*, p. 442.

Children play with it.[1] Yet no one prizes it, though, next to the human soul, it is the most beautiful and most precious thing upon earth and has power to pull down kings and princes. Nevertheless, it is esteemed the vilest and meanest of earthly things. . . .'[2] Leaving aside the rich symbolism of this Stone, we may add that the ubiquity and universality of the *Lapis Philosophorum* are a fundamental theme in alchemical literature. A small book which appeared in London in 1652—*The Names of the Philosopher's Stone*—records more than 170 names for it, among which are: the Virgin's Milk, the Shade of the Sun, Dry Water, Saliva of the Moon, etc. Pernety, in his *Dictionnaire mytho-hermétique* (Paris, 1787), gives an incomplete alphabetical list of about 600 names. A fragment, attributed to Zosimos, speaks of 'this Stone which is not a stone, a precious thing which has no value, a thing of many shapes which has no shapes, this unknown which is known of all'.[3] But, as Hortulanus writes, quoted by the *Rosarium Philosophorum*, 'only he who knows how to make the Philosopher's Stone understands the words which relate to it'.[4] And the *Rosarium* warns us that these questions must be transmitted mystically (*talis materia debet tradi mystice*), just as poetry uses fables and parables.[5] According to some, there was even an 'oath not to divulge the secret in books'.[6]

What we are dealing with here is a 'secret language' such

---

[1] An obvious reference to the *ludus puerorum*, an important symbolism in hermetism (cf. Hartlaub, *Arcana Artis*, pp. 296 sq.). Probably an allusion to the spontaneity and facility of the *opus alchymicum*, which must be performed 'naturally' like a child's game. The alchemical symbolism is identifiable with the image of the Infant in the Gospels.

[2] A. E. Waite, *The Hermetic Museum. Restored and Enlarged* (London, 1891), I, p. 180; Read, *Prelude to Chemistry*, p. 130.

[3] Quoted by Read, *op. cit.*, p. 129.

[4] Quoted by Jung, *Psychologie der Übertragung* (American edn.), p. 288.

[5] Jung, *ibid.*, p. 286, n. 15.

[6] Zadith Senior, quoted by Jung, *op. cit.*, p. 215, n. 7. Agrippa de Nettesheim also speaks of the 'oath of silence', *ibid.*, p. 215 and note 7. The secret language is already employed in Mesopotamian technical recipes of the eighteenth century B.C. Cf. R. J. Forbes, *Studies in Ancient Technology* (Leyden, 1955), I, p. 125. On the 'trade secrets', cf. *ibid.*, p. 127.

as we meet among the shamans and secret societies and among the mystics of the traditional religions. This 'secret language' is at once the expression of experiences not otherwise communicable by the medium of daily speech, and the cryptic communication of the hidden meaning of symbols.[1] We must also point out that this paradoxical ubiquity and inaccessibility of the Philosopher's Stone reminds one of the general dialectic of things sacred. The hierophanies, owing to the very fact that they manifest the sacred, change the ontological régime of things: base or insignificant, a stone, a tree, a stream, as soon as they incorporate the element of the sacred, become prized by those who take part in this religious experience. The alchemist's emergence on another spiritual plane, with the aid of the Philosopher's Stone, may be compared with the experience of the *homo religiosus* who assists in the transmutation of the cosmos by the revelation of the sacred. The paradox of the hierophany consists in the fact that it manifests the sacred and incarnates the transcendental in a 'base thing'; in other words, it brings about a break in level. The same paradox is evident in the Philosopher's Stone: it is beyond the comprehension of the uninitiated, though children may play with it or servants throw it into the streets; although it is everywhere, it is also the most elusive of things.

Alchemical experience and magico-religious experience share common or analogous elements. The use of religious terms by Western alchemists was not necessarily a safeguard against censure by the Church. The *opus alchymicum* had profound analogies with the mystic life. Georg von Welling writes: 'that our intention is not directed towards teaching anyone how to make gold but towards something much higher, namely how Nature may be seen and recognized as

[1] See Eliade, *Le Chamanisme*, pp. 99 sq. *Le Yoga*, pp. 251 sq., 394 sq., and *Techniques de l'Extase et Langages Secrets*. Cf., too, René Alleau, *Aspects de l'Alchimie traditionelle*, pp. 91 sq.

coming from God, and God in Nature'.[1] A disciple of Paracelsus, Oswald Croll, declares that alchemists are 'holy men who by virtue of their Deifick Spirit have tasted the First fruits of the Resurrection in this life and have had a foretaste of the Celestial Country'.[2] In the mind of many alchemists, the procuring of the Philosopher's Stone is equated with the perfect knowledge of God. This, moreover, is why the Stone makes possible the identification of opposites. According to Basil Valentine, 'evil must become the same as good'. Starkey describes the Stone as 'the reconciliation of Contraries, a making of friendship between enemies' (texts quoted by Gray, *op. cit.*, p. 34). We are here face to face with the very old symbolism of the *coincidentia oppositorum*, universally widespread, well attested in primitive stages of culture, and which served more or less to define both the fundamental reality (the *Urgrund*), and the paradoxical state of the totality, the perfection and consequently the sacredness of God.

Nevertheless, the first virtue of the Stone is its capacity to transmute metals into gold. In the words of Arnold of Villanova, 'there abides in Nature a certain pure matter which, being discovered and brought by Art to perfection, converts to itself all imperfect bodies that it touches' (quoted by J. Read, *op. cit.*, p. 119). Here then, very much alive, is the primitive idea that the Stone or the Elixir completes and consummates the work of Nature. Frate Simone da Colonia wrote in his *Speculum minus Alchimiae*: 'This art teaches us to make a remedy called the Elixir, which, being poured on imperfect metals, perfects them completely, and it is for this reason that it was invented.'[3] And an alchemistic *codex* studied

---

[1] Preface to the *Opus Mago-Cabbalisticum*, quoted by R. D. Gray, *Goethe the Alchemist*, p. 19.

[2] Oswald Croll, *Philosophy Reformed and Improved* (London, 1657), p. 214, quoted by Gray, *op. cit.*, p. 21.

[3] Manuscript in the library of the University of Bologna, quoted by G. Carbonelli, *Sulle fonti storiche della chimica et dell'alchimia in Italia*, p. 7.

by Carbonelli tells us that: 'this matter, if it had been better conducted by Nature into the viscera of the Earth and had not inadvertently been mixed with impurities, would have been the Holy Sun and the Moon' (*op. cit.*, p. 7). The notion that the Stone accelerates the temporal rhythm of all organisms and quickens growth is to be found in the *Pratique* by Lully: 'In spring, by its great and marvellous heat, the Stone brings life to the plants: if thou dissolve the equivalent of a grain of salt in water, taking from this water enough to fill a nutshell, and then if thou water with it a vinestock, thy vinestock will bring forth ripe grapes in May.'[1]

Arabian alchemists were the first to ascribe therapeutic properties to the Stone, and it was through Arabian alchemy that the conception of the *Elixir Vitae* came to the West.[2] Roger Bacon, without actually using the expression, speaks in his *Opus Majus* of a 'medicine which gets rid of impurities and all blemishes from the most base metal, can wash unclean things from the body and prevents decay of the body to such an extent that it prolongs life by several centuries'. In the words of Arnold of Villanova: 'the Philosopher's Stone cures all maladies. In one day it cures a malady which would last a month, in twelve days a sickness which would last a year, and a longer one in a month. It restores youth to the old.'[3] The alchemical concept of the Elixir, which had come to the West via Arab writers, supplanted the myth of the miraculous herb or drink of immortality—a myth to be found among all European peoples from earliest times, and whose antiquity is beyond doubt. The Elixir was therefore a novelty in Europe only to the extent that it was identified with the alchemical *opus* and the Philosopher's Stone.

[1] Fragment reproduced by W. Ganzenmüller, *L'Alchimie au Moyen Age*, p. 159.
[2] On the Elixir made of gold, in Western alchemy, see J. Ruska, *Das Buch der Alaun und Salze*, pp. 64 sq.; *Le Livre des Alauns et des Sels* is an Arab text of the twelfth century, attributed to Ibn Râzi.
[3] Texts quoted by Ganzenmüller, *op. cit.*, p. 158.

Moreover, as was to be expected, the image of the Stone finally integrated all the magical beliefs. The man who carried the Stone was deemed to be invulnerable, and the *Book of the Very Holy Trinity* tells us that 'the Stone held in the palm of the hand renders the holder invisible. If it is sewn in fine linen and the linen worn tightly round the body so that the Stone becomes hot, then one may be raised into the air as high as one desires. In order to descend, it is sufficient to relax the linen slightly'.[1]

We can here recognize the famous *siddhi* of the yogi and the Indian alchemists: invisibility, levitation, magic flight (see above, pp. 127 sq.). Yoga, like shamanism, places them among the 'miraculous powers' side by side with 'mastery of fire'.[2] But that does not necessarily imply the oriental origin of the powers of the European magicians and alchemists. Miracles of the fakir type were known in Europe where they very probably derived from a local tradition.[3] In this case, as in that of the Elixir, alchemy merely took the place of very old beliefs which had their roots in prehistory.

---

[1] Quoted by Ganzenmüller, *op. cit.*, p. 159. On this text see Denis Duveen, *Le Livre de la Très Sainte Trinité* (Ambix, 1948, pp. 26–32).
[2] See Eliade, *Le Yoga*, pp. 276 sq., 324 sq., and *Le Chamanisme*, pp. 365 sq.
[3] See *La Chamanisme*, p. 380.

15

Alchemy and Temporality

IN so few pages we of course make no claim to have stated the essential elements of so vast a subject, so many aspects of which are a closed book to us. Our intention was not to summarize the history of Asiatic and Western metallurgy and alchemy. We had no other purpose than to follow the development of a few symbols and myths, offshoots of those primitive techniques thanks to which man assumed a growing responsibility towards matter. If our analysis and interpretation are well founded, alchemy prolongs and consummates a very old dream of *homo faber*: collaboration in the perfecting of matter while at the same time securing perfection for himself. We have described some principal phases of this collaboration and we shall not now return to it. One common factor emerges from all these tentative probings: in taking upon himself the responsibility of changing Nature, man put himself in the place of Time; that which would have required millennia or aeons to 'ripen' in the depths of the earth, the metallurgist and alchemist claim to be able to achieve in a few weeks. The furnace supersedes the telluric matrix; it is there that the embryo-ores complete their growth. The *vas mirabile* of the alchemist, his furnaces, his retorts, play an even more ambitious role. These pieces of apparatus are at the very centre of a return to primordial chaos, of a rehearsal of the cosmogony. Substances die in them and are revived, to be finally transmuted to gold. We have sufficiently brought out the spiritual aspect of the alchemical operation to be in a position to consider it from the outside as an endeavour aimed at the modification of Matter. In this aspect of the work, the operation was a continuation of the aspirations of the *artifex* of prehistoric times who played with fire in order to change Nature, to create new forms, in short, to collaborate with the Creator, to perfect his creation. The mythical figure of the African smith-civilizing-hero has not yet lost the religious significance attaching to metallurgical work: the Celestial Smith, as we have seen, completes creation, organizes the world, lays the foundation of culture and guides human beings towards the knowledge of the mysteries.

It is through fire that 'Nature is changed', and it is significant that the mastery of fire asserts itself both in the cultural progress which is an offshoot of metallurgy, and in the psycho-physiological techniques which are the basis of the most ancient magics and known shamanic mystiques. From the time of this very primitive phase of culture, fire is used as the transmuting agent: the incombustibility of the shamans proclaims that they have gone beyond the human condition, that they have something of the condition of 'spirits' (hence the ritual setting of the *fire-tricks*: it confirms and establishes the shaman's prestige). As an instrument of transmutation, fire also plays its part in certain initiations, certain traces of which persist even in Greek myth and legend. It is possible that the rite of incineration itself symbolized the hope of transmutation by fire. In all these magico-religious contexts 'the mastery of fire' indicates the interest in what we shall designate as a near-'spirituality'; the shaman and later the yogi or mystic are specialists in the soul, the mind, the inner life. An extremely complex symbolism associates the terrifying fire-theophanies with the sweetest flames of mystic love and with the luminous manifestations of the divine as well as with the innumerable 'combustions' and 'passions' of the soul. At many levels, fire, flame, dazzling light, inner heat, express spiritual experiences, the incarnation of the sacred, the proximity of God.

And so, like the alchemists, the smelters and smiths, too, were 'masters of fire'. All, by aiding the work of Nature, accelerated the tempo of things and, in the final instance, were substitutes for Time itself. The alchemists were not of course all aware that their 'work' did the work of Time. But this is not important: the essential point is that their work, transmutation, involved, in one form or another, the elimination of Time. In the words of Ben Jonson's characters:

> *Subtle:* The same we say of lead, and other metals, which would be gold, if they had time.
> *Mammon:* And that Our Art doth further. (See p. 51.)

But strong in the conviction that they were working in conjunction with God, the alchemists considered their work as a perfecting of Nature, tolerated if not encouraged by God. Far removed though they were from the ancient metallurgists and smiths, they nevertheless continued the same attitude *vis-à-vis* Nature. For the primitive miner, as for the Western alchemist, Nature is a hierophany. It is not only 'alive', it is also 'divine'; it has, at least, a divine dimension. It is, moreover, thanks to this sacred quality of Nature—revealed in the 'subtle' aspect of substances—that the alchemist thought he could obtain his transmuting agent, the Philosopher's Stone, as well as his Elixir of Immortality. We shall not return to the subject of the initiatory structure of the *opus alchymicum*. Suffice it to recall that the freeing of Nature from the laws of Time went hand in hand with the deliverance of the alchemist himself. In Western alchemy, much later, the redemption of Nature, as demonstrated by Jung, completed the redemption of man by Christ.

The Western alchemist completed the last stage of the very ancient programme, begun by *homo faber*, the moment he undertook to transform a Nature which from various viewpoints he regarded as sacred or capable of being revealed as sacred. The concept of alchemical transmutation is the fabulous consummation of a faith in the possibility of changing Nature by human labours (labours which always had some liturgical significance).

The survival of the alchemist's ideology does not become immediately evident just when alchemy disappears from the pages of history and all its empirically valid chemical knowledge is being integrated into chemistry. The new science of chemistry makes use only of those empirical discoveries which do not represent—however numerous and important one may suppose them to be—the true spirit of alchemy. We must not believe that the triumph of experimental science reduced to nought the dreams and ideals of the alchemist. On the contrary, the ideology of the new epoch, crystallized around the myth of infinite progress and boosted by the experimental sciences and the progress of industrialization which dominated and inspired the whole of the nineteenth century, takes up and carries forward—despite its radical secularization—the millennary dream of the alchemist. It is in the specific dogma of the nineteenth century, according to which man's true mission is to transform and improve upon Nature and become her master, that we must look for the authentic continuation of the alchemist's dream. The visionary's myth of the perfection, or more accurately, of the redemption of Nature, survives, in camouflaged form, in the pathetic programme of the industrial societies whose aim is the total transmutation of Nature, its transformation into 'energy'. It is in this nineteenth century, dominated by the physico-chemical sciences and the upsurge of industry, that man succeeds in supplanting Time. His desire to accelerate the natural tempo of things by an ever more rapid and efficient exploitation of mines, coal-fields and petrol deposits, begins to come true. Organic chemistry, fully mobilized to wrest the secrets of the mineral basis of life, now opens the way to innumerable 'synthetic' products. And one cannot help noticing that these synthetic products demonstrate for the first time the possibility of eliminating Time and preparing, in factory and laboratory, substances which it would have taken Nature thousands and thousands of years to produce. And we know full well to what extent the 'synthetic preparation of life', even in the modest form of a few cells of protoplasm, was the supreme dream of science throughout the whole second half of the nineteenth century and the beginning of the twentieth. This was the alchemist's dream too—the dream of creating the homunculus.

On the plane of cultural history, it is therefore permissible to say that the alchemists, in their desire to supersede Time, anticipated what is in fact the essence of the ideology of the modern world. Chemistry has received only insignificant fragments of the alchemical heritage. The bulk of this heritage is to be found elsewhere—in the literary ideologies of Balzac and Victor Hugo, in the work of the naturalists, in the systems of political economy, whether capitalist, liberal or Marxist, in the secularized theologies of materialism, positivism and infinite progress—everywhere, in short, where there is faith in the limitless possibilities of *homo faber*; everywhere where the eschatological significance of labour, technology and the scientific exploitation of Nature reveals itself. The more one reflects, the more one discovers that this frantic enthusiasm feeds on a certitude: by conquering Nature through the

physico-chemical sciences, man can become Nature's
rival without being the slave of Time. Henceforth science and
labour are to do the work of Time. With what he recognizes
to be most essential in himself—his applied intelligence and
his capacity for work—modern man takes upon himself the
function of temporal duration; in other words he takes on the
role of Time.

It is not our purpose to develop these few observations
concerning the ideology and situation of *homo faber* in the
nineteenth and twentieth centuries. It was simply our intention to point out that it is in this faith in experimental
science and grandiose industrial projects that we must look
for the alchemist's dreams. Alchemy has bequeathed much
more to the modern world than a rudimentary chemistry; it
has left us its faith in the transmutation of Nature and its
ambition to control Time. It is true that this heritage has
been interpreted and realized by modern man in a totally
different way from that of the alchemist. The alchemist was
still continuing the behaviour of primitive man, for whom
Nature was the source of sacred revelations and work a ritual.
But modern science could only come into its own by
divesting Nature of these sacred attributes. Scientific phenomena are only revealed at the cost of the disappearance of the
hierophanies. Industrial societies have nothing to do with the
liturgical activity identifiable with craft-rites. That kind of
work was useless in a factory, even if only for lack of any
industrial initiation or 'tradition'.

It is worth recalling another fact. Although he put himself
in the place of Time, the alchemist took good care not to assume its role. His dream was to accelerate the tempo of things,
to create gold more quickly than Nature; but like the good
'philosopher' or mystic that he was, he was afraid of Time. He
did not admit himself to be an essentially temporal being, he

longed for the beatitude of paradise, aspired to eternity and pursued immortality, the *elixir vitae*. In this respect, too, the alchemist was behaving like pre-modern man. By all sorts of means he tried to conceal from himself his awareness of the irreversibility of Time, either by regenerating it periodically by a re-enactment of the cosmogony, or by sanctifying it in the liturgy, or even by 'forgetting' it, that is, by refusing to acknowledge the secular intervals between two significant (and hence sacred) acts. Above all we must bear in mind that the alchemist became master of Time when, with his various apparatus, he symbolically reiterated the primordial chaos and the cosmogony (see p. 156) or when he underwent initiatory 'death and resurrection'. Every initiation was a victory over death, i.e. temporality; the initiate proclaimed himself 'immortal'; he had forged for himself a post-mortem existence which he claimed to be indestructible.

But the moment the individual dream of the alchemist might have been realized by a whole society, and on the plane on which it was collectively realizable (the sphere of the physico-chemical sciences and industry), the defence against Time ceased to be possible. The tragic grandeur of modern man is bound up with the fact that he was the first to take on the work of Time in relation to Nature. We have seen how his spectacular conquests fulfil, on a different plane, the longings of the alchemists. But there is more yet: man in modern society has finally assumed the garb of Time not only in his relations with Nature but also in respect to himself. On the philosophical plane he has recognized himself to be essentially, and sometimes even uniquely, a temporal being, taking his existence from Time and bound by actuality. And the modern world, to the extent to which it asserts its own greatness and fully accepts its dramatic role, feels at one with Time in the way that nineteenth-century science and industry urged it to be. For they proclaimed that man can achieve things better and faster than Nature if he, by means of his intelligence, succeeds in penetrating to her secrets and supplementing, by his own operations, the multiple temporal durations (the geological, botanical, animal rhythms) required by Nature in order to bring her work to fruition. The temptation was too great to resist. Through innumerable millennia man has dreamed of improving upon Nature. It was inconceivable that he should hesitate when confronted by the fabulous perspectives opened out to him by his own discoveries. But the price had to be paid. Man could not stand in the place of Time without condemning himself implicitly to be identified with it, to do its work even when he would no longer wish to.

The work of Time could be replaced only by intellectual and manual (especially manual) work. Of course, Man has from time immemorial been condemned to work. But there is a difference, and it is a fundamental one. To supply the necessary energy to the dreams and ambitions of the nineteenth century, work had to be secularized. For the first time in his history, man assumed this very harsh task of 'doing better and quicker than Nature', without now having at his disposal the liturgical dimension which in other societies made work bearable. And it is in work finally secularized, in work in its pure state, numbered in hours and units of energy consumed, that man feels the implacable nature of temporal duration, its full weight and slowness. All in all, one may say that man in modern society has taken on, in the literal sense of the word, the role of Time, exhausting himself by so doing and becoming a uniquely temporal being. And since the irreversibility and vacuity of Time has become a dogma for the modern world (or more exactly, for those who do not recognize themselves as being at one with the Judaeo-Christian ideology), the temporality assumed and experienced by man is translated, on the philosophical plane, into the tragic awareness of the vanity of all human existence. Happily, passions, images, myths, games, distractions, dreams—not to mention religion, which does not belong to the proper spiritual horizon of modern man—are there to prevent this tragic consciousness from imposing itself on planes other than the philosophic.

These considerations are no more a criticism of the modern world than they are a eulogy of other, primitive or exotic societies. One may criticize many aspects of modern society as one can those of other societies, but this is not our concern. It has been our desire simply to show in what direction the guiding ideas of alchemy, rooted in protohistory, have continued into the ideology of the nineteetnth century, and with what results. As for the crises of the modern world, we must bear in mind that this world inaugurates a completely new type of civilization. It is not possible to foresee its future developments. But it is useful to remember that the only revolution comparable to it in the past history of humanity, that is, the discovery of agriculture, provoked upheavals and spiritual breakdowns whose magnitude the modern mind finds it well-nigh impossible to conceive. An ancient world, the world of nomadic hunters, with its religions, its myths, its moral conceptions, was ebbing away. Thousands and thousands of years were to elapse before the final lamentations of the old world died away, forever doomed by the advent of agriculture. One must also suppose that the profound spiritual crisis aroused by man's decision *to call a halt and bind himself to the soil*, must have taken many hundreds of years to become completely integrated. It is impossible to imagine the upheaval of all values caused by the change-over from the nomadic to the sedentary life and to appreciate its psychological and spiritual repercussions. The technical discoveries of the modern world, its conquest of Time and Space, represent a revolution of similar proportions, the consequences of which are still very far from having become part of us. The secularization of work is like an open wound in the body of modern society. There is, however, nothing to indicate that a re-sanctification may not take place in the future. As for the temporality of the human condition, it presents an even more serious discovery. But a reconciliation with temporality remains a possibility, given a more correct conception of Time. But this is not the place to deal with these problems. Our aim was simply to show that the spiritual crisis of the modern world includes among its remote origins the demiurgic dreams of the metallurgists, smiths and alchemists. It is right that the historiographic consciousness of Western man should be at one with the deeds and ideals of his very remote ancestors—even though modern man, heir to all these myths and dreams, has succeeded in realizing them only by breaking loose from their original significance.

THE FORGE AND THE CRUCIBLE:
A POSTSCRIPT

Mircea Eliade

METALLURGY AND ALCHEMY AS "RELIGIOUS" PHENOMENA

SINCE no author can afford to rewrite his books every ten or twenty years, he is at least obliged to inform his readers of the progress made by recent research. I tried such a critical and bibliographical *mise au point* while preparing the second edition of my *Shamanism*.[1] In the following notes I intend to make a similar *mise au point* with regard to the religious meanings of archaic and traditional metallurgical practices and the original significance of alchemy. I have discussed these problems more than once since 1935,[2] but I will refer mostly to *The Forge and the Crucible*.[3]

Approaching the subject from the perspective of a historian of religions, I will not insist on the vast literature published by historians of metallurgical techniques and ancient chemistry. Among such contributions, I will refer only to those containing materials or information

[1] Mircea Eliade, "Recent Works on Shamanism: A Review Article," *History of Religions*, I, No. 1 (Summer, 1961), 152–86.

[2] See my *Alchimia Asiatică*, Vol. I (Bucharest, 1935); *Cosmologie si Alchimie babiloniană* (Bucharest, 1937); and "Metallurgy, Magic and Alchemy," *Zalmoxis*, I (1938), 85–129.

[3] M. Eliade, *Forgerons et alchimistes* (hereafter cited as "*F. & A.*") (Paris, 1956); *The Forge and the Crucible* (hereafter cited as "*F. & C.*"), trans. Stephen Corrin (New York and London, 1962).

relevant to the themes discussed in *The Forge and the Crucible*. In fact, my investigations on the early history of mining, metallurgy, and alchemy were only a part of a more ambitious project which has nothing to do with the endeavor of the historians of techniques and natural sciences, though it is partly based on the results of their research. In short, I wanted to study the mythology of the *homo faber* in order to understand the meaning and the function of his conquest of the material world before the rise of scientifical thought. In a youthful monograph, *Cunoștințele botanice în vechea Indie,*[4] I tried to elucidate the structure and the purpose of botanical observations and classifications in ancient and medieval India. In other words, my endeavor was to analyze that stage in the history of Indian thought when the botanical world was no longer considered "magically and mythologically," but had not yet become the object of "scientific" study, as in post-Linnaean times. In a paper read in the section of History of Sciences at the International Congress of Historians (Bucharest, 1932), I discussed what I called, following Masson-Oursel, "le caractère qualitatif de la physique indienne," that is, the effort of Sāmkhya and Vaiśeșika to construct a physics based on the systematic definition and classification of qualities, while almost ignoring quantities.[5]

But the main effort was concentrated on the study of

[4] *Buletinul Societății de Științe,* Cluj, V (1931), 221–37.

[5] Related to such an analysis, but investigating the "prehistory" of the arts, not that of the techniques and natural sciences, is a series of monographs which I wrote on the ecstatic "origins" of lyric and epic poetry ("Techniques de l'extase et langages secrets," *Conferenze, Istituo Italiano per il Medio ed Estremo Oriente,* Vol. II [Rome, 1953]; "Littérature orale," *Histoire des litteratures, Encyclopédie de la Pléiade,* I [Paris, 1956], 3–26) and on the religious origins of architecture and urbanistics ("Centre du monde, temple, maison," *Le symbolisme cosmique des monuments religieux* [Rome, 1957], pp. 57–82).

the magico-religious contexts of metallurgy and alchemy. (See a summary of the previous publications in *F. & C.*, pp. 13–14, and *F. & A.*, p. 14). Without negating the concrete, "objective" results of the discovery of metals and the progress of mining and metallurgical practices—results admirably, but exclusively, studied by the historians of sciences—I emphasized some aspects of this fabulous enterprise that were usually ignored or depreciated. Seeking to comprehend the *whole* cultural history of mankind, not only the scientific progress, I attempted to investigate also the *imaginary world (univers imaginaire)* which came into being through the discovery of metals. A history neglecting this imaginary world—which is, in fact, a world of meaning—not only is incomplete; it is also "subjective," and thus non-scientific, for the purely empirical or rationalistic approach to mines, metals, and metallurgy represents a recent stage in the evolution of Western culture. In fact, the discovery of metals and the progress of metallurgy radically modified the human mode of being in the universe. Not only did the manipulation of metals contribute considerably to man's conquest of the material world; it also changed his world of meaning. The metals opened for him a new mythological and religious universe.

A similar, though even more radical, modification was effectuated through the discovery of agriculture. I cite this example because it better illustrates what I mean by saying that an important technological discovery "opens" for man a new spiritual world. It is useless to insist on the revolutionary character of the discovery of agriculture and on its economic, technological, and social consequences. They are evident, and are laboriously repeated in all the books and textbooks on the subject. But no less important are the "spiritual" consequences of the discovery of agriculture.[6] A new world of meaning was grasped through agricultural work. A number of analogies and homologies suggested themselves "naturally": for instance, the relations between women, field, sexual life, human fertility, agriculture, lunar phases, death and rebirth, etc. The early farmer expressed his specific mode of being in the world through plant symbolism and in vegetal terminology—and we still conserve something of this archaic heritage in our language, allegory, and symbolism.

A historian of religions is interested in all these spiritual values and *univers imaginaires* brought about by empirical discoveries, because they played an important role in the history of the human mind. It is not only the agricultural and metallurgic techniques that made Neolithic man the first "chain inventor" in history but also the religious and mythological creations which became possible through the discovery of agriculture and metallurgy. The symbologies, mythologies, and rituals accompanying these technological discoveries played a no less important role in shaping post-Neolithic man the first "chain inventor" in history but also the religious and mythological creations which became possible through the discovery of agriculture and metallurgy. The symbologies, mythologies, and rituals accompanying these technological discoveries played a no less important role in shaping post-Neolithic man than did the empirical discoveries themselves.

For such reasons, alchemy cannot be reduced to a protochemistry. In fact, when it became an elementary

---

[6] See M. Eliade, *Patterns in Comparative Religion* (New York, 1958), pp. 331 ff.

chemistry, the alchemical world of meaning was on the verge of disappearing. Everywhere we find alchemy, it is always intimately related to a "mystical" tradition: in China with Taoism, in India with Yoga and Tantrism, in Hellenistic Egypt with gnosis, in Islamic countries with hermetic and esoteric mystical schools, in the Western Middle Ages and Renaissance with Hermetism, Christian and sectarian mysticism, and Cabala. Consequently, to understand the meaning and function of alchemy, we must *not* judge the alchemical texts by the possible chemical insights which they may contain. Such an evaluation would be tantamount to judging—and classifying—great poetical creations by their scientific data or their historical accuracy.

That the alchemists *did* contribute also to the progress of the natural sciences is certainly true. But they did this indirectly and only as a consequence of their concern with mineral substances and living matter. For they were "experimenters," not abstract thinkers or erudite scholastics. Their inclination to "experiment," however, was not limited to the natural realm. As I tried to show in *The Forge and the Crucible,* the experiments with mineral or vegetal substances pursued a more ambitious goal: to change the alchemist's own mode of being.

These few introductory observations are not intended as a summary of my book or a defense of its methodology.[7] I wanted only to emphasize once more the interest of such studies for the historian of religions, not to mention the historian of culture of the next generation, that intrepid scholar who will have assimilated the historiographical progress alluded to at the end of this postscript.

[7] Among the most comprehensive and sympathetic reviews, I would like to cite those of S. H. Nasr in *Isis*, XLIX (1958), 450–53, and of W.-E. Peuckert in *Zeitschrift für Volkskunde*, LVII, No. 1 (1961), 146–48.

ALCHEMY AND THE PROBLEM OF ITS "ORIGINS"

The recent literature related to alchemy and early chemistry *(F. & C.,* pp. 195 ff.; *F & A.,* pp. 198 ff.) has been conveniently presented by Allen G. Debus in "The Significance of the History of Early Chemistry" *(Cahiers d'histoire mondiale,* IX, No. I [1965], 39–58). The monumental *History of Chemistry* by J. R. Partington, in four volumes (London, 1961), with extremely rich bibliographies, deserves special mention; see also H. M. Leicester's *The Historical Background of Chemistry* (New York, 1956), John Read's *Through Alchemy to Chemistry* (London, 1957), E. J. Holmyard's *Alchemy* (Penguin Books, 1957), and especially Robert P. Multhauf's *The Origin of Chemistry* (London, 1966).

A review of some recent works on the origin and the significance of alchemy was published by Wolfgang Schneider in "Probleme und neuere Ansichten in der Alchemiegeschichte" *(Chemiker-Zeitung/Chemische Apparatur,* LXXXV, No. 17 [1961], 643–51); see also his "Die geschichtlichen Beziehungen der Metallurgie zu Alchemie und Pharmazie" *(Archiv für das Eisenhüttenwesen,* XXXVII, No. 7 [July 1966], 533–38). Dr. Schneider, who published, among many other works, a *Lexicon Alchemistische-Pharmazeutisches Symbole* (Weinheim, 1962), is one of the historians of chemistry who accepts the approach and the conclusions of *The Forge and the Crucible.* Important contributions to the understanding of alchemical terminology are to be found in Maurice P. Crossland's *Historical Studies in the Language of Chemistry* (Cambridge, Mass., 1962). Some of W. Ganzenmüller's more important contributions have been brought together in his volume *Beiträge zur Geschichte der Technologie und der Alchemie* (Weinheim, 1956).

SMITHS AND THEIR SUPERNATURAL MODELS

On the folklore of smiths (*F. & C.*, pp. 87 ff.; *F. & A.*, pp. 89 ff.), see Frederick W. Robins' *The Smith. The Traditions and Lore of an Ancient Craft* (London, 1953). The magic cunning of the smith is admitted even in St. Patrick's hymn: "I summon to-day all . . . virtues (of God) between me (and these evils) against spells of women and smiths and wizards" (*The Tripartite Life of Patrick*, quoted by E. E. Hlinger, "Magic Weapons in Celtic Legends," *Folklore*, LVI [1945], 295–307, esp. p. 299). The "evolution of the smith" has been investigated by R. J. Forbes in *Metallurgy in Antiquity* (Leiden, 1950), pages 62–104. New and relevant information was introduced by Karl Jettmar in his article "Schmiede/brauchtum im östliche Hindukush" (*Mitteilungen der Anthropologische Gesselschaft in Wien*, LXXXVII [1957], 22–31). See also R. Goris' "The Position of the Blacksmiths" (*Bali. Studies in Life, Thought and Ritual* [The Hague, 1960], pp. 289–300) and D. Veerkamp's " 'Stummer Handel' in Schmiedesagen Europas und Südasiens" (*Zeitschrift für Ethnologie*, Vol. LXXX [1955]).

Significant progress has been made recently in understanding the mythologies and rituals of African smiths (*F. & C.*, pp. 55 ff.; *F. & A.*, pp. 60–61, 96–97). The socioeconomic explanation of the ambivalent attitude toward the smiths proposed, among others, by P. Clement ("Le forgeron en Afrique Noire. Quelques attitudes du groupe à son égarde," *Revue de Géographie humaine et d'Ethnologie*, I [1948], 35–58); has been criticized by Luc de Heusch ("Le symbolisme du forgeron en afrique" (*Reflets du monde*, No. 10 [July, 1956], pp. 57–70). The author emphasized that if the African smith is sometimes feared and honored, sometimes despised, this is due to the fact that he is looked upon as both a "master of the fire" and a mythical solar hero as well as a magically dangerous personage, who is a producer of weapons, and is responsible for bloodshed. A brilliant analysis of the Dogon smith's religious status has been recently made by Germaine Dieterlen in "Contribution à l'étude des forgerons en Afrique occidentale" *(Ecole Pratique des Hautes Études. Section des Sciences Religieuses: Annuaire 1965–1966,* LXXIII [Paris, 1965], 3–28, esp. pp. 16–18). The myths of the primordial smith, presented by Griaule in *Dieu d'eau* (Paris, 1948, pp. 101–6), are now elaborately discussed by M. Griaule and G. Dieterlen in *Le renard pâle,* Volume I: *Le myths cosmogonique* (Paris, 1965). See also Geneviève Calame-Griaule's *Ethnologie et langage: La parole chez les Dogon* (Paris, 1965), pages 275 ff, etc. (see Index, *s.v.* forge, *forgeron*).

On the initiation of the African smith, see Ernesta Cerulli's "L'iniziazione al mestiero di fabro in Africa" *(Studi e materiali di storia delle religioni,* XXVII [1956], 87–101). See also E. C. Lanning's "Genital Symbols on Smiths' Bellows in Uganda" *(Man,* LIV, No. 262, 167–69).

The religious functions of the Tibetan and Central Asiatic blacksmiths, their rituals and mythologies, and their rapports with the shamans *(F. & C.,* pp. 81 ff.; *F. & A.,* pp. 83 ff.) have been investigated by René de Nebesky-Wojkowitz *(Oracles and Demons of Tibet* [The Hague, 1956], pp. 153 ff., 337 ff., 467, 539), R.-A. Stein *(Recherches sur l'épopée et le barde au Tibet* [Paris, 1959], pp. 81, 150–51, 189, 361 ff., etc.), Siegbert Hummel ("Der götliche Schmied in Tibet," *Folklore Studies,* XIX [1960], 251–72), and F. Altheim *(Geschichte der Hunen,* I [Berlin, 1959], 195–215).

MINING AND METALLURGY: BELIEFS AND TECHNIQUES

On the thunderstorms (*F. & C.*, pp. 20 ff.; *F. & A.*, pp. 19 ff., see Georg Holtker's "Der Donnerkeilglaube vom steinzeitlichen Neuguinea ausgesehen" (*Acta Tropica*, I [1944], 30–51; it contains an extremely rich Bibliography, pp. 40–50).

On the mythology of the Iron Age (*F. & C.*, pp. 27 ff.; *F. & A.*, pp. 26 ff.), see *Le fer à travers les âges: Actes du Colloque International, Nancy, 3–6 Octobre, 1955* (*Annales de l'Est*, Mémoire No. 16 [Nancy, 1955], especially Jean Leclant's "Le fer dans l'Egypte ancienne, le Soudan et l'Afrique" (pp. 85–91).

On mining and its mythology and folklore (*F. & C.*, pp. 43 ff.; *F. & A.*, pp. 44 ff.), see Georg Schreiber's *Der Bergbau in Geschichte, Ethos und Sakralkultur* (Cologne and Opladen, 1962).

On *Bergbüchlein* (*F. & C.*, pp. 44 ff.; *F. & A.*, pp. 50 ff.), see W. Pieper's *Ulrich Rülein von Calw und seine Bergbüchlein* (Berlin, 1955); see also Dorothy Wyckoff's "Albertus Magnus on Ore Deposits" (*Isis*, XLIX [1958], 109–122); Lazarus Ercker's *Treatise on Ores and Assaying*, translated by A. G. Sisco and C. S. Smith (Chicago, 1951); and *Bergwerk- und Probierbüchlein*, translated and annotated by A. G. Sisco and C. S. Smith (New York: American Institute of Mining and Metallurgical Engineers, 1949).

The Mesopotamian documents (*F. & C.*, pp. 71 ff.; *F. & A.*, pp. 75 ff.) have been systematically investigated by Martin Levey in his *Chemistry and Chemical Technology in Ancient Mesopotamia* (Amsterdam, 1959); see also the same author's "Gypsum, Salt and Soda in Ancient Mesopotamian Chemical Technology" (*Isis*, XLIX [1958], 336–41).

RECENT WORKS ON HELLENISTIC AND ISLAMIC ALCHEMY

H. J. Shepard sees in Gnosticism the main source of alchemical mysticism; see his "Gnosticism and Alchemy" (*Ambix,* VI [1957], 86–101); see also his "Egg Symbolism in Alchemy" (*Ambix,* VI [1958], 140–48), "The Redemption Theme and Hellenistic Alchemy" (*Ambix,* VII [1959], 42–76), "A Survey of Alchemical and Hermetic Symbolism" (*Ambix,* VIII [1960], 35–41), and "The Ouroboros and the Unity of Matter in Alchemy: A Study in Origins" (*Ambix,* X [1962], 83–96).

On Islamic alchemy (*F. & C.,* pp. 196–97; *F. & A.,* p. 199), see the bibliographical references in Debus (*op. cit.,* p. 45, n. 17). Of special importance is H. E. Stapleton's "Two Alchemical Treatises Attributed to Avicenna" (*Ambix,* X [1962], 41–82) and Henry Corbin's *Avicenna and the Visionary Recital,* translated from the French by Willard R. Trask (New York, 1960), especially pages 212 ff.

The History of Hindu Chemistry, by P. C. Ray (*F. & C.,* p. 192; *F. & A.,* p. 196), was reprinted in 1956 (Calcutta: Indian Chemical Society); see the review by J. Filliozat in *Isis,* XLIX (1958), 362–63.

While preparing *Forgerons et alchimistes,* I did not know of Maung Hsin Aung's article "Alchemy and Alchemist in Burma" (*Folklore,* XLIV [1933], 346–54). One becomes a *zawgyee* (a term derived from *yogi*) by introducing into his body the proper metal compounds, prepared from mercury or iron; halfway through his training the postulant obtains the "stone of live metal." Its possession enables him to fly through the air and travel under the earth; he becomes invulnerable and can live hundreds of years. The stone cures all sickness and transforms, by touch, brass or silver into gold. The postulant continues to experiment until he obtains the required compounds. When he swallows the stone, he becomes unconscious for seven days. Usually he retires into a cave, and after seven days he emerges as a *zawgyee*. Henceforth he is like a god: he can live millions of years, restore the dead to life, and become invisible (pp. 346–47). A *zawgyee* is forbidden to eat meat and drink intoxicating beverages. He is allowed to have sexual relations, not with women, but with certain fruits in the shape and size of young maidens. The *zawgyee* animates them and make them his wives. See also Maung Hsin Aung's "Burmese Alchemy Beliefs" (*Journal of the Burmese Research Society*, XXXV, 83–91). The similarity with the Indian yogi-alchemist is evident; see my book *Yoga. Immortality and Freedom* (New York, 1958), pages 274 ff.

ALCHEMY DURING THE RENAISSANCE AND REFORMATION

On Paracelsus and Renaissance iatrochemistry (*F. & C.*, p. 198; *F. & A.*, p. 200), see Walter Pagel's *Paracelsus: An Introduction to Philosophical Medicine in the Era of the Renaissance* (Basel, 1958), *Das Medizinische Weltbild des Paracelsis, seine Zusammenhänge mit Neuplatonismus und Gnosis* (Wiesbaden, 1962), and "Paracelsus and the Neoplatonic and Gnostic Tradition" (*Ambix*, VIII [1960], 125–60); Allen G. Debus's *The English Paracelsians* (London, 1965) and "The Significance of the History of Early Chemistry," pages 48 ff. (with its rich bibliography); and Wolfgang Schneider's "Paracelsus und die Entwicklung der pharmazeutischen Chemie" (*Archiv der Pharmazie*, CCXCIX, No. 9 [1966], 737–46).

With regard to Jonson's *Alchemist* (*F. & A.*, p. 54 ff.; *F. & C.*, pp. 51 ff.), I neglected an excellent article by Edgar Hill Duncan, "Jonson's *Alchemist* and the Literature of Alchemy" (*PMLA*, LXI [September, 1946], 699–710). The author illustrates abundantly Jonson's remarkable knowledge of alchemy, "a knowledge greater than that of any other major English literary figure, with the possible exceptions of Chaucer and Donne" (Duncan, *op. cit.*, p. 699). The same author discussed Chaucer's knowledge of alchemy in "The Yeoman's Canon's *Silver Citrinacioun*" (*Modern Philology*, XXXVII [1940], 241–62); see also his articles "Donne's Alchemical Figures" (*ELH*, IX [1942], 257–85) and "The Alchemy in Jonson's *Mercury Vindicated*" (*Studies in Philology*, XXXIX [1942], 625–37). A general survey is found in H. Fisch's "Alchemy and English Literature" (*Proceedings of the Leeds Philosophical and Literary Society*, VII, 123–36).

Luther's attitude toward alchemy and the relations between Lutheran theology and alchemy have been investigated by J. W. Montgomery ("Cross, Constellation, and Crucible: Lutheran Astrology and Alchemy in the Age of the Reformation," *Transactions of the Royal Society of Canada*, Vol. I, Ser. 4 [June, 1963], Sec. II, pp. 251–700; see also the French translation, "L'astrologie et l'alchimie luthériennes à l'époque de la Réforme," *Revue d'histoire et de philosophie réligieuses* [1966], pp. 323–45). It is worth quoting Luther's fullest statement on the subject:

The science of alchemy (*ars alchimica*) I like very well, and, indeed, it is truly the natural philosophy of the ancients. I like it not only for the many uses it has in decorating metals and in distilling and sublimating herbs and liquors, but also for the sake of the allegory and secret signification, which is exceedingly fine, touching the resurrection of the dead at the Last Day. For, as in a furnace the fire retracts and separates from a substance the other portions, and carries upward the spirit, the life, the sap, the strength, while the unclean matter, the dregs, remains at the bottom, like a dead and worthless carcass [here Luther uses the further illustrations of the preparation of wine, cinnamon, and nutmeg], even so God, at the day of judgment, will separate all things through fire, the righteous from the ungodly [*Tischreden*, Weimar edition, I, 1149, quoted by Montgomery, *op. cit.*, p. 263].

The author emphasizes the Lutheran ideas implicit in the alchemical works of Andreas Libavius (1550–1616) and Khunrath (1560–1605) and in the *Chymical Wedding* of J. V. Andreae (1586–1650).

In a short paper, "Prima materia. Das Geheimnis eines Gemäldes von Giorgione" (*Die BASF. Aus der Arbeit der Badischen Anilin und Soda Fabrik*, IX [1959], 50–54), G. F. Hartlaub suggests an alchemical interpretation of the well-known picture by Giorgione, "The Three Philosophers." The author sees in these personages, not the three Magi from the East, but the personifications of the ranks of a secret society. According to him, the picture probably represents a symbolical veneration of the interior of the earth, where the *prima materia* was sought (*visita interiora terrae*, etc.). See also by the same author *Der Stein der Weisen* (Munich, 1959), "Chymische Märchen" (*BASF*, Vol. IV, Nos. 2 and 3 [1954]; Vol. V, No. 1 [1955]), and "Symbole der Wandlung" (*BASF*, IX [1959], 123–28).

Among the many photographic reprints of ancient editions of Western alchemical works (*F. & C.*, pp. 198–99; *F & A.*, pp. 201–2; see Debus, "The Significance of the History of Early Chemistry," p. 46, nn. 21–26), a special mention is due the series of texts brought out by the publishing house "Archè," of Milan, in limited editions of 110 copies. Especially interesting are Giovan Battista Nazari's *Della tramutatione metallica sogni tre* (Brescia, 1599); Giovanni Braccesco's *La espositione di Geber filosofo, Seguito da Il legno della vita Dialoghi due* (reproduction of the edition printed in Venice, 1562); and

Huginus à Barmâ's *Le rêgne de Saturne changé en Siècle d'Or* (reproduction of the Parisian edition, 1780). The last represents the French translation of a very rare Paracelsian work, *Saturnia regna in aurea saecula conversa,* first published in Paris in 1657. The "Archè" editions are accompanied by short introductions, bibliographies, and historical commentaries.

THE ORIGINS OF ALCHEMY

On the origin of alchemy, see Wolfgang Schneider's "Ueber den Ursprung des Wortes 'Chemie' " (*Pharmazeutische Industrie,* XXI [1959], 79–81), his "Probleme und neuere Ansichten in der Alchemiegeschichte," and Homer H. Dubs's "The Origin of Alchemy" (*Ambix,* IX [1961], 23–36). In a series of articles, S. Mahdihassan has tried to prove the Chinese origin of the term *kimia*. He claims that "there is in South China the term Kim-Iya, meaning Gold (making)-fresh plant juice. Pre-Islamic Arabs transported it from China to Alexandria, the trade emporium of the time, where kimiy was transliterated as Chemia, but actually pronounced kimiya" (S. Mahdihassan, "A Triple Approach to the Problem of the Origin of Alchemy," *Scientia,* LX [1966], 444–55, esp. p. 445). See also, by the same author, "Chinese Origin of Alchemy" (*United Asia,* V [1953], 241–44), "Alchemy and Its Connections with Astrology, Pharmacy, Magic and Metallurgy" (*Janus, XLVI* [1956], 81–103), and "Alchemy and Its Chinese Origin as Revealed by its Etymology, Doctrines and Symbols" (*Iqbal Review* [Karachi] [October, 1966], pp. 22–58). In the last of these papers just mentioned, the author summarizes his views on the "origins" of alchemy: "Primitive society had to face hard life from limited availability of foodstuffs. The aged males were felt as burdens on bread winners and were inclemently handled. In India . . . they had to retire as solitary denizens of a forest. But the human mind, reluctant to resign to death, made these ascetics live on dreams of rejuvenation. . . . The use of fresh plants had been the system of medicine at the time. . . . The Chinese herbalists . . . believed not only in Animism but more so in Dualism" (p. 23). Further references could be made, but these citations suffice to illustrate the author's methodological approach.

CHINESE ALCHEMY

Important contributions to the understanding of Chinese alchemy (*F. & C.*, pp. 109 ff; *F. & A.*, pp. 113 ff.) have been made by Joseph Needham and his collaborators. Although the fifth volume of Needham's *Science and Civilization in China,* devoted to the history of Chinese chemistry and industrial chemistry, is not yet published, we have two monographs of considerable interest: Ho Ping-Yü and Joseph Needham's "The Laboratory Equipment of the Early Medieval Chinese Alchemist" (*Ambix,* VII [1959], 57–115) and Ts'ao T'ien Ch'in, Ho Ping-Yü, and Joseph Needham's "An Early Medieval Chinese Alchemical Text on Aqueous Solutions" (*Ambix,* VII [1959], 122–58). See also Needham's "Remarks on the History of Iron and Steel Technology in China" (in *Le fer à travers les âges.* [Nancy, 1956], pp. 93–102).

No less important is the complete translation of a classical alchemical treatise, the *Nei P'ien* of Ko Hung (Pao-p'u-tzu), known until now only in a fragmentary form in the translations of Tenney L. Davis and Eugen Feifel (*F. & C.*, pp. 188 ff.; *F. & A.*, pp. 193–94); see James R. Ware trans. and ed.), *Alchemy, Medicine, and Religion*

in the China of A. D. 320: The Nei P'ien of Ko Hung
(Cambridge, Mass., 1966). Professor Ware introduces this
famous treatise with the translation of Ko Hung's auto-
biography (*ibid.*, pp. 6–21). One regrets, however, the
absence of explanatory notes and commentaries. The
reader seemingly is expected to know something of the
vast folklore of tortoises and cranes and its reinterpretation by the Chinese alchemists (*ibid.*, pp. 53 ff.; see Eliade,
Alchimia Asiatică [cited in n. 1], I, 15 ff.). But one wonders if the following quotations can be understood without a commentary:

> Take the elixir and preserve unity:
> With all heaven together end.
> Revert your sperm, breathe like fetus:
> Protract longevity peaklessly.
>
> WARE (trans. and ed.), *op. cit.*, p. 59

The return of the semen and the so-called embryonic
respiration are intricate techniques, with a long history—
one may even say a "prehistory"—in China and India
(see *F. & C.*, pp. 124 ff.; *F. & A.*, pp. 122 ff.). The allusion
to the circulation of the breaths (Ware [trans. and ed.],
op. cit., p. 69) is incomprehensible without some quotations from the texts studied and translated by H. Maspéro (see M. Eliade's *Le Yoga* (Paris, 1955), pp. 75 ff.;
Yoga. Immortality and Freedom, pp. 59 ff.; *F. & C.*, pp.
125 ff.; *F. & A.*, pp. 129 ff.). Also the role of gold and jade
in the preservation of a corpse (Ware [trans. and ed.], *op.
cit.*, p. 62; see Elliade, *Alchimia Asiatică*, I, 18 ff.; *F. & C.*,
pp. 119 ff.; *F. & A.*, pp. 118 ff.) and the importance of
cinnabar in alchemy as wel as in Taoist lore (Ware [trans.
and ed.], *op. cit.*, pp. 74 ff.; *F. & C.*, pp. 117 ff.; *F. & A.*,
pp. 121 ff.) should have been commented upon.

Hopefully, someday we will have an extensive source

book of Chinese alchemical texts, profusely annotated, so as to make them accessible to a large public. One of the main interests of the Chinese alchemy for the history of culture consists in its utilization and reinterpretation of many archaic and "popular" techniques (dietary recipes as well as sexual respiratory techniques for prolongation of life, methods of meditation, etc.). Rolf Stein and Max Kaltenmark[8] have investigated the "prehistory" of many Taoist and alchemical practices and have shown their parallels in Indochina (see *F. & C.*, pp. 117 ff; *F. & A.*, pp. 121 ff.). On the theme of the grotto (or the calabash) into which magicians and alchemists retreat for initiation, a theme brilliantly studied by R.-A. Stein in his monograph "Jardins en miniature d'Extrème-Orient," see also Michel Soymié's "Le Lo-Feou Chan, étude de géographie réligieuse" (*Bulletin de l'École Française de l'Extrème Orient* [Saigon], XLVIII [1956], 1–139, esp. pp. 88–96 ["La grotteciel"] and 97–103 ["Le soleil de minuit"]).

ALCHEMY AND THE HISTORY OF IDEAS

The researches of C. G. Jung have contributed considerably to making alchemy significant for modern culture (see *F. & C.*, pp. 199–209; *F. & A.*, pp. 201–4). His last important work, which took him more then ten years to complete, was recently translated into English: *Mysterium coniunctionis. An Inquiry into the separation and Synethesis of Psychic Opposites in Alchemy* (London and New York, 1963; the two volumes of the German original were published in Zurich in 1955–56). The reader familiar with Jung's previous works devoted to alchemy[9] will find in *Mysterium coniunctionis* the same methodological

---

[8] See also a brilliant summary by Max Kaltenmark, *Lao Tseu et le taoïsme* (Paris, 1965), pp. 165–74.

presuppositions: as a psychologist, and like Herbert Silberer forty years before him, Jung sees in alchemical symbolism and techniques the projection of a process which takes place in the unconscious. The subject matter of the present volume is the alchemical procedure of uniting the opposites. Jung interprets this extremely complicated and enigmatic operation as a representation of what he calls the individuation process, "though with the not unimportant difference that no single individual ever attains to the richness and scope of the alchemical symbolism" (*ibid.*, p. 555).

Whether this purely psychological approach is accepted or not—and some readers without a personal knowledge of analytical psychology may find it difficult to accept—is without consequence. For *Mysterium coniunctionis* is a rich and valuable book, bringing together an amazing amount of obscure and hard to obtain alchemical, Gnostic, and mystical texts; and, what is even more important, it elucidates their symbolism in the light of comparative religion and analytical psychology. The cultural impact of *Mysterium coniunctionis* may prove to be independent of Jung's psychological theory. Ultimately, such a work may help the public rediscover the fascination of alchemical symbolism and grasp the historical importance of the alchemists' dream.

The third volume of *Mysterium coniunctionis,* published in Zurich in 1957, contained an edition and a study by Marie-Louise von Franz of *Aurora consurgens,* a thirteenth-century text traditionally attributed to

---

⁹ See the Bibliography in *F. & C.*, pp. 199–200; *F. & A.*, pp. 201–2. Vol. XIV of the English translation of Jung's collected works is entitled *Alchemical Studies* (New York, 1967) and comprises, among other texts, the hitherto untranslated studies "Paracelsus as a Spiritual Phenomenon" (1942) and "The Arbor Philosophica" (1945/1954).

Thomas Aquinas and rediscovered by Jung. The work
was recently translated into English by R. F. C. Hull and
A. S. B. Glover: *Aurora consurgens. A Document Attributed to Thomas Aquinas on the Problem of Opposites in
Alchemy* (London and New York, 1966). The English
translation is superior to the German original, not only
because of the corrections of various errors, incomplete
quotations, and wrong references, but also because of a
short but important Foreword by Marie-Louise von
Franz.

Aurora consurgens is unique among alchemical treatises. Only about a half-dozen of the "classics" of alchemy
are quoted, and technical instruction and chemical recipes
are lacking (*ibid.*, p. 400). On the other hand, the mystical element is strongly emphasized. In some manuscripts
it is stated to be a work by Aquinas, but scholars have
rejected this tradition. It is well known that Thomas'
master, Albertus Magnus, was interested in alchemy and
occultism in the very years he met his disciple (1245–50).
As to Thomas himself, he thought that alchemy was "a
true art, but difficult on account of the occult influences
of the celestial powers" (*ibid.*, p. 418). Dr. von Franz is
inclined to think that *Aurora consurgens* might very well
be a transcript of Thomas' last words, his last "seminar,"
while lying on his deathbed, in the monastery of St. Mary
at Fossanova. As such, the treatise would be related to
Thomas' mystical illumination, following his ecstatic experience in the chapel of St. Nicholas in Naples; and it
would not reflect his philosophical and theological system,
which Thomas laboriously constructed in his previous
writings but which he considered after his *raptus* "as
worthless as straw."

Most probably, this hypothesis will not be accepted by

the specialists. But the interest of the text will not diminish. Moreover, the long commentary (*ibid.*, pp. 153–431) constitutes in itself a very learned contribution to the understanding of alchemical and mystical symbolism.

As we have pointed out, Jung's interest in alchemy was aroused mainly for psychological reasons. His approach contrasted radically with that of the historian of science, who concentrated almost exclusively on the scientific value of what he considers to be a protochemistry. Finally, there are some modern authors for whom alchemy is still a "traditional science" (*ars regia*): they understand the *elixir* and the *lapis* both as symbols and concrete substances (*F. & C.*, p. 198; *F. & A.*, pp. 200–201). But there is room for a broader and more comprehensive approach, namely, to study the alchemists' universe of meaning in itself and for itself. The research of Stein and Kaltenmark, for example, has disclosed the *univers imaginaire* of the Chinese alchemists and Taoists. Their discoveries are not only extremely important for the understanding of the Chinese mind but are also of value in themselves for revealing a world of meaning which is independent of man's historical transformations. In other words, such studies widen our understanding of man, regardless of the historical context of the specific *univers imaginaire* which is hermeneutically presented.

No less important and significant for the broadening of the Western historiographical consciousness are some recent works on Hermetism and its relations with Renaissance science, art, and philosophy. We may quote as an example the superb monograph of Frances Yates, *Giordano Bruno and the Hermetic Tradition* (Chicago, 1965); it brilliantly illustrates the progress realized in the last years in *understanding* a world of meaning which was neglected, or despised, by the Renaissance historiography of the previous generation. The importance of the Hermetic *univers imaginaire* in the victory of Copernian heliocentrism and in the development of Italian Renaissance philosophy is overwhelming. Similar progress has been made in the understanding of literary history. One may think, for example, of Auguste Viatte's *Les sources occultes du romantisme: Illuminisme-Théosophie* (Paris, 1927), a work which opened the way to a series of studies which, by demonstrating the importance of occultism, esoterism, and alchemy, renewed completely the interpretation of French Renaissance poetry (Albert-Marie Schmidt) and French Romanticism (Albert Béguin, *L'Ame romantique et le rêve* [Marseille, 1937]), and contributed considerably to discovering and elucidating the relations between Illuminism, Rosicrucianism, Freemasonery, and the literature of the first half of the nineteenth century.

Such studies disclose a series of *univers imaginaire*, whose role in the formation of the modern Western mind was not even suspected. One can only hope that in the near future the world of meaning of the alchemists will be investigated and comprehended with learning, acumen, and sympathetic understanding similar to that illustrated by the recent studies in Renaissance Hermetism and French Romanticism.

Appendices

METEORITES, THUNDERSTONES,
BEGINNINGS OF METALLURGY

Concerning the myth of the celestial vault of stone, cf. Uno Holmberg, 'Der Baum des Lebens' (*Annales Academiae Scientiarum Fennicae*, Série B., vol. XVI, Helsinki, 1922–3), p. 40; H. Reichelt, 'Der Steinerne Himmel' (*Indogermanische Forschungen*, 32, 1913, pp. 23–57), maintained that the conception of stone and metal skies was common to the Indo-Europeans. R. Eisler, 'Zur Terminologie und Geschichte der jüdischen Alchemie' (*Monatschrift für Geschichte und Wissenschaft des Judentums*, 1926, N.F., vol. 26, pp. 194–201), held that meteorites had given rise to the idea that the skies were made of different metals (iron, copper, gold, silver, etc.). On the connection between skies, metals and colours, cf. Holmberg, *op. cit.*, p. 49; A. Jeremias, *Handbuch der altorientalischen Geisteskultur* (2nd Edn., Berlin, 1929), pp. 180 sq. But R. J. Forbes, *Metallurgy in Antiquity* (Leyden, 1950), remarks that precise allusions to the relation between metals, colours and planets are rarer than is generally believed, even in the Babylonian epoch.

Concerning the 'thunderstones', see Richard Andrée, *Ethnograpische Parallelen, Neue Folge* (Leipzig, 1889), pp. 30–41 (*Der Donnerkeil*); P. Sébillot, *Le Folklore de France*, vol. I (Paris, 1904), pp. 104–5; W. W. Skeat, 'Snakestones'

(*Folklore*, 23, 1912, pp. 45–80); P. Saintyves, *Corpus de Folklore préhistorique en France et dans les colonies françaises*, vol. II (Paris, 1934); *Le Folk-lore des outils de l'âge de la pierre*, pp. 107–202.

Concerning the role of metals in the life and religion of primitive peoples, the reader may consult Richard Andrée's comprehensive volume, *Die Metalle bei den Naturvölkern mit Berücksichtigung prähistorischer Verhältnisse* (Leipzig, 1884). On the folklore of lead, cf. Leopold Schmidt, *Das Blei in seiner volkstumlichen Geltung* (Mitt. d. Chemischen Forschungsinstitutes der Oesterreiches, II, 4–5, 1948, pp. 98 sq.). On the history of metallurgy and its cultural aspects, see T. A. Rickard, *Man and Metals. A History of Mining in relation to the development of civilization* (New York, 1932, 2 vols.; there is also a French translation), and J. R. Partington, *Origins and Development of Applied Chemistry* (London, 1935). The state of the latest research on metallurgy in antiquity is conscientiously established by R. J. Forbes, *Metallurgy in Antiquity, A notebook for archaeologists and technologists* (Leiden, 1950), with full bibliography. Cf. also by the same author, *Bibliographia Antiqua, Philosophia Naturalis* (First part, Mines, Leyden, 1940; second part, Metallurgy, Leyden, 1942). See also Charles Singer, E. J. Holmyard and A. R. Hall, *A History of Technology*, vol. I (Oxford, 1955).

On AN. BAR: Hommel, *Grundriss der Geographie und Geschichte Vorderasiens* (Berlin, 1908–22), p. 13; G. G. Boson, *Les Métaux et les pierres dans les inscriptions assyro-babyloniennes* (inaugural dissertation, Munich, 1914), pp. 11–12; Axel W. Persson, *Eisen und Eisenbereitung in ältester Zeit, Etymologisches und Sachliches* (*Bulletin de la Société Royale de Lettres de Lund*, 1934, pp. 111–27), p. 114; Forbes, Metallurgy in Antiquity, p. 465.

On *parzillu*: Persson, *op. cit.*, p. 113; Forbes, p. 465.

On the industry and commerce of copper and bronze in the ancient Near East, cf. R. Dussaud, *La Lydie et ses voisins aux hautes époques* (Paris, 1930), pp. 76 sq.

On the vocabulary of bronze, Georges Dossin, 'Le Vocabulaire de Nuzi Smn' (*Revue d'Assyriologie*, 1947–8), pp. 26 sq.

On the question of iron in ancient Egypt and the term *biz-n.pt*, cf. G. A. Wainwright, 'Iron in Egypt' (*The Journal of Egyptian Archaeology*, 18, 1932, pp. 3–15; summed up in Persson's article, pp. 2–3); id., 'The Coming of Iron' (*Antiquity*, 10, 1936, pp. 5–25); E. Wyndham Hulme, 'Early Iron-smelting in Egypt' (*Antiquity*, II, 1937, pp. 222–3); Forbes, *Metallurgy in Antiquity*, pp. 425 sq. H. Quiring, who has summed up his researches in the article 'Die Herkunft des ältesten Eisens und Stahl' (*Forschungen und Fortschritte*, 9, 1933, pp. 126–270), thinks he has proved that the iron ores later used by the Egyptians came from the sands of Nubia which contained magnetite in grains with more than 60 per cent of iron.

On the subject of iron in Minoan Crete: H. R. Hall, *The Civilization in the Bronze Age* (London, 1928), p. 253; A. W. Persson, p. 111; Forbes, pp. 456 sq.

NOTE B

MYTHOLOGY OF IRON

Apotropaic iron against demons and spirits: I. Goldziher, 'Eisen als Schutz gegen Dämonen' (*Archiv für Religionwissenschaft*, 10, 1907, pp. 41–6); S. Seligmann, *Der Böse Blick* (Berlin, 1910), vol. I, pp. 273–6; vol. II, pp. 8–9, etc.; id., *Die magischen Heil—und Schutzmittel* (Stuttgart, 1927), pp. 161–9 (this last volume is the expansion of a few chapters of the *Böse Blick*); Frazer, *Tabu and the Perils of the Soul*, pp. 234 sq.

(French translation, pp. 195 sq.); Tawney-Penzer, *The Ocean of Story*, vol. II (London, 1924), pp. 166–8; J. J. Meyer, *Trilogie altindischer Machte und Feste der Vegetation* (Zürich-Leipzig, 1937), vol. I, pp. 130 sq., vol. II, pp. 118 sq.; G. Dumezil, 'Labrys' (*Journal Asiatique*, 1929, pp. 237–54), pp. 247 sq. (iron knives keep demons away; Caucasian beliefs); J. Filliozat, *Le Kumâratantra* (Paris, 1937), p. 64 (magic role of the knife). Cf. also *Handwörterbuch der Deutsche Aberglauben*, under *Eisen*.

Iron as protector of crops (north-eastern Europe): A. V. Rantasalo, *Der Ackerbau im Volksaberglauben der Finnen und Esten mit entsprechenden Gebrauchen der Germanen verglichen* (5 vol., *FF Communications*, Sontavala–Helsinki, 1919–25), vol. III, pp. 17 sq.

NOTE C

ANTHROPOGONIC THEMES

Creation of man from clay or earth: S. Langdon, *Le Poème sumerien du Paradis, du Déluge et de la Chute de l'homme* (Paris, 1919, trans. C. Virolleaud), pp. 22–3, 31–2; id. *Semitic Mythology* (Boston, 1931), pp. 111–12; in the Oceanian traditions, cf. R. B. Dixon, *Oceanic mythology* (Boston, 1916), p. 107 (man created from dust with the blood of the god); see also Sir James Frazer, *Folk-Lore of the Old Testament* (London, 1919), vol. I, pp. 3–44; id. *Creation and Evolution in Primitive Cosmogonies* (London, 1935), pp. 3–35 (written in 1909 and hence not as full as the previous). On Egyptian traditions, cf. E. A. Wallis Budge, *From Fetish to God in Ancient Egypt* (Oxford, 1934), pp. 143, 434 (man created from the tears of god); Adolf Erman, *Der Religion der Aegypter* (Berlin, 1934), p. 66; Sandman Holmberg, *The God Ptah* (Lund–Copenhagen, 1946), pp. 31 sq.

For a general view of anthropogonic themes, see Stith Thompson, *Motif-Index of Folk-Literature*, vol. I (Helsinki, 1932, FF *Communications* Nr. 106), pp. 150–9. For later translations of the Babylonian Poem of the Creation, see G. Furlani, *II Poema della Creazione* (Bologna, 1934), pp. 100 sq. (cf. pp. 34–5 for similar Mesopotamian traditions); R. Labat, *Le Poème babylonien de la Création* (Paris, 1935). For a direct connection with the metallurgical problem, cf. the tradition found among the Toradja: the god *Pue ne Palabru* fashions each child in the forge (Kruyt, quoted by J. W. Perry, *The Children of the Sun*, 2nd edition, London, 1927, p. 207).

NOTE D

ARTIFICIAL FERTILIZATION AND ORGIASTIC RITES

On artificial fertilization in Mesopotamia, cf. A. H. Pruessen, 'Date Culture in Ancient Babylonia' (*Journal of the American Oriental Society*, 36, 1920, pp. 213–32); George Sarton, 'The artificial fertilization of date-palms in the time of Ashur-Nasir-Pal' (*Isis*, 21, Nr. 60, April, 1934, pp. 8–14); id. 'Additional note on date culture in ancient Babylonia' (*ibid.*, Nr. 65, June, 1935, pp. 251–2; these two articles include a complete bibliography on the question); Hélène Danthine, *Le Palmier-dattier et les arbres sacrés dans l'iconographie de l'Asie occidentale ancienne* (Paris, 1937), pp. 111–21.

On similar traditions among the Hebrews and Arabs, see Salomon Gandz, 'Artificial fertilization of date-palms in

Palestine and Arabia' (*Isis*, 33, Nr. 65, June 1935, pp. 245–50). On orgiastic practices connected with the grafting of citrus trees, according to the writings of Ibn Wahshya, cf. S. Tolkowsky, *Hesperides, A History of the Culture and Use of Citrus Fruits* (London, 1938), pp. 56, 129 sq.

NOTE E

SEXUAL SYMBOLISM OF FIRE

The sexual symbolism of fire in ancient India is investigated by K. F. Johansson, *Über die altindische Göttin Dhisanâ* (Skrifter utgifna Vetenskapssafundet i Uppsala, Uppsala–Leipzig, 1917), pp. 51–5. On traditions in modern India, cf. W. Crooke, *Religion and the Folklore of Northern India* (Oxford, 1926), p. 336; J. Abbot, *The Keys of Power, A study of Indian Ritual and Belief* (London, 1932), p. 176.

On the symbolism of the hearth (= the vulva) in protohistoric cultures, see Oscar Almgren, *Nordische Felszeichnungen als religiöse Urkunden* (Frankfurt a.M., 1934), pp. 244 sq. Among the ancient Germans and in northern Europe: J. Grimm, *Deutsche Mythologie* (4e Ausgabe, 1876, vol. III, p. 175.

On the sexual symbolism of the production of fire among 'primitives', cf. Sir James Frazer, *The Magic Art and the Origin of Kings*, vol. II, pp. 208 sq.; id., *Mythes sur l'origine du feu* (French trans., Paris, 1931), pp. 62 sq. Examples of sexual orgies at the solemn kindling of a fire, *ibid.*, p. 64 (among the Marind-Anim, after Wirz).

On the cosmological symbolism of the lighting of the fire and the ideas of regeneration by Time, see my work *Le Mythe de l'Éternel Retour* (Paris, 1949), pp. 107 sq.

On the symbolism of the 'centre', *ibid.*, pp. 30 sq.; and *Images et Symboles* (Paris, 1952), pp. 33 sq.

NOTE F

SEXUAL SYMBOLISM OF THE TRIANGLE

On the sexual symbolism of the *delta*, see R. Eisler, *Kuba-Kybele*, pp. 127, 135 sq., and Uberto Pestalozza, *Religione Mediterranea* (Milan, 1951), p. 246, n. 65. On the 'triangle'-'door'-'woman' relationship, cf. H. C. Trumbull, *The Threshold Covenant* (New York, 1892), pp. 252–7 (information from Greek, Chinese, Jewish, etc., sources). On the *arché geneseoas*, cf. Franz Dornseiff, *Das Alphabet in Mystik and Magie* (Leipzig, 2nd Ed., 1925), pp. 21–2. On the symbolism of the triangle in India: G. Tucci, *Tracce di culto lunare in India* (*Rivista di Studi Orientali*, XLL, 1929–30, pp. 419–27), p. 422 and note on tantric symbolism; J. J. Meyer, *Trilogie altindischer Machte und Feste der Vegetation* (Zürich-Leipzig, 1937), vol. III, pp. 133–294.

R. Eisler, *Kuba-Kybele* (*Philologus*, vol. 68, 1909, pp. 118–51, 161–209), p. 135, gives an unfortunate interpretation of the sexual symbolism of the Ka'aba: as the *tetragonos lithos*, the sacred stone of Mecca, was (according to him) the 'house' of a *pyramis* or of an obelisk (Konische Phallostein). It should be remembered, however, that, in 1909, when Eisler was writing this study, psychoanalysis was scarcely known and those scholars who had any knowledge of it were very easily led astray by pan-sexual symbolisms.

PETRA GENITRIX

On myths about men born from stone, cf. B. Nyburg, *Kind und Erde* (Helsinki, 1931), pp. 61 sq.; M. Eliade, *Traité d'Histoire des Religions*, p. 208. On fertilizing stones and the rite of the 'slide' or 'sliding' rites, cf. *Traité*, pp. 194 sq.

On the birth of gods from a *petra genitrix* (Great Goddess = *matrix mundi*), cf. R. Eisler, *Weltmantel und Himmelszelt* (Munich, 1910), vol. II, pp. 411, 727 sq., etc.; id., 'Kuba-Kybele' (*Philologus*, vol. 68, 1909, pp. 118–51, 161–209), pp. 196 sq.

On paleosemitic traditions concerning men issued from stones, cf. W. Robertson Smith, *The Religion of the Semites*, 3rd Ed. (London, 1927), p. 86 (Arab legend); Hans Schmidt, *Die Erzählung von Paradies und Sundefall* (Tubingen, 1931), p. 38, n. 1 (Old Testament).

On the birth of Christ from a stone in Rumanian religious folklore, see Alexandre Rosetti, *Colindele Romanilor* (Academia Romana, Bucharest, 1920), p. 68.

BABYLONIAN 'ALCHEMY'

R. Campbell Thompson's translations of the Assyrian documents, *On the Chemistry of the Ancient Assyrians* (London, 1925, 158 typewritten pages); Bruno Meissner, *Babylonien und Assyrien*, vol. II (Heidelberg, 1925), pp. 382 sq.; Robert Eisler, *Der Babylonische Ursprung der Alchemie* (*Chemiker-Zeitung*, No. 83, 11th July 1925, pp. 577 sq.; N. 86, 18th July

1925, pp. 602 sq.); id., *Die chemische Terminologie der Baby-lonier* (*Zeitschrift für Assyriologie*, Bd. 37, April 1926, pp. 109–31); id., 'L'origine babylonienne de l'alchimie' (*Revue de Synthèse Historique*, 1926, pp. 1–25). On the mineralogical and chemical terminology, see also R. C. Thompson, *A Dictionary of Assyrian Chemistry and Geology* (Oxford, 1936). R. C. Thompson has summarized his researches in his article: *A Survey of the Chemistry of Assyria in the seventh century B.C.* (*Ambix*, II, 1938, pp. 3–16).

Robert Eisler's interpretation has been rejected for differ-ent reasons by the assyriologist H. Zimmern, *Assyrische chemisch-technische Rezepte, insbesondere für Herstellungen farbigen glasierter Ziegel in Umschrift und Übersetzung* (*Zeit-schrift für Assyriologie*, Bd. 36, September 1925, pp. 177–208); id., *Vorläufige Nachtrag zu den assyrischen chemisch-technischen Rezepten* (*ibid.*, Bd. 37, September 1926, pp. 213–14); by the historian of science Ernst Darmstaedter, *Vorläufige Bemer-kungen zu den assyrischen chemisch-technischen Rezepten* (*Zeitschrift für Assyriologie*, 1925, pp. 302–4); id., 'Nochmals babylonische Alchemie' (*ibid.*, 1926, pp. 205–13); the Arabic scholar and historian of science, Julius Ruska, 'Kritisches zu R. Eisler's chemie-geschichtlicher Methode' (*Zeitschrift für Assyriologie*, Bd. 37, 1926, pp. 273–88).

R. Eisler's hypothesis has been accepted by Abel Rey, *La Science orientale avant les Grecs* (Paris, 1930), pp. 193 sq.; see also R. Berthelot, *La Pensée de l'Asie et l'astrobiologie* (Paris, 1938), pp. 43 sq.

In the second volume of Edmund von Lippmann's *Entstehung und Ausbreitung der Alchemie* (Berlin, 1931), pp. 51 sq., the author maintains a somewhat negative attitude without committing himself categorically; see, too, vol. III (Weinheim, 1954), p. 40. One would have liked to see the problem tackled by Forbes in his comprehensive work.

CHINESE ALCHEMY

For a general incursion into the history of Chinese scientific thought as part of the universal history of science, see George Sarton, *An Introduction to the History of Sciences*, vols. I–III, five volumes (Washington, 1926–48).

On the history of the metallurgical and chemical arts in ancient China, see Li Ch'iao Ping, *The Chemical Arts of Old China* (Easton, 1948). B. Laufer has shown that the paste *liu li* (used in the manufacture of glass windows), as well as kaolin, were first experimented with by Taoist alchemists: cf. *The Beginnings of Porcelain in China* (Chicago, 1917, Field Museum), pp. 142, 118, etc. The salts of arsenic with which alchemists worked have found their uses in agriculture and various industries: cf. M. Muccioli, 'L'arsenico presso i Cinesi' (*Archivio di Storia della Scienza*, VIII, pp. 65–76, particularly pp. 70–1). On the application of alchemical discoveries to ceramic and metallurgical techniques, see E. von Lippmann, *Entstehung und Ausbreitung der Alchemie*, I, p. 156; II, pp. 45, 66, 178, etc.

On Chinese alchemy, the essential material will be found in the bibliography to my book *Le Yoga, Immortalité et Liberté* (Paris, 1954), pp. 399–400. The most notable works on the subject are: O. Johnson, *A Study of Chinese Alchemy* (Shanghai, 1928; see too B. Laufer's review, *Isis*, 1929, vol. XII, pp. 330–2); A. Waley, *Notes on Chinese Alchemy* (Bulletin of School of Oriental Studies, VI, 1930, pp. 1–24); W. H. Barnes, 'Possible reference to Chinese Alchemy in the Fourth or Third Century B.C.' (*The China Journal*, vol. XXIII, 1935, pp. 75–9); Homer H. Dubs, 'The Beginnings of Alchemy' (*Isis*, vol. XXXVIII, 1947, pp. 62–86).

Among the translations of alchemical texts the following may be especially noted: Lu-Ch'iang Wu and Tenney L. Davis, 'An Ancient Chinese Treatise on alchemy entitled Ts'an T'ung Ch'i, written by Wei Po-Yang about A.D. 142' (*Isis*, 1932, vol. XVIII, pp. 210–89); id., 'Ko Hung on the Yellow and the White' (*Proceedings of the American Academy of Arts and Sciences*, vol. LXX, 1935, pp. 221–84). This last work includes the translation of chapters 4 and 6 of the treatise by Ko Hung (Pao Pu'tzu); chapters 1–3 are translated by Eugen Feifel, *Monumenta Serica*, vol. VI, 1941, pp. 113–211 (see *ibid.*, vol. IX, 1944, a new translation of chapter 4 again by Feifel), and chapters 7 and 11 by T. L. Davis and K. F. Chen, 'The Inner Chapters of Pao Pu'tzu' (*Proceedings of the American Academy of Arts and Sciences*, vol. LXXIV, 1940–42, pp. 287–325). See also Roy C. Spooner and C. H. Wang, 'The Divine Nine Turn "Tan Sha" Method, a Chinese alchemical Recipe' (*Isis*, 1947, vol. XXXVIII, pp. 235–42).

H. H. Dubs believes that the origin of alchemy is to be sought in the China of the fourth century B.C. According to Dubs, alchemy could only have come into being where gold was unknown or where methods of assaying gold were unknown; now, in Mesopotamia these methods had been widely known since the fourteenth century B.C., which would throw doubt on the Mediterranean origins of alchemy (Dubs, pp. 80 sq.). However, this opinion does not appear to have been accepted by the historians of alchemy (see F. Sherwood Taylor, *The Alchemists*, New York, 1949, p. 75). Dubs is of the opinion that alchemy found its way to the West via Chinese travellers (*op. cit.*, p. 84). However, it is not excluded that in China, 'scientific' alchemy represents a foreign influence (cf. Laufer, *Isis*, 1929, pp. 330–1). On the penetration of Mediterranean ideas into China, see Dubs, *op. cit.,* pp. 82–3, notes 122–3. On the probable Mesopotamian origin of Chinese alchemical ideology, cf. H. E. Stapleton, *The Antiquity of Alchemy* (*Ambix*, V, 1953, pp. 1–43), pp. 15 sq.

On the alchemical symbolism of respiration and the sexual act, cf. R. H. van Gulik, *Erotic colour prints of the Ming period, with an essay on Chinese sex life from the Han to the Ch'ing dynasty, 206 B.C.–A.D. 1644* (privately published in fifty copies, Tokyo, 1951), pp. 115 sq.

NOTE J

MAGIC TRADITIONS AND ALCHEMICAL FOLKLORE IN CHINA

On the 'magic flight' of the yogi and alchemist, see M. Eliade, *Le Yoga,* p. 397. On 'magical flight' in China, cf. Eliade, *Le Chamanisme,* pp. 394 sq.; on the flight of the Taoist Immortals, cf. Lionel Giles, *A Gallery of Chinese Immortals* (London, 1948), pp. 22, 40, 43, 51, etc.; Max Kaltenmark, *Le Lie-sien tchouan* (*Biographies legendaires des Immortels taoistes de l'antiquité*), translated and annotated (Pekin, 1953), pp. 51, 54, 82, 146, 154.

A large number of very ancient myths and beliefs concerning immortality and the means of achieving it were taken up and given new significance by the Chinese alchemists. The tortoise and the crane were regarded as symbols of immortality. In the ancient writers cranes are always to be found in the company of the Immortals (J. J. de Groot, *The Religious System of China,* Leiden, 1892, vol. IV, pp. 232–3, 295); cranes are shown on funeral chariots to suggest the passage to immortality (*ibid.,* vol. IV, p. 359). In the pictures depicting the eight Immortals en route for the supernatural island, it is the crane which bears the boat upwards in the air (cf. Werner, *Myths and Legends of China*, London, 1924, p. 302). Pao Pu'tzu (Ko Hung) declares that one's vital energies may be increased by drinking beverages made with the eggs of cranes or the shell of the tortoise (text quoted by Johnson, *Chinese Alchemy*, p. 61). The tradition is very old: the *Lieh Hsien Ch'uan* relates that *Kuei-fu* fed himself on cinnamon and sunflower mixed with the brains of the tortoise (Kaltenmark, p. 119).

Among the vegetable species capable of procuring longevity, Chinese tradition singled out the herb '*chih*' (the herb of immortality), the pine, the cypress and the peach. The pine and cypress were considered to be rich in *yang* substances (cf. J. J. de Groot, *op. cit.*, vol. IV, pp. 294–324). By eating pine seeds Yo Ts'iuan was able to fly in the air. 'The people of that time who received and ate them, all reached the age of two or three hundred years' (M. Kaltenmark, *Lie-sien tchouan*, p. 54; cf. *ibid.*, pp. 81, 136, 160). Concerning the pine trees of longevity, cf. Rolf Stein, *Jardins en miniature d'Extrême-Orient, Le Monde en petit. (Bulletin de l'École française d'Extrême-Orient*, 42, Hanoi, 1943, pp. 1–104, especially pp. 84 sq.). Pao Pu'tzu, for his part, writes that if one rubs one's heels with the sap of the cypress, one 'may walk upon water without sinking'; if one rubs the entire body, one becomes invisible. The fruit of the cypress, dried, reduced to a powder and placed in a torch, will shine with superlative brilliance, and if there happens to be gold or jade buried nearby the flame will become blue and turn towards the earth. The man who feeds on this powder of the cypress-fruits may live to a thousand (text reproduced by De Groot, vol. IV, p. 287). As for the peach tree, its resin, according to Pao Pu'tzu, renders the human body luminous.

Other plants and simples are also reputed to confer

longevity and to convey magical powers. The *Lieh Hsien Ch'uan* mentions the leek (p. 97), cinnamon (pp. 82, 119), agaric (p. 82), seeds of crucifers (p. 79), of aconite (p. 154), of angelica (p. 154), of the sunflower (p. 119), etc. There appears to be an unbroken continuity of folklore traditions, Taoism and alchemy: the Taoist alchemist is the successor of the hunter of medicinal remedies, who, from time immemorial, went off into the mountains with a calabash to collect magic seeds and plants. Cf., on this theme, R. Stein, *Jardins en miniature*, pp. 56 sq. and *passim*.

NOTE K

INDIAN ALCHEMY

On Indian alchemy and pre-chemistry, see P. C. Ray, *A History of Hindu Chemistry*, vol. I (2nd edn., Calcutta, 1925); cf. too Rasacharya Kaviraj Bhudeb Mookerjee, *Rasajala-nidhi* or *Ocean of Indian Medicine, Chemistry and Alchemy*, 2 vols. (Calcutta, 1926–7); this is not a very valuable compilation but it contains a wealth of quotations from traditional alchemical works. For an exposé of the doctrine of the alchemist *siddha*, see V. V. Raman Sastri, *The Doctrinal Culture and Tradition of the Siddhas* (*Cultural Heritage of India*, Sri Ramakrishna Centenary Memorial, Calcutta; s.d. vol. II, pp. 303–19); Shashibhusan Dasgupta, *Obscure Religious Cults as background of Bengali Literature* (Calcutta, 1946), pp. 289 sq.; Mircea Eliade, *Le Yoga, Immortalité et Liberté*, pp. 229 sq.

On the relationship between Tantrism, Hathayoga and alchemy, see M. Eliade, *Le Yoga*, pp. 274 sq., 398 sq. (bibliographies). See also A. Waley, 'References to Alchemy in

Buddhist scriptures' (*Bulletin of the School of Oriental Studies*, London, vol. VI, pp. 1102–3). Allusions to alchemy may also be found in *Mahāyāna-saṁgrahabhasya* (Nanjio, 1171; trans. into Chinese by Hsuan-tsang, about 650) and in *Abhidharma Mahavibhasa* (Nanjio, 1263, trans. Hsuang-tsang 656–9). Cf. too O. Stein, 'References to Alchemy in Buddhist scriptures' (*Bull. School Orient. Studies*, vol. VII, 1933, pp. 262 sq.).

On the alchemist Nâgârjuna, see latest state of research and bibliographies in my *Le Yoga*, p. 398.

On Albiruni, cf. J. Filliozat, *Albiruni et l'alchimie indienne* (*Albiruni Commemoration Volume*, Calcutta, 1951, pp. 101–5).

On the role of mercury in Indian alchemy, P. C. Ray, *op. cit.*, I, p. 105, of the introduction; E. von Lippmann, *Entstehung und Ausbreitung der Alchemie* (Berlin, 1919), p. 435; vol. II (Berlin, 1931), p. 179; Jolly, *Der Stein der Weisen* (*Windisch-Festschrift*, Leipzig, 1914), pp. 98–106. On the Tamil *sittar*, cf. A. Barth, *Oeuvres*, I (Paris, 1914), p. 185; J. Filliozat, *Journal Asiatique*, 1934, pp. 111–12; the *sittar* divided the *saraku* (substances, ingredients) into *ân* and *pensarakhu*, male and female ingredients, which recall the *yin-yang* binomism of Chinese speculation. L. Wieger (*Histoire des croyances religieuses et des opinions philosophiques en Chine*, 2nd edn., Hien-hien, 1927, p. 395) thinks that the Taoist alchemist Ko Hung (Pao Pu'tzu) of the third century had imitated the treatise *Rasaratnākara* attributed to Nâgârjuna. In that case the Rasaratnākara which was considered to belong to the seventh or eighth century (cf. E. Lamotte, *Traité de la Grande Vertu de Sagesse*, I, Louvain, 1944, p. 383, n. 1), 'might go back to the period of the Buddhist Nâgârjuna of the second century' (J. Filliozat, *La Doctrine classique de la médicine indienne*, Paris, 1949, p. 10). There is also the possibility that Tamil alchemy underwent Chinese influence (cf.

J. Filliozat, 'Taoisme et Yoga', in *Dan Viet-Nam*, No. 3, August 1949, pp. 113–20, esp. p. 120).

On alchemical manuscripts in the Cordier Bequest, see J. Filliozat, *Journal Asiatique*, 1934, pp. 156 sq.

NOTE L

SAL AMMONIAC IN ORIENTAL ALCHEMY

The Sanskrit name for sal ammoniac is *navasāra*, the Iranian name *nôshâdar*. H. E. Stapleton has attempted to explain these terms by the Chinese *nau-sha*: see *Sal Ammoniac of study in primitive Chemistry (Memoirs of the Asiatic Society of Bengal*, vol. I, no. 2, pp. 25–42, Calcutta, 1905); cf. Stapleton and R. F. Azo, *Chemistry in Iraq and Persia in the Xth Century A.D. (Memoirs of the Asiatic Society of Bengal*, vol. VIII, no. 61, 1927), p. 346, note 1. B. Laufer has shown up the inconsistency of this hypothesis; see *Sino-Iranica* (Field Museum, Chicago, 1919), p. 505. Sal ammoniac was used for the first time in Iranian alchemy and from there made its way to Chinese, Indian and Arab alchemy. On this question, see Julius Ruska, *Sal Ammoniacus, Nusadir and Salmiak* (Sitzungs-berichte der Heidelberger Akademie der Wissen-schaften, Heidelberg, 1925); id., *Das Buch der Alaune and Salze* (Berlin, 1931), pp. 111, 195 sq. The Arab term *nushadir* derives from the Iranian *noshadar*. It is possible that the discovery and alchemical application of sal ammoniac are traceable to one of the 'alchemical schools of the Sassanid empire'; cf. Henri Corbin, *Le Livre Glorieux de Jabir ibn Hayyan* (Eranos-Jahrbuch, XVIII, Zürich, 1950, pp. 47–114), p. 53, n. 15. Sal ammoniac is well attested in Assyrian cunei-form texts; cf. Campbell Thompson, *Dictionary of Assyrian*

Chemistry and Geology, p. 12. See also J. R. Partington, *Origins and Development of Applied Chemistry* (London, 1935), pp. 147, 317; H. E. Stapleton, *The Antiquity of Alchemy* (Ambix, V, 1953, pp. 1–43), p. 34, n. 68; E. von Lippmann, *Entstehung und Ausbreitung der Alchemie*, III (Weinheim, 1954), p. 116.

NOTE M

GRAECO-EGYPTIAN, ARAB AND WESTERN ALCHEMY

ESSENTIAL BIBLIOGRAPHY

The majority of Greek works on alchemy have been edited and translated by Marcelin Berthelot, *Collection des alchimistes grecs*, 3 vols. (Paris, 1887). The texts of Stephanos of Alexandria, not included by Berthelot in his collection, have been recently edited and translated by F. Sherwood Taylor, 'The Alchemical works of Stephanos of Alexandria' (*Ambix*, I, 1937, pp. 116–39; II, 1938, pp. 39–49). The chemical papyri have been published by O. Lagercrantz, *Papyrus Graecus Holmiensis* (Uppsala, 1913), and Marcelin Berthelot, *Archeologie et Histoire des Sciences* (Paris, 1906). For the list of manuscripts see *Le Catalogue des manuscrits alchimiques grecs* (Brussels, 1924).

The essential documentation and history of Alexandrian alchemy will be found in M. Berthelot, *Les Origines de l'Alchimie* (Paris, 1885); id., *Introduction à l'étude de la Chimie des Anciens et du Moyen Age* (Paris, 1889); Edmund von Lippmann, *Entstehung und Ausbreitung der Alchemie*, I (Berlin, 1919), II (Berlin, 1931), III (Weinheim, 1954); Arthur John Hopkins, *Alchemy, Child of Greek Philosophy*

(Columbia University Press, New York, 1934); R. P. Festugière, O.P., Alchymica (*L'Antiquité Classique*, VIII, 1939, pp. 71–95); id., *La Révélation d'Hermes Trismégiste*, I (Paris, 1944), pp. 216–82; F. Cumont and J. Bidez, *Les Mages hellénisés* (Paris, 1938), I, pp. 170 sq., 198 sq.; II, 309 sq.; F. Sherwood Taylor, 'The Origins of Greek Alchemy' (Ambix, I, 1937, pp. 30–47); id., *The Alchemists* (New York, 1949); R. Pfister, 'Teinture et alchimie dans l'Orient hellénistique' (*Seminarium Kondakovianum*, VII, Prague, 1935, pp. 1–59); J. Bidez, 'Dernières recherches sur l'histoire de l'alchimie en Grece, à Byzance et en Égypte (*Byzantion*, 13, 1938, pp. 383–8); G. Goldschmidt, 'Der Ursprung der Alchemie' (*Ciba Zeitschrift*, V, 1938, pp. 1950–88); A. Rehm, 'Zur Überlieferung der griechischen Alchemisten (*Byzantinische Zeitschrift*, 39, 1939, pp. 394–434); W. J. Wilson, 'Origin and Development of Graeco-Egyptian alchemy' (*Ciba Symposia*, III, 1941, pp. 926–60); W. Ganzenmüller, 'Wandlungen in der geschichtlichen Betrachtungen der Alchemie' (*Chymia*, III, 1950, pp. 143–55); R. J. Forbes, 'The Origin of Alchemy' (*Studies in ancient Technology*, I, Leiden, 1955, pp. 121–44); cf. too C. A. Browne, 'Rhetorical and Religious aspects of Greek Alchemy' (*Ambix*, II, 1946, pp. 129–37; III, 1948, pp. 15–25); Egon Wellesz, 'Music in the treatises of Greek Gnostics and Alchemists' (*Ambix*, IV, 1951, pp. 145–58).

For the history of Arab alchemy, the reader will refer mainly to J. Ruska's studies and editions of texts (bibliography will be found in the *Festgabe zu seinem 70 Geburtstage*, Berlin, 1937, pp. 20–40). The most important are: *Arabische Alchemisten*, I–II (Heidelberg, 1924); *Tabula Smaragdina* (Heidelberg, 1926); *Turba Philosophorum* (Berlin, 1931); *Das Buch der Alaune und Salze* (Berlin, 1935). Cf. too the general exposé given by Ruska in two articles: 'Quelques Problèmes de

Littérature alchimique' (*Annales Guebhard-Sèverine*, Neuchâtel, VII, 1931, pp. 156–73) and 'Methods of Research in the History of Chemistry' (*Ambix*, 1937, pp. 21–9).

On Jâbîr, see E. J. Holmyard, *The Arabic Works of Jâbîr ibn Hayyân* (Paris, 1928), and especially Paul Kraus, *Jâbîr ibn Hayyân, contribution à l'histoire des idées scientifiques dans l'Islam*, I–II (*Le Claire*, 1942–3, *Mémoires présentés à l'Institut d'Égypte*, tomes 44–5).

On Razi: Gerard Heym, 'Al-Razi and Alchemy' (*Ambix*, I, 1938, pp. 184–91); J. R. Partington, 'The Chemistry of Razi' (*ibid.*, pp. 192–6).

Cf. too J. W. Fück, 'The Arabic Literature on Alchemy according to An-Nadim, *A.D.* 987' (*Ambix*, IV, 1951, pp. 81–144); Henri Corbin, 'Le Livre Glorieux de Jabir ibn Hayyan. Alchimie et Archetypes' (*Eranos-Jahrbuch*, XVIII, Zürich, 1950, pp. 47–114); H. E. Stapleton, R. F. Azo and H. Hussain, 'Chemistry in Iraq and Persia' (*Memoirs of the Asiatic Society of Bengal*, VIII, 1927, pp. 340 sq.).

There is no need to mention here the enormous literature on the alchemy of the Middle Ages and the Renaissance. The reader will refer to the three volumes by M. Berthelot, *La Chimie au moyen âge* (Paris, 1893), to the classic work of Edmund von Lippmann, to A. Ganzenmüller, *Die Alchemie in Mittelalter* (Paderborn, 1938, French trans., Paris, 1940); cf. also Aldo Mieli, *Pagine di Storia della Chimica* (Roma, 1922); John Read, *Prelude to Chemistry, An Outline of Alchemy, its Literature and Relationships* (London, 1939); F. Sherwood Taylor, *The Alchemists* (New York, 1949); Albert-Marie Schmidt, *La Poésie scientifique en France au seizième siècle* (Paris, 1938), pp. 317 sq. (Three alchemist-poets: Beroalde de Verville, Christofle de Gamon, Clovis Hesteau de Nuysement); Lynn Thorndike, 'Alchemy during the first half of the sixteenth century' (*Ambix*, II, 1938, pp. 26–38); Robert

Amadou, *Raymod Lulle et l'Alchimie* (Paris, 1953; this constitutes the introduction to the Codicille, newly translated
by Leonce Bouysson).

On Paracelsus, see Ernst Darmstaedter, *Arznei und
Alchemie. Paracelsus-Studien* (Leipzig, 1931); A. F. Titley,
'Paracelsus. A résumé of some controversies' (*Ambix*, I, 1938,
pp. 166–83); C. G. Jung, *Paracelsica* (Zürich, 1942); T. P.
Sherlock, 'The Chemical Work of Paracelsus' (*Ambix*, III,
1948, pp. 33–63); A. Koyré, *Mystiques, Spirituels, Alchimistes
du XVIᵉ siècle allemand* (Paris, 1955), pp. 45 sq.

Gerard Heym had begun an 'Introduction to the Bibliography of Alchemy' (*Ambix*, I, 1937, pp. 48–60); this work
was unfortunately not completed.

The works of George Sarton, *An Introduction to the
History of Science*, 5 vols., and of Lynn Thorndike, *A History
of Magic and Experimental Science*, 6 vols. (New York, 1929–
41), include full bibliographies. See also the critical reviews
published in *Isis* (founder George Sarton).

On alchemy considered from the 'traditional' point of
view, see Fulcanelli, *Les demeures philosophales et le symbolisme
hermetique dans ses rapports avec l'Art sacré et l'esoterisme du
Grand-Oeuvre* (Paris, 1930); J. Evola, *La Tradizione ermetica*
(Bari, 1931; seconda edizione riveduta, 1948); Eugene Can-
seliet, *Deux logis alchimiques* (Paris, 1945); Alexander von
Bernus, *Alchymie und Heilkunst* (Nurnberg, 1940); Rene
Alleau, *Aspects de l'Alchimie traditionelle* (Paris, 1953, pp.
223–36, bibliographies); Maurice Aniane, *Notes sur l'alchimie*,
'*Yoga*' cosmologique de la chrétienté médiévale (in the volume
Yoga. Science de l'homme intégral, texts and studies published
under the direction of Jacques Masui, Paris, 1953, pp. 243–73);
Claude D'Ygé, *Nouvelle Assemblée des Philosophes Chymiques.
Aperçus sur le Grand-Oeuvre des Alchimistes* (Paris, 1954; this
includes the complete text of the *Parole delaissée* by Bernard

Le Trevisan and of the *Explication très curieuse* by Gobineau de Montluisant; pp. 225–32, bibliography).

C. G. JUNG AND ALCHEMY

Professor Jung's researches owe nothing to an interest in the history of chemistry or to the attraction of hermetic symbolism in itself. As physician and analyst he was investigating the structure and behaviour of the psyche with strictly therapeutic intentions. If he was gradually led to the study of mythology and religion, rites and gnoses, it was in order to understand more fully the processes of the mind and so ultimately to help his patients to recover. In the course of his work he was struck by the analogy between the symbolism and dreams of some of his patients and the symbolism of alchemy. This induced Jung to begin the serious study of alchemical literature. This he did over a period of fifteen years but he never referred to it, either to his patients or to his immediate collaborators. He was careful to avoid any possible suggestion or auto-suggestion. It was not until 1935 that he delivered a lecture to *Eranos* in Ascona on the symbolism of dreams and the process of individuation ('Traumsymbole des Individuations-prozesses', *Eranos-Jahrbuch*, III, Zürich, 1936), followed, in 1936, by a further lecture: 'Die Erlösungsvorstellungen in der Alchemie' (*Eranos-Jahrbuch*, IV, 1937). In the first, Jung compares a series of dreams, showing the stages in the process of individuation, with the successive operations of the *opus alchymicum*. In the second he endeavours to offer a psychological interpretation of certain central symbols in alchemy giving special emphasis to the symbolic complex of the redemption of matter. Both texts, elaborated and considerably amplified, were published in 1944 in book form with the title *Psychologie und Alchemie* (Zürich, Rascher, 2nd edn. revised, 1952). After the Ascona lectures, allusions to alchemy become more and more frequent in Jung's writings. The following studies deserve special note: 'Die Visionen des Zosimos' (*Eranos-Jahrbuch*, V, 1937, pp. 15–54; a fuller version has been published in the recent volume, *Von den Wurzeln des Bewusstseins*, Zürich, Rascher, 1954, pp. 139–216); *Die Psychologie der Übertragung* (Zürich, 1946), prolegomena to the monumental *Mysterium Coniunctionis*, the first volume of which appeared in 1955; *Der Philosophische Baum* (a first draft was published in the *Verhandlungen der Naturforschenden Gesellschaft*, Basle, Bd. LVI, 1945, pp. 411 sq.; the text, completely revised, was taken up again in the volume *Von den Wurzeln des Bewusstseins*, pp. 353–496).

When Professor Jung began his researches into alchemy there was only one really serious book on the subject in which alchemy was tackled from the viewpoint of depth psychology; *Probleme der Mystik und ihre Symbolik* (Vienna, 1914), by Herbert Silberer, one of Freud's most brilliant disciples. When he began his researches, Jung did not feel he had the right to step outside the strictly psychological boundaries of the subject; he was dealing with 'psychic facts' and the relationship which he was in the process of discovering between them and certain symbols and operations in alchemy. The 'hermetists' and 'traditionalists' later reproached Jung for having translated into psychic terms, symbolisms and operations which were in their essence trans-psychic. Similar reproaches were made by theologians and philosophers. They found it difficult to forgive him for interpreting religious or metaphysical notions in terms of psychology. Jung's reply to such objections is well known. Trans-psychology is not the affair of the psychologist; every spiritual experience implies a psychic actuality and this actuality has a certain content and structure with which it is the psychologist's right and duty to concern himself.

It was the novelty and importance of Jung's researches that they established the following fact: the unconscious undergoes processes which express themselves in alchemical symbolism tending towards psychic results corresponding to the *results of hermetic operations*. It would be difficult to underestimate the bearing and scope of such a discovery. Leaving aside for a moment the purely psychological interpretation suggested by Jung, his discovery amounted in substance to this: in the very depths of the unconscious, processes occur which bear an astonishing resemblance to the stages in a spiritual operation—gnosis, mysticism, alchemy— *which does not occur in the world of profane experience*, and which, on the contrary, makes a clean break with the profane world. In other words, we are in the presence of a strange solidarity of structure between the products of the 'unconscious' (dreams, awakened dreams, hallucinations, etc.) and those experiences which, by the very fact that they are outside the categories of the profane and desanctified world, may be considered as belonging to a 'trans-consciousness' (mystical, alchemical experiences, etc.). But Jung had observed at the outset of his researches that the series of dreams and *rêves éveillés*, the alchemical symbolism of which he was in the process of investigating, accompanied a process of psychic integration which he calls the process of individuation. Such products of the unconscious, therefore, were neither anarchic nor gratuitous; they pursued a precise goal, individuation, which, for Jung, represents the supreme ideal of every human being, namely, the discovery of the possession of his own Self. But if we bear in mind that the goal of the alchemist was the Elixir Vitae and the Philosopher's Stone, that is, the conquest of immortality and absolute freedom (possession of the Stone permitted, among other things, transmutation into gold and hence the freedom to change the world, to 'save' it), it becomes clear that the process of individuation, assumed by the unconscious without the 'permission' of the conscious, and mostly against its will, and which leads man towards his own centre, the Self—this process must be regarded as a pre-figuration of the *opus alchymicum*, or more accurately, an 'unconscious imitation', for the use of all beings, of an ex-tremely difficult initiation process reserved only for a small spiritual élite. Consequently, one is led to the conclusion that there are several levels of spiritual fulfilment, interdependent and interrelated—if looked upon from a certain frame of reference, in this case, the psychological one. The uninitiated person who has alchemical dreams and comes close to a psychic integration, also goes through the ordeal of an 'initiation': however, the result of this initiation is not the same as that of a ritual or mystic initiation, although, functionally, they are akin. Indeed at the level of dreams and other unconscious processes, we are dealing with a spiritual reintegration which has, for the 'uninitiated,' the same importance as an 'initiation' on the ritual or mystical level. Every symbolism is polyvalent. Jung has shown an analogous polyvalence in 'alchemical' or 'mystic' operations: these are applicable at multiple levels and achieve corresponding results. Imagination, dream, hallucination—all disclose a similar alchemical symbol—and by this very fact place the patient in *an alchemical situation*—and achieve an amelioration which, at the psychic level, corresponds to the results of the alchemical operation.

Jung interprets his own discoveries in another way. To him as a psychologist, alchemy, with all its symbolisms and operations, is a projection on to Matter, of archetypes and processes, of the collective unconscious. The *opus alchymicum* is in reality the process of individuation by which one becomes the Self. The *elixir vitae* would be the attainment of the Self; for Jung had observed that 'the manifestations of the Self, that is, the appearance of certain symbols which are part and parcel of the Self, bring with them something of the intemporality of the unconscious which finds expression in a feeling of eternity and immortality' (*Psychologie der Übertragung*). Hence the alchemists' quest for immortality corresponds, on the psychological level, to the process of individuation, to the integration of the Self. As for the Philosopher's Stone, Jung gives its symbolism several meanings. Let us recall, first of all, that for Jung the alchemical operations are *real*: but this reality is not physical but psychic. Alchemy represents the projection of a drama, at once cosmic and spiritual, in laboratory terms. The aim of the *opus magnum* was at once the freeing of the human soul and the healing of the cosmos. In this sense alchemy is a continuation of Christianity. In the eyes of the alchemists, observes Jung, Christianity saved man but not nature. It is the alchemist's dream to heal the world in its totality; the Philosopher's Stone is conceived as the *Filius Macrocosmi* who heals the world, whereas, according to the alchemists, Christ is the Saviour of the Microcosm, that is, of man only. The ultimate goal of the *opus* is Cosmic Salvation; for that reason, the *Lapis Philosophorum* is identified with Christ. In Jung's view, what the alchemists called 'Matter' was in reality the Self. The 'soul of the world', the *'anima mundi'*, identified by the alchemists with the *'spiritus mercurius'*, was imprisoned in 'Matter'. For this reason, the alchemists believed in the reality of 'Matter' which was, in effect, their own psychic self. The aim of the *opus* was to free this 'Matter', to 'save' it, in short, to obtain the Philosopher's Stone, that is, the 'glorious body', the *'corpus glorificationis'*.

See my article on Jung and Alchemy (*Le Disque Vert*, 1955, pp. 97–109). We may note that the historians of science have favourably received Jung's theses on Alchemy; cf. Walter Pagel, 'Jung's Views on Alchemy' (*Isis*, 39, pp. 44–8) and Gerard Heym's review (*Ambix*, III, 1948, pp. 64–7).

NOTE O

ALCHEMY IN THE PERIOD OF THE RENAISSANCE AND THE REFORMATION

The enthusiasm provoked by the rediscovery of Neoplatonism and Hellenistic Hermetism at the beginning of the Italian Renaissance continued for the following two centuries. We know now that Neoplatonic and Hermetic doctrines had a profound and creative impact on philosophy and the arts and also played a major role in the development of alchemical chemistry, medicine, the natural sciences, education and political theory.[1]

With regard to alchemy, we must keep in mind that a number of its basic presuppositions—such as the growth of ores, the transmutation of metals, the Elixir and the obligatory secrecy—were carried over from the Middle Ages to the Renaissance and the Reformation. Scholars of the seventeenth century did not question, for instance, the natural growth of metals; rather they inquired whether the alchemist might assist Nature in this process and 'whether those who claimed to have

[1] See W. Pagel, *Paracelsus* (London, 1958); Frances Yates, *Giordano Bruno and the Hermetic Tradition* (Chicago, 1964); idem, *The Rosicrucian Enlightenment* (Chicago, 1972).

done so already were honest men, fools or imposters.'[1]
Herman Boerhaave (1664–1739), usually considered to be the
first great rational chemist, famous for his empirically conducted experiments, still believed in transmutation. And we
shall shortly discuss the importance of alchemy in Newton's
scientific revolution. But under the impact of Neoplatonism
and Hermetism, the traditional alchemy, i.e. arabic and
Western medieval alchemy, enlarged its frame of reference.
The Aristotelian model was replaced by a Neoplatonic one,
which emphasized the role of spiritual intermediaries between
man, cosmos and the Supreme Deity. The old and universally
diffused conviction of the alchemist's collaboration with
Nature now received a Christological significance. The alchemists came to believe that, as Christ redeemed man through
his death and resurrection, the *opus alchymicum* would redeem
Nature. The sixteenth century Hermetist Heinrich Khunrath
identified the Philosopher's Stone as Jesus Christ, the 'Son of
Macrocosm', and thought that its discovery would reveal the
true nature of the macrocosm, just as Christ bestowed whole-
ness on the microcosm, man.[2]

C. G. Jung has rightly insisted on this aspect of Renaissance
and Reformation alchemy. In particular, he carefully investigated the parallel between Christ and the Philosopher's Stone.[3]
In the eighteenth century, the Benedictine monk Don Pernety
summarized as follows the alchemical interpretation of the
Christian *Mysterium*:[4] 'Their Elixir is originally a part of the
World's universal Spirit, embodied in a Virgin earth, from

---

[1] Betty J. Teeter Dobbs, *The Foundation of Newton's Alchemy* (Cambridge, 1976),
p. 44.
[2] *Ibid.*, p. 54.
[3] Cf. especially *Psychology and Alchemy*, translated by R. F. C. Hull, 2nd ed.
(Princeton, 1968), pp. 345 ff. ('The Lapis–Christ Parallel').
[4] Dom A. J. Pernety, *Dictionnaire mytho-hermétique* (Paris, 1758; reprint, collection
'Archè', Milan, 1969), p. 349.

which he [i.e. the Spirit] must be extracted, in order to undergo all the necessary operations before reaching the goal: the glorious and immutable perfection. In the first operation [*preparatio*], the Spirit is tortured until he sheds his blood; in the [stage of] *putrefactio* he dies; when the white color [*albedo*] succeeds the black one [*nigredo*], he comes forth from the darkness of his tomb and resuscitates in glory, ascends to heaven as a pure quintessence; from there he judges the living and the dead,' the 'dead' corresponding to that part of man which, being impure and subject to alteration, cannot resist the fire and is thus annihilated in Gehenna.

From the Renaissance onward, both the old operational alchemy and this more recent 'mystical' and Christological reinterpretation played a decisive role in the astonishing cultural metamorphosis that made possible the triumph of the natural sciences and the industrial revolution. The hope of redeeming man and nature through the alchemical *opus* prolonged the nostalgia for a radical *renovatio* that had obsessed Western Christendom since Giacchino da Fiore. Regeneration, that is, the 'spiritual rebirth', was the Christian goal par excellence, but for many reasons became ever less present in institutionalized religious life. Rather, this nostalgia for an authentic 'spiritual rebirth', the hope for a collective *metanoia* and transfiguration of history, inspired the Medieval and Renaissance popular millenarian movements, prophetic theologies and mystical visions, as well as Hermetic Gnosis.

What is even more significant is the fact that a similar hope inspired what can be called the chemical reinterpretation of the *opus alchymicum*. The famous alchemist, mathematician and encyclopedic scholar John Dee (b. 1527), who assured the Emperor Rudolf II that he possessed the secret of transmutation, thought that a world reform could be achieved through the spiritual powers released by occult—especially alchemical—

operations.[1] The English alchemist Elias Ashmole, like many of his contemporaries, considered alchemy, astrology and natural magic as the saviours of the sciences of their days. Indeed, for the followers of Paracelsus and van Helmont, only through the study of 'chemical philosophy' (i.e. the new alchemy) or 'true medicine' could Nature be understood.[2] Chemistry and not astronomy was considered to be the key that would unlock the secrets of heaven and earth. Alchemy had a divine significance. Since the Creation was understood as a chemical process, both earthly and celestial phenomena were interpreted in chemical terms. On the basis of macrocosm-microcosm relationships, the 'chemical philosopher' could learn the secrets of earthly as well as heavenly bodies. Thus Robert Fludd gave a chemical description of the circulation of the blood, which paralleled the circular motion of the sun.[3]

Like many of their contemporaries, the Hermetists and the 'chemical philosophers' were expecting—and some of them actively preparing—a radical and general reform of all religious, social and cultural institutions. The first, indispensable stage of this universal *renovatio* was the reform of learning. The *Fama Fraternitatis*, a short book published anonymously in 1614 which launched the Rosicrucian movement, called for a new type of learning. The mythical founder of the order, Christian Rosenkrantz, was reputed to have mastered the true secrets of medicine and thus all science. He then wrote a number of books which are kept secret and are studied only by the members of the Rosicrucian order.[4] Thus at the beginning of

---

[1] Cf. Peter French, *John Dee* (London, 1972); R. J. W. Evans, *Rudolf II and his World* (Oxford, 1973), pp. 218–28. On John Dee's influence upon Khunrath, cf. Frances Yates, *The Rosicrucian Enlightenment*, pp. 37–38.

[2] A. G. Debus, 'Alchemy and the Historian of Science', p. 134.

[3] A. G. Debus, *The Chemical Dream of the Renaissance* (Cambridge, 1968), pp. 7, 14–15.

[4] Debus, *The Chemical Dream*, pp. 17–18. *Fama Fraternitatis* is reprinted in Yates, *The Rosicrucian Enlightenment*, pp. 238–51. A French translation of *Fama*, the

the seventeenth century we are confronted again with the old,
familiar, mythical scenario: a primordial revelation written
down by a fabulous personage and hidden for centuries, which
was lately rediscovered and is communicated only to a secret
group of initiates. And, as was the case with many Chinese,
Tantric and Hellenistic texts, the rediscovery of the primordial
revelation, although still inaccessible to profane men, is
announced to the world in order to attract the attention of
those who honestly search for truth and salvation. Indeed, the
author of the *Fama Fraternitatis* asked all the learned scholars
of Europe to examine their art and to join the Rosicrucian
Brotherhood in the reformation of learning; in other words, to
hasten the general *renovatio*. The response to this appeal was
tremendous, and in less than ten years, several hundred books
and tracts appeared, debating the merits of the secret group.

In 1619, Johann Valentin Andreae, who is supposed by
some historians to be the author of the *Fama*, published
Christianopolis, a book that probably influenced Bacon's *New
Atlantis*.[1] In *Christianopolis*, Andreae suggested that a proper
community be formed in order to elaborate a new method of
learning based on 'chemical philosophy'. In that Utopian
city, the center for such studies would be the laboratory; there
the 'sky and the earth are married together', and the 'divine
mysteries impressed upon the land are discovered'.[2] Among
the defenders of *Fama Fraternitatis* and thus of the Rosicrucian
order was Robert Fludd, a fellow of the Royal College of
Physicians, who was also an adept of mystical alchemy. He

Confessio Fraternitatis R.C. (1615) and *The Chymical Marriage of Christian Rosen-
creutz* of J. V. Andreae (1586–1654) was brought out by Bernard Gorceix, *La Bible des
Rose-Croix* (Paris, 1970).
    [1] Cf. Andreae, *Christianopolis: An Ideal State of the Seventeenth Century*, translated
by Felix Emil Held (New York and London, 1916). See also Yates, *The Rosicrucian
Enlightenment*, pp. 145—46; Debus, *The Chemical Dream*, pp. 19–20; John Warwick
Montgomery, *Cross and Crucible: Jonathan Valentin Andreae (1586–1654), Phoenix
of the Theologians*, I–II (The Hague, 1973).
    [2] *Christianopolos* (trans. Held), pp. 196–97.

emphatically stated that it was impossible for anyone to attain the highest knowledge of natural philosophy without serious training in the occult sciences. For him, the 'true medicine' was the very basis of natural philosophy. Our knowledge of the microcosm, i.e. the human body, will teach us the structure of the universe, and will thus lead us to our Creator. Similarly, the more we learn of the universe, the more we will known about ourselves.[1]

Recent studies, especially those of Debus and Frances Yates, have thrown a new light on the consequences of this search for a new learning based on 'philosophical chemistry' and the occult sciences. The importance conferred on the experimental probing of alchemical recipes in well-equipped laboratories prepared the way for a rationalistic chemistry. The continuous systematic exchange of information among the practitioners of the occult sciences brought on the creation of many academies and learned societies. But the myth of the 'true alchemy' did not lose its impact, even on the authors of the scientific revolution. In an essay published in 1658, Robert Boyle advocated the free communication of alchemical as well as medical secrets.[2] On the other hand, Newton thought that it was not safe to make alchemical secrets public and wrote to the Secretary of the Royal Society that Boyle should keep 'high silence' on these matters.[3]

Newton never published the results of his alchemical

[1] Robert Fludd, *Apologia Compendiaris Fraternitatem de Rosea Cruce Suspicionis et Infamiae Maculis Aspersam, Veritatis quasi Fluctibus abluens et abstergens* (Leiden, 1616), pp. 89–93, 100–103; quoted by Debus, *op. cit.*, pp. 22–23.

[2] The essay was reprinted, with commentary, by Margaret E. Rowbottom, 'The earliest published writing of Robert Fludd', *Annals of Science* 6 (1950): 376–89. 'If . . . the Elixir be a secret, that we owe wholly to our Makers Revelation, not our own industry, methinks we should not so much grudge to impart what we did not labour to acquire, since our Saviours prescription in the like case was this: *Freely ye have received, freely give*', etc.; Rowbottom, p. 384. The above quotation is reproduced by Dobbs, *The Foundations of Newton's Alchemy*, pp. 68–69.

[3] Fragments of this letter to Henry Oldenburg, April 26, 1676 (= Newton, *Correspondence*, II, pp. 1–3) are quoted by Dobbs, *op. cit.*, p. 195.

studies and experiments, although he declared that some of his experiments were successful. His innumerable alchemical manuscripts, however—which were neglected until 1940—have been thoroughly investigated by Professor Dobbs in her book *The Foundations of Newton's Alchemy*.[1] According to Dobbs, Newton probed 'the whole vast literature of the older alchemy as it has never been probed before or since' (p. 88). Newton sought in alchemy the structure of the small world to match his cosmological system. The discovery of the force which held the planets in their orbits did not satisfy him completely. But in spite of his intensive experiments from about 1668 to 1696, he failed to find the forces which govern the action of small bodies. However, when in 1679–80 he began to work seriously on the dynamics of orbital motion, he applied his chemical ideas of attraction to the cosmos.[2]

As McGuire and Rattans have shown, Newton was convinced that in earliest times 'God had imparted the secrets of natural philosophy and of the true religion to a select few. This knowledge was subsequently lost but partially recovered later, at which time it was incorporated in fables and mythic formulations where it would remain hidden from the vulgar. In modern days it could be more fully recovered from experience.'[3] For this reason, Newton usually turned to the most esoteric sections of alchemical literature, hoping that the real secrets were hidden there. It is highly significant that the founder of modern mechanical science did not reject the theology of the primordial secret revelation, nor did he reject the principle of transmutation, the basis of all alchemies. He wrote in his

[1] The history of Newton's alchemical manuscripts until their partial recovery by John Maynard Keynes in 1936–39 is related by Dobbs, p. 6 f.

[2] Richard S. Westfall, 'Newton and the Hermetic Tradition', in *Science, Medicine and Society in the Renaissance: Essays to Honor Walter Pagel*, edited by Allen G. Debus (New York, 1972), II, pp. 183–98, esp. pp. 193–94; Dobbs, p. 211.

[3] Dobbs, p. 90, referring to E. McGuire and P. M. Rattansi, 'Newton and the "Pipes of Pan"', *Notes and Records of the Royal Society of London* 21 (1966): 108–43.

treatise on *Opticks*: 'The changing of Bodies into Light, and Light into Bodies, is very conformable to the course of Nature, which seems delighted with Transmutation.'[1] According to Professor Dobbs, 'Newton's alchemical thoughts were so securely established on their basic foundations that he never came to deny their general validity, and in a sense the whole of his career after 1675 may be seen as one long attempt to integrate alchemy and the mechanical philosophy'.[2]

When the *Principia* was published, Newton's opponents emphatically declared that Newton's forces were in fact occult qualities. Professor Dobbs admits that his critics were right: 'Newton's forces were very much like the hidden sympathies and antipathies found in much of the occult literature of the Renaissance period. But Newton had given forces an ontological status equivalent to that of matter and motion. By so doing, and by quantifying the forces, he enabled the mechanical philosophies to rise above the level of imaginary impact mechanism' (p. 211). In his book *Force in Newton's Physics*, Professor Richard Westfall came to the conclusion that it was the *wedding* of the Hermetic tradition with the mechanical philosophy which produced modern science as its offspring.[3]

In its spectacular development, 'modern science' has ignored or rejected its Hermetic heritage. In other words, the triumph of Newton's mechanics abolished Newton's own scientific ideal. As a matter of fact, Newton and his contemporaries had expected quite another type of scientific revolution. Prolonging and expanding on the hopes and objectives of the neoalchemist of the Renaissance—that is, on the endeavor to redeem Nature—men as different as Paracelsus, John Dee,

---

[1] Newton, *Opticks* (London, 1704; reprint of the 4th edition [1730], New York, 1952), p. 374; quoted by Dobbs, p. 231.

[2] *Op. cit.*, p. 230.

[3] Richard S. Westfall, *Force in Newton's Physics: The Science of Dynamics in the Seventeenth Century* (London and New York, 1971), pp. 377–91; Dobbs, *op. cit.*, p. 211.

Comenius, J. V. Andreae, Ashmole, Fludd and Newton saw in alchemy the model for a more ambitious enterprise: namely, the perfection of man through a new method of learning. In their view, such a method would integrate a supraconfessional Christianity with the Hermetic tradition and the natural sciences, i.e. medicine, astronomy and mechanics. This ambitious synthesis was in fact a new religious creation, specifically Christian, and is comparable with the results of the previous integration of Platonic, Aristotelian and Neoplatonic metaphysical constructs. The type of 'learning' elaborated in the seventeenth century represented the last holistic enterprise attempted in Christian Europe. Such holistic systems of knowledge were proposed in ancient Greece by Pythagoras and Plato, but they characterize especially the Chinese culture, where no art, science or technology was intelligible without its cosmological, ethical and 'existential' presuppositions and implications.

Index

235